MS-900: Microso

Study Guide with Practice Questions & Labs

Second Edition

Document Control

Proposal Name	:	Microsoft 365 Fundamentals
Document Edition	:	Second
Document Release Date	:	21st April 2023
Reference	:	MS-900

Feedback:
If you have any comments regarding the quality of this book or otherwise alter it to suit your needs better, you can contact us through email at info@ipspecialist.net
Please include the book's title and ISBN in your message.

About IPSpecialist

Our philosophy is to treat our customers like family. We want you to succeed and are willing to do everything possible to help you make it happen. We have the proof to back up our claims. We strive to accelerate billions of careers with great courses, accessibility, and affordability. We believe continuous learning and knowledge evolution are the most important things to keep re-skilling and up-skilling the world.

Planning and creating a specific goal is where IPSpecialist helps. We can create a career track that suits your visions and develop the competencies you need to become a professional Network Engineer. We can also assist you with the execution and evaluation of your proficiency level based on the career track you choose, as they are customized to fit your specific goals.

We help you STAND OUT through our detailed IP training content packages.

Course Features:

- ❖ Self-Paced Learning
    - Learn at your own pace and in your own time
- ❖ Covers Complete Exam Blueprint
    - Prep for the exam with confidence
- ❖ Case Study-Based Learning
    - Relate the content to real-life scenarios
- ❖ Subscriptions that Suit You
    - Get more and pay less with IPS subscriptions
- ❖ Career Advisory Services
    - Let the industry experts plan your career journey
- ❖ Virtual Labs to test your skills
    - With IPS vRacks, you can evaluate your exam preparations
- ❖ Practice Questions
    - Practice questions to measure your preparation standards
- ❖ On Request Digital Certification
    - On request: digital certification from IPSpecialist LTD.

About the Authors:

This book has been compiled with the help of multiple professional engineers. These engineers specialize in different fields, e.g., Networking, Security, Cloud, Big Data, IoT, etc. Each engineer develops content in their specialized field that is compiled to form a comprehensive certification guide.

About the Technical Reviewers:

Nouman Ahmed Khan

AWS-Architect, CCDE, CCIEX5 (R&S, SP, Security, DC, Wireless), CISSP, CISA, CISM is a Solution Architect working with a major telecommunication provider in Qatar. He works with enterprises, mega-projects, and service providers to help them select the best-fit technology solutions. He also works closely as a consultant to understand customer business processes and helps select an appropriate technology strategy to support business goals. He has more than 14 years of experience working in Pakistan/Middle-East & UK. He holds a Bachelor of Engineering Degree from NED University, Pakistan, and an M.Sc. in Computer Networks from the UK.

Abubakar Saeed

Abubakar Saeed has more than twenty-five years of experience, Managing, Consulting, Designing, and implementing large-scale technology projects, extensive experience heading ISP operations, solutions integration, heading Product Development, Presales, and Solution Design. Emphasizing adhering to Project timelines and delivering as per customer expectations, he always leads the project in the right direction with his innovative ideas and excellent management.

Dr. Fahad Abdali

Dr. Fahad Abdali is a seasoned leader with extensive experience managing and growing software development teams in high-growth start-ups. He is a business entrepreneur with more than 18 years of experience in management and marketing. He holds a Bachelor's Degree from NED University of Engineering and Technology and a Doctor of Philosophy (Ph.D.) from the University of Karachi.

Mehwish Jawed

Mehwish Jawed is working as a Senior Research Analyst. She holds a Master's and Bachelor of Engineering degree in Telecommunication Engineering from NED University of Engineering and Technology. She also worked under the supervision of HEC Approved supervisor. She has more than three published papers, including conference and journal papers. She has a great knowledge of TWDM Passive Optical Network (PON). She also worked as a Project Engineer, Robotic Trainer in a private institute and has research skills in communication networks. She has the technical knowledge and industry-sounding information, which she effectively utilizes when needed. She also has expertise in cloud platforms, such as AWS, GCP, Oracle, and Microsoft Azure.

Hareem Khan

Hareem Khan is currently working as a Technical Content Developer, having command over networking and security. She has completed training in CCNA and Cybersecurity. She holds a BE in Telecommunications Engineering from NED University of Engineering and Technology. She has strong knowledge of all the basics of IP and Security Networks and Routing and Switching Protocols. She has worked on various certification courses of Azure, Microsoft and GCP. She is part of content development team and has expertise on labs of Azure, Microsoft, Security and GCP.

Free Resources:

For Free Resources: Please visit our website and register to access your desired Resources Or contact us at: info@ipspecialist.net

Career Report: This report is a step-by-step guide for a novice who wants to develop his/her career in computer networks. It answers the following queries:

- What are the current scenarios and prospects?
- Is this industry moving toward saturation, or are new opportunities knocking at the door?
- What will the monetary benefits be?
- Why get certified?
- How to plan, and when will I complete the certifications if I start today?
- Is there any career track I can follow to accomplish the specialization level?

Furthermore, this guide provides a comprehensive career path toward being a specialist in networking and highlights the tracks needed to obtain certification.

IPS Personalized Technical Support for Customers: Good customer service means helping customers efficiently and in a friendly manner. It is essential to be able to handle issues for customers and do your best to ensure they are satisfied. Good service is one of the most important things that can set our business apart from others.
Excellent customer service will attract more customers and attain maximum customer retention.

IPS offers personalized TECH support to its customers to provide better value for money. If you have any queries related to technology and labs, you can ask our technical team for assistance via Live Chat or Email.

2023 BONUS MATERIAL! FREE SURPRISE VOUCHER

1. Get **350** UNIQUE Practice Questions (online) to simulate the real exam.

OR

2. Get FREE **Exam Cram Notes** (online access)

Get the Coupon Code from the **References** Section

Our Products

Study Guides

IPSpecialist Study Guides are the ideal guides to developing the hands-on skills necessary to pass the exam. Our workbooks cover the official exam blueprint and explain the technology with real-life case study-based labs. The content covered in each workbook consists of individually focused technology topics presented in an easy-to-follow, goal-oriented, step-by-step approach. Every scenario features detailed breakdowns and thorough verifications to help you completely understand the task and associated technology.

We extensively used mind maps in our workbooks to visually explain the technology. Our workbooks have become a widely used tool to learn and remember information effectively.

Practice Questions

IP Specialists' Practice Questions are dedicatedly designed from a certification exam perspective. The collection of these questions from our Study Guides is prepared to keep the exam blueprint in mind, covering not only important but necessary topics. It is an ideal document to practice and revise your certification.

Exam Cram

Our Exam Cram notes are a concise bundling of condensed notes of the complete exam blueprint. It is an ideal and handy document to help you remember the most important technology concepts related to the certification exam.

Hands-on Labs

IPSpecialist Hands-on Labs are the fastest and easiest way to learn real-world use cases. These labs are carefully designed to prepare you for the certification exams and your next job role. Whether you are starting to learn technology or solving a real-world scenario, our labs will help you learn the core concepts in no time.

IPSpecialist self-paced labs were designed by subject matter experts and provide an opportunity to use products in a variety of pre-designed scenarios and common use cases, giving you hands-on practice in a simulated environment to help you gain confidence. You have the flexibility to choose from topics and products about which you want to learn more.

Companion Guide

Companion Guides are portable desk guides for the IPSpecialist course materials that users (students, professionals, and experts) can access at any time and from any location. Companion Guides are intended to supplement online course material by assisting users in concentrating on key ideas and planning their study time for quizzes and examinations.

Content at a glance

Table of Contents

About Microsoft 365 Certifications

The Microsoft 365 Certification is created to demonstrate to customers that an app has passed scrutiny against controls taken from top industry standard frameworks and that adequate security and compliance procedures have been implemented to safeguard client data. There are two stages to the Microsoft 365 Certification: Attestation and Certification.

Attestation

The attestation phase focuses on a lengthy questionnaire describing an app's security, data handling, and compliance features. The information given by Independent Software Vendors (ISVs) comprises the following and covers all of the app functionality that is exposed when it is active in a company's Microsoft 365 platform:

1. **Data handling:** How an application gathers and manages organizational data and the degree to which an organization has control over that data.

2. **Security:** The policies, practices, and procedures that an application must follow to safeguard data, identify and thwart cyberattacks, and more.

3. **Compliance:** The application's conformity to the necessary industry norms and requirements.

4. **Privacy:** How well the app complies with relevant, applicable privacy laws.

5. **Identity:** The application's compliance with identity management and access control guidelines.

Certification

An extensive security examination of the application and its underlying infrastructure is the main focus of the certification process. The app will be examined in relation to several security measures taken from well-known industry standard frameworks such as SOC 2, PCI DSS, and ISO 27001. Microsoft encourage you to share those reports if your software has previously achieved a SOC 2, PCI DSS, or ISO 27001 certification. They are not necessary, but they may be utilized to satisfy some of the controls without requiring further proof. Microsoft do ask that you give us explicit proof (papers, screenshots, etc.) that you meet all the necessary controls if you do not have any external certifications. Apps that have received certifications have proven that they have effective security and compliance procedures in place to safeguard user information.

Value of Microsoft 365 Certifications

Microsoft emphasizes sound conceptual knowledge of its entire platform and hands-on experience with the Azure infrastructure and its many unique and complex components and services.

For Individuals

- Demonstrate your expertise in designing, deploying, and operating highly available, cost-effective, and secured applications on Microsoft 365
- Gain recognition and visibility of your proven skills and proficiency with Azure
- Earn tangible benefits such as access to the Microsoft Certified Community, get invited to Microsoft Certification Appreciation Receptions and Lounges, obtain Microsoft Certification Practice Exam Voucher and Digital Badge for certification validation, and Microsoft Certified Logo usage

- Foster credibility with your employer and peers

For Employers

- Identify skilled professionals to lead IT initiatives with Cloud technologies
- Reduce risks and costs in implementing your workloads and projects on the Azure platform
- Increase customer satisfaction

Types of Certification

Role-based Certification

- *Fundamental* - Validates overall understanding of the Azure Cloud
- *Associate*- Technical role-based certifications. No pre-requisite required
- *Expert*- Highest level technical role-based certification

About Microsoft 365 Certified: Fundamentals

Exam Questions	Case study, short Answer, repeated Answer, MCQs
Number of Questions	40-60
Time to Complete	45-60 minutes
Exam Fee	99 USD

This certification exam assesses your capacity to suggest Microsoft 365 solutions that deal with typical corporate IT problems. You ought to be aware of how Microsoft 365 solutions raise output, promote teamwork, and enhance communications.

You should be able to distinguish Microsoft 365 solutions from the competitors in the market as an exam candidate if you possess the necessary expertise. Additionally, you should be knowledgeable about Microsoft 365 licenses, deployment and migration assistance, and support choices for businesses trying to get the most out of their cloud investments.

This exam measures your ability to accomplish the following technical tasks:

- Describe cloud concepts (5–10%)
- Describe Microsoft 365 apps and services (45–50%)
- Describe security, compliance, privacy, and trust in Microsoft 365 (25–30%)
- Describe Microsoft 365 pricing, licensing, and support (10–15%)

Recommended Knowledge

- Describe the different types of cloud services available
- Describe the benefits of and considerations for using cloud, hybrid, or on-premises services
- Describe productivity solutions in Microsoft 365
- Describe collaboration solutions in Microsoft 365
- Describe endpoint modernization, management concepts, and deployment options in Microsoft 365

- Describe analytics capabilities in Microsoft 365
- Explain zero-trust security principles for Microsoft 365
- Describe identity and access management solutions in Microsoft 365
- Describe threat protection solutions in Microsoft 365
- Describe trust, privacy, and compliance solutions in Microsoft 365
- Plan, predict, and compare pricing
- Identify licensing options available in Microsoft 365
- Describe the Microsoft 365 service lifecycle
- Describe support offerings for Microsoft 365 services
- Describe Mobile Device Management
- Discover Microsoft 365 Apps

The following general domains and their weights on the exam are included in this exam curriculum:

	Domain	Percentage
Domain 1	Describe cloud concepts	10-15%
Domain 2	Describe Microsoft 365 apps and services	45-50%
Domain 3	Describe security, compliance, privacy, and trust in Microsoft 365	25-30%
Domain 4	Describe Microsoft 365 pricing, licensing, and support	10-15%

Course Introduction

Microsoft 365 Fundamentals - Course Introduction

The fundamentals of cloud computing and the Software as a Service (SaaS) cloud model are covered in this course, focusing on Microsoft 365's cloud service offerings. You will start by learning about the principles of cloud computing, including an introduction to Microsoft cloud services. You will learn about Microsoft Azure and look at how Microsoft 365 and Office 365 differ. After that, you will thoroughly examine Microsoft 365, which will include a comparison of Microsoft on-premises services and Microsoft 365 cloud services, a look at enterprise mobility in Microsoft 365, and a look at how Microsoft 365 services support collaboration.

The course then examines how Microsoft 365 handles security, compliance, privacy, and trust before reviewing subscriptions, licenses, invoicing, and support for Microsoft 365.

User Profile

This course is intended for business decision-makers and IT professionals who want to deploy cloud services within their company or just want to learn the foundations of cloud computing. With a general focus on Microsoft 365 cloud service offerings, this includes the factors to consider and the advantages of implementing cloud services in general and the SaaS cloud model in particular.

Prerequisites

Candidates must be familiar with the following to pass the MS-900: Microsoft 365 Fundamentals Certification exam.

- The choices that are open to you and the advantages of   using Microsoft's 365 Cloud Service products
- The approaches that need to be suggested to handle the organization's frequent IT problems
- What could set it apart from other market competitors, are Microsoft 365 Solutions
- Grouping together different Microsoft services and goods, including Azure, Dynamics 365, and Microsoft 365
- Provision of services and cost-effective licensing optimization
- There are many organizational support possibilities

Chapter 01: Introduction to Microsoft 365

Introduction

The productivity cloud Microsoft 365, which offers cutting-edge and intelligent experiences, in-depth organizational insights, and a dependable platform to help people and businesses get more done, is covered in this session. Microsoft 365, an evolution of Office 365, provides much more than just the standard office tools you may be accustomed to. Microsoft 365 offers a subscription for every organization because each has different needs. Register for your trial environment to experience how Microsoft 365 enables individuals and organizations to perform at their highest level.

What is Cloud Computing?

Cloud Computing is storing data and accessing computers over the internet. It delivers computing services like servers, software, analytics, databases, and storage via the internet. Computing resources are delivered on-demand through a cloud service platform with pay-as-you-go pricing. The companies that are providing services are termed "Cloud Providers." There are several cloud providers, the major ones being Amazon, Google, and Azure.

Benefits of Cloud Computing

We all know that cloud computing has brought a great change in the traditional business thinking for IT resources. There are many benefits of cloud computing. Some of which are:

1. **Cost**

   Cloud computing eliminates the capital cost of buying hardware and software and building and running in-house data centers – server racks, 24-hour electricity for power and cooling, etc.

2. **Scale Globally**

   Cloud computing services have the capacity to scale with elasticity. In the cloud, IT resources are provided with more or less computing power, storage, and bandwidth – as per requirement and from the right place.

3. **Increase Speed and Agility**

   New IT resources are readily available so that resources can be scaled up infinitely according to demand. This leads to a dramatic increase in agility for organizations.

4. **Reliability**

   Cloud computing allows data backup, disaster recovery, and business continuity as data can be replicated in the network of the cloud supplier on multiple redundant sites.

5. **Security**

   The protection of their data is one of the main problems for any organization, regardless of its size and industry. Infringements of data and other cyber crimes can devastate a company's revenue,

customer loyalty, and positioning. Cloud provides many advanced security features to strengthen the security of the overall company. It also helps in protecting your data, application, and infrastructure.

The Economy of Cloud Computing

Cloud reduces the Capital Expenditure (CapEx) cost and has many other benefits. In the traditional environment of organizations, as there is a need for large investments in CapEx, the cloud is the best way to switch to the pay-as-you-go model. With cloud computing, you can easily move toward Operational Expenditure (OpEx).

> **EXAM TIP:** Capital Expenditure (CapEx) is the expenditure to maintain or acquire fixed assets by spending money. This includes land, equipment, etc.
>
> Operational Expenditure (OpEx) is the cost of a product or a system that is running on a day-to-day basis, like electricity, printer papers, etc.

Technical Terms

To understand Cloud Computing, you need to understand some technical terms.

- **High Availability (HA)** - It is the core of cloud computing. As we know, in traditional server environments, companies own a number of hardware, and the workload is limited to this hardware capacity. In case of additional load, capacity cannot be increased, whereas sometimes this hardware seems extra for the workload. In the cloud, you do not own any hardware, and adding servers is just a click away. With this method, you get high availability for your servers by replacing the failed server instantly with the new one. HA depends on the number of VMs that you set up to cover in case one goes down

- **Fault Tolerance** - For resilience in the cloud, fault tolerance is also an essential factor. Fault tolerance gives you zero downtime, meaning that if there is any fault from the Microsoft side, then it is immediately mitigated by Microsoft itself

- **Disaster Recovery (DR)** – This is used in case of any catastrophic disaster like a cyber-attack. DR recovers your business from these critical systems or in normal operation if such an event occurs. DR has designated time to recover and a recovery point

- **Scalability** - In cloud computing, scalability means adding or removing resources in an easy and quick way as per demand. It is crucial in such a situation where you do not know the actual number of resources that are needed. Auto-scaling is an approach for scalability depending on your requirement by defining the threshold

- **Elasticity** - Elasticity is the capacity to dynamically extend or minimize network resources to respond to autonomous working load adjustments and optimize the use of resources. This can contribute to overall cost savings for services

- **Agility** - Agility is the capability to adapt quickly and efficiently to changes in the business environment. Agility also refers to the ability to quickly develop, test and deploy business-led software applications. Instead of providing and managing services, Cloud Agility lets them concentrate on other issues such as security, monitoring, and analysis

> **EXAM TIP:** From the Exam perspective, one must be familiar with all the terms like HA, Fault Tolerance, DR, Elasticity, Scalability, and Agility.

Types of Cloud Computing

Cloud computing is a broad word that refers to a set of services that provide organizations with a low-cost way to expand their IT capacity and usefulness.

Businesses can choose where, when, and how they employ cloud computing to ensure an efficient and dependable IT solution based on their needs.

Infrastructure as a Service (IaaS), Platform as a Service (PaaS), and Software as a Service (SaaS) are the three basic cloud computing service models. Although there are evident distinctions between the three and what they can offer a business regarding storage and resource sharing, they can also interact to build a single cloud computing paradigm.

Software as a Service

Cloud providers take over both servers and code. Cloud providers host and maintain the applications and underlying infrastructure for SaaS and handle updates such as software upgrades and security patches. Users link the app over the internet, usually through their phone, tablet, or PC through their web browser.

The first offering is Software as a Service (SaaS), and it is now thought to be the biggest and most well-liked cloud computing application. It is expanding as web-based alternatives are used in place of conventional on-device software. The need to install client software is quickly eliminated by shifting applications to the cloud, frequently utilizing a subscription-based model, and making the software browser-accessible. In many cases, this makes the software cross-platform and usable on the variety of devices that we use today. Gmail, Google Drive, Power BI, Microsoft Office 365 and others are a few examples.

Platform as a Service

Cloud computing platforms that provide an on-demand environment to build, test, deliver and manage software applications are called Platform as a Service. PaaS facilitates the fast development of web or mobile apps for developers without setting or maintaining the underlying server, storage, network, and database infrastructure needed for development.

Platform as a Service (PaaS) is a platform, which runs on a single VM and is designed to support the complete application life cycle, typically for website building, testing, deploying, managing, and updating. This service allows you to avoid the expense and complexity of buying, installing, and managing software licenses. Instead, you manage the applications and services you deploy, and the cloud service provider typically manages everything else.

Infrastructure as a Service

An Infrastructure as a Service (IaaS) enables a server in the cloud or VM instance that you would have complete control over. This offering is closer to an on-premises VM. IaaS requires you to manage the operating system and the virtual machine's disk and networking attributes. Hardware management is taken care of, and a remote desktop is utilized to manage the VM. IaaS is a great solution where multiple applications running on a single VM are needed to fulfill the needs of third-party software.

> **Note:** IaaS gives you a basic IT infrastructure for Cloud IT like VMs, Data Storage, Networks, and OS on a pay-as-you-go model.

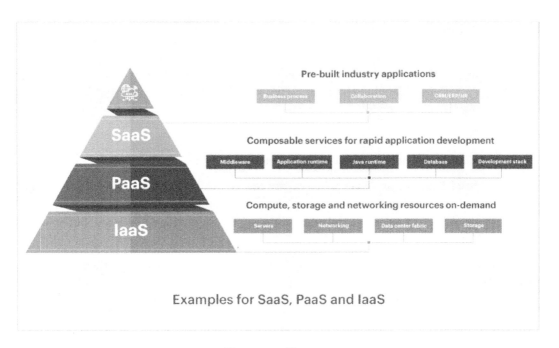

Figure 1-01: Features

Serverless

Overlapping PaaS, serverless computing concentrates on creating application functionality without continually spending time maintaining the required server and infrastructure. The cloud provider is responsible for configuration, capacity planning, and server governance. The highly scalable and event-based serverless architectures only use resources when a particular task or trigger occurs.

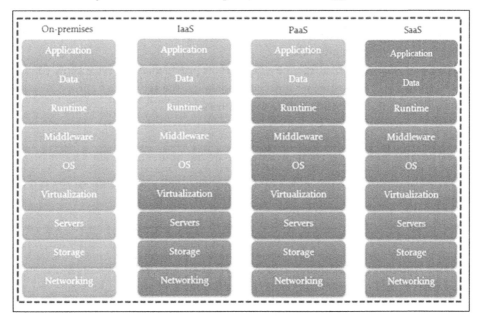

Figure 1-02: Overview of SaaS, PaaS, and IaaS

SaaS: Common Scenarios

Software as a Service (SaaS) allows you to use built-in cloud-based applications over the internet. The most common examples include email and sophisticated business apps like Customer Relationship Management (CRM), Enterprise Resource Planning (ERP), etc. This service allows you to only pay for the app you use according to the pay-as-you-go model.

Advantages

There are several advantages of SaaS. These include, but are not limited to:

Easy access to cloud-based apps – SaaS provides easy access to the cloud-based app without installing and updating hardware and software. This service gives access to sophisticated applications such as CRM and ERP, making it affordable for businesses and organizations. They do not have to worry about how to manage and deploy applications.

Use free client software – Most clients can run the application directly from their browser without downloading and installing it.

Global access – With this cloud-based service, all data is directly stored in the cloud with some security. Users and clients can access the information and required data from any device connected to the internet.

PaaS: Common Scenarios

PaaS provides a complete deployment environment in the cloud. You can build, deploy, and run simple to complex applications. You can use and scale services and resources according to the pay-as-you-go model and access them over the secure and reliable internet.

The following are common scenarios that use PaaS:

- **Development Framework** – PaaS provides a framework that enables you to deploy and run simple to complex cloud-based applications over a secure internet connection. Cloud features provide high availability, reliability, scalability, and multi-tenant capabilities used by PaaS to reduce the coding overhead in deploying a framework
- **Analytics and Business Intelligence** – Some tools provided as a service allow you to examine big data. Organizations and businesses most commonly use the service to improve forecasting, product decision, investment frameworks, project workflows, etc.

Advantages

There are several advantages of PaaS. These include, but are not limited to:

Reduces deployment time – PaaS provides a lot of pre-coded built applications so you can quickly deploy new applications.

Option for multiple platforms – This service offers you an opportunity to deploy services and resources for various platforms.

Use of artificialized tools – As PaaS follows the pay-as-you-go approach, most organizations and business intelligence can use sophisticated tools they could not afford to purchase.

Supports geographically distributed teams – With PaaS, you can make an online   development framework. Multiple development teams can work together on the same idea from anywhere in the world.

Manages application lifecycle – PaaS cloud service enables you to efficiently manage the application lifecycle, such as building, testing, managing, deploying, etc.

IaaS: Common Scenarios

IaaS enables you to quickly meet demand by scaling the resources according to need. It avoids having to buy and maintain physical architecture and infrastructure. Each service is offered as a separate component, and you only pay for the service you use.

The following are some common scenarios that use IaaS:

- **Hosting a Website** – You get more control than traditional website hosting when you host a website or run a website over IaaS
- **Web Apps** – IaaS supports the infrastructure of web apps, including storage, web, and application server. An organization can deploy web apps on IaaS and scale resources to meet the demand
- **Storage, Backup, and Recovery** – Storage management sometimes become very complex. IaaS makes it easy to manage, simplify, backup, and recover data
- **High-Performance Computing** – When working with traffic requiring high-performance computing, you can run these workloads in the cloud while avoiding hardware complexities and paying only for what you use
- **Big Data Analysis** – IaaS provides the processing power for big data analysis

Advantages

There are several advantages of IaaS.

Reduced Costs – This service eliminates the up-front hardware cost and allows you to only pay for the resources and services you use. Businesses looking for new ideas often use this cloud service that enables them to deploy computing infrastructure quickly.

Better Business Continuity and Disaster Recovery – This service is better for disaster recovery because it allows scaling resources and services to meet demand. This service is also best suited for business continuity and high availability.

Fast Response – You can deploy and deliver apps to the user faster with IaaS managing the underlying infrastructure.

Scalable, Reliable, and Flexible – IaaS cloud services provide scalable, reliable, and flexible services that meet the Service Level Agreement (SLA).

EXAM TIP: Cloud computing provides the resources and services to meet demands over the internet. It provides services using three service models.
SaaS: Delivers cloud-based applications.
PaaS: Provides the deployment and development environment for users to use this environment for their cloud-based applications.
IaaS: Allows you to manage and scale resources to meet demand and use resources according to the pay-as-you-go model without any underlying hardware infrastructures.

Services	Advantages	Disadvantages
SaaS	Allows comprehensive access Available at any place A unique feature for collaboration work	Restrictions Dictate overall execution due to internet coverage
PaaS	Low cost Developed as publicly and privately Easy for web apps	No control over virtual machines Problem of relocation
IaaS	Automate the installation of hardware Easier for users to install cloud services	Very Expensive

Table 1-01: SaaS, PaaS, and IaaS

Cloud Computing Deployment Models

We know that all clouds are not the same, and not every business requirement for cloud computing is the same. Therefore, to meet the requirements, different models, types, and services have been used. Firstly, you must decide how the cloud service is being applied by finding the cloud deployment type or Architecture.

When you shift some of the on-premises applications to the cloud, the next decision you have to make is how to deploy them. There are four ways to deploy and integrate cloud services into your application architecture and infrastructure:

- Public Cloud
- Private Cloud
- Hybrid Cloud
- Community Cloud

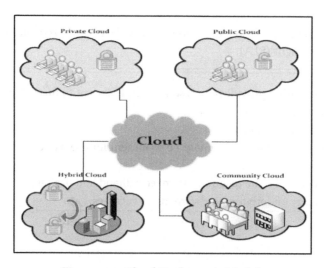

Figure 1-03: Cloud Deployment Models

Public Cloud

The public cloud is the most common approach that is open to all organizations. All resources, such as servers and disks, are owned and managed by the cloud provider in the public cloud. Microsoft Azure is an example. The cloud service provider carries out the maintenance, operation, and monitoring. The physical hardware is shared with other organizations, and your view is virtualized. Your data is secure and isolated. However, the cloud provider decides where it is stored and where your logic runs. The primary advantage of this approach is the lower cost, scalability, and flexibility. You are only required to pay for what you use, you scale on-demand based on your need, and there is no need to purchase and maintain expensive hardware.

Why Public Cloud?

Several applications allow you to use the public cloud:

- **Service Consumption** – Service consumption, through an on-demand or subscription model, charges you only for the CPU usage, storage, and other resources that you have used or reserved for use in the future
- **No hardware requirement** – With the public cloud, there is no requirement to purchase, maintain, or manage the physical architecture and infrastructure
- **Automation** – It provides a quick response by using a web portal or scripts
- **Geographical distribution** – With this cloud approach, you can store data in the location nearest to your user without having to maintain data centers
- **Minimize Hardware Monitoring** – You are free from hardware maintenance with a public cloud, as the service provider is responsible for this

Private Cloud

The second approach is called a private cloud. This is where computing resources are used exclusively by a business or organization. It can be physically located on-premises or managed by a cloud provider. The maintenance, operation, and monitoring come under the private network owned by that organization. In addition to scalability and reliability, it has very high-level security.

Why Private Cloud?

Several applications allow you to use the private cloud:

- **Pre-Existing Environment** – Private cloud allows using an existing operating environment with solution expertise
- **Legacy Application** – Private cloud can be used to handle business-critical legacy applications
- **Data Authority and Security** – Private cloud can be used to secure data

Hybrid Cloud

A hybrid cloud allows users to access both public and private cloud resources within a single access environment. In a hybrid cloud, some of your data and applications run on your private infrastructure and some run on Cloud Service Provider (CSP) on the public cloud. This cloud model can be used in various ways, such as a migration approach to gradually transition your app and services from your private data center into CSP. This allows for better testing and easier migration. This cloud model can also be used for segmenting work. You can connect to the environment with a secure private network to pass data back and forth. Part of the data is processed in your local private infrastructure, and another is processed in the cloud. In this case, the hybrid cloud can be used for cloud bursting. You can upload work to the cloud when your internet data

center hits the maximum workload. You can then scale and burst workloads to leverage CSP, then drop back down to internal resources when the load returns to normal.

Why Hybrid Cloud?

Several applications allow you to use a hybrid cloud:

- **Existing Hardware Investment** – Most businesses prefer to use their existing hardware and operating environment
- **Use for Regulation** – Most regulatory frameworks require their data to remain physically located
- **Easy Migration** – With this cloud, you can shift data from on-premises to the cloud when required

Community Cloud

This model allows the user to access the group of organizations for its services. It can provide a sharing mechanism, but its security is high compared to a public cloud and low compared to a private cloud.

Microsoft 365

A cloud-based subscription service called Microsoft 365 includes a portfolio of integrated goods like Office applications, Teams, Windows, top-notch security, and more. Any size of an organization, including yours, may benefit from Microsoft 365. It represents the workplace of the future. Whether at home, in the office, out in the field, or on the go, these Microsoft 365 features help enhance productivity, collaboration, and communication securely across numerous devices. Microsoft 365 ensures a trustworthy, secure, and contemporary experience for every employee   anytime, anywhere thus integrating everyone into the digital revolution.

Microsoft 365 Fundamentals

Your gateway and guide to everything Microsoft 365 is Microsoft 365 Fundamentals. Three understanding routes make up Microsoft 365 fundamentals, introducing you to the platform's many features through its range of products and services.

The three learning paths are outlined in the list below:

- Describe the basic features and principles of Microsoft 365. Learn how Microsoft 365's productivity, collaboration, and business management tools enable individuals and companies to do more
- Demonstrate a fundamental understanding of the security and compliance features of Microsoft 365. Discover how Microsoft's security, compliance, and identity solutions assist individuals and companies in securing their entire digital footprint, streamlining compliance, and lowering risk
- Show that you are knowledgeable about Microsoft 365 licensing, service, and support. Find out how adoption guidance, ongoing support, and license options that suit your needs can help people and businesses make the most of their Microsoft 365 investments

Microsoft 365 productivity in the cloud

Organizations are heading toward digitization, profoundly changing when, where, and how we work. Employees seek more job flexibility while still   feeling connected to their coworkers. Employees are expected to sync and operate across various devices, including personal devices, making management and security

tough. Organizations strive to remain competitive in a constantly changing economic environment and prepare for economic turbulence. They want to help their staff reach their maximum potential without inducing burnout. Organizations seek to automate processes, but their employees use too many apps, resulting in a fragmented experience. They want to be safe against security risks, but do not have the resources to keep up with the sophistication of attacks. Organizations seek top-line growth, cost-cutting, and improved customer service. Below are the benefits of Microsoft 365.

Benefits of Microsoft 365

1. **Problem-solving and provision of security**: Microsoft 365 can help you overcome today's productivity and security concerns by allowing you to work securely from anywhere. All you need are the proper tools and technologies in a single, cost-effective package.

2. **Stimulation of productivity**: Be more productive from anywhere with Microsoft 365. Enable your team to do their best work with cloud technology to improve team collaboration, whether at the office, out in the field, or at home. Microsoft Teams allows you to feel closer to your coworkers through chat, voice, and video. Create content with built-in Office apps and use Artificial Intelligence (AI) to improve your work. Utilize integrated technologies to streamline work and automate manual tasks, allowing you to focus on what matters most. With Microsoft Viva, you can create a culture that helps your people achieve their best from anywhere. With clever mobile apps, you can easily transition from your PC to your mobile devices, allowing you to stay productive while on the road.

3. **Security through modern technology:** Through Microsoft 365, you can protect your company with technology you can trust. You can improve and modernize your security, manage risk, and meet compliance standards on Microsoft's trusted cloud. Ensure only the right users have access to Azure Active Directory, multifactor authentication, and biometric access, like Windows Hello. With Microsoft Endpoint Manager, you can deploy a seamless, end-to-end management solution and gain insight across all connected devices. Microsoft 365 Defender can defend your company against sophisticated cyberattacks. With Microsoft Secure Score, you can get a real-time assessment of your existing security posture.

4. **Cost-effective solutions:** With Microsoft 365, you can get a single, cost-effective solution. Rather than buying multiple platforms for different capabilities, consolidate them to a single platform. Workflows, dashboards, and AI can help you save money on automation and process improvements. Enhance your security and compliance posture to lower your overall cost of risk so that IT can focus on strategy and better manage hardware and software. Reduce hard costs, like real estate and travel, through flexible work from anywhere.

Microsoft 365 Enables Hybrid And Flexible Work Strategies

The pandemic has changed how we work, do business, and meet client needs, among other things. So much more can be done remotely than we ever imagined. Organizations are attempting to negotiate this new way of working, which includes hybrid and flexible work. Changes are needed to assist entirely remote personnel who choose to come into the office, who must remain onsite, such as frontline staff, and who do both.

Frontline workers have borne the brunt of the strain during the last few years. Frontline employees make up the majority of the workforce and are in positions where they are the first to interact with consumers, see products and services in action, and represent your brand. For all major sectors, they are the backbone of

hybrid operations. These workers have typically been underserved by technology, despite their critical importance in every business.

Microsoft wants you and your company to succeed in today's hybrid world. Hybrid work is unavoidable, so fostering the right culture to support it is critical. Organizations should establish a clear, flexible work policy that allows workers of all types to choose how, when, and where they work.

Microsoft 365 has the capabilities to help your company fulfill the different needs of your employees by allowing them to work onsite or remotely:

1. **Staying connected:** Stay connected at all times and from anywhere in the world. Your employees have access to:
    *   Your Microsoft 365 subscription which includes cloud-based services and data
    *   On-premises application data centers, that provide organizational resources
2. **Securing sign-ins:** Microsoft 365 and Windows have built-in security measures that protect against malware, malicious attacks, and data loss. Secure sign-ins with Multi-Factor Authentication (MFA) and built-in security features to guard against malware, malicious attacks, and data loss.
3. **Management of hybrid workers' devices:** Manage the devices of your hybrid workers from the cloud by configuring security, allowing certain apps, and enforcing system compliance.
4. **Collaborative and productive:** Be extremely collaborative while being equally productive as on-premises with:
    *   Online   meetings, chats, and push-to-talk conversations using Teams
    *   Shared work areas for OneDrive and SharePoint allow for real-time collaboration and worldwide access to cloud-based file storage
    *   Workflows and shared tasks to divide and complete the work

> EXAM TIP: Your Microsoft 365 subscription includes cloud-based services and data. On-premises application data centers, for example, provide organizational resources.

Differences between Office 365, Microsoft 365, and Windows 365

The evolution of Office 365 to Microsoft 365

Microsoft introduced Office 365, the software-as-a-service you might be familiar with and might have used, more than ten years ago. Office 365, developed from Microsoft's Business Productivity Online Suite (BPOS), was created to integrate the company's current online products into a continuously updated cloud service. It brought together essential productivity programs like Word, Excel, PowerPoint, OneNote, and Outlook with teamwork and communication programs like Exchange, SharePoint, and Skype for Business. Office 365 was a strategy for the company to expand its communication and collaboration services while also growing its Office-centric business. Updated versions of Office 365 subscriptions were later produced, focusing on consumers, smaller enterprises, and schools after initially catering to corporate users. New features like OneDrive were present in these versions. Microsoft 365 was created because Microsoft's cloud productivity services expanded   significantly over the past few years beyond what people typically think of as "Office." By changing the name of Office 365 to Microsoft 365, it is clear that additional features and advantages have been added. Office 365 is a subset of Microsoft 365, which includes Windows, Teams, and additional cloud-based security and device management products and services in addition to all you already know about Office

365. With cutting-edge apps, clever cloud services, and top-notch security, Microsoft 365 helps people and companies do more. Microsoft 365, a subscription service like Office 365, ensures that you always have access to the most recent contemporary productivity and collaboration tools.

> **Note:** You can always access tech assistance and the most recent features, fixes, and security updates. Plans for Microsoft 365 subscriptions are available for usage by individuals, households, small and big businesses, schools, and more. No action is required on your part if you already have an office 365 subscription; it will automatically convert to a Microsoft 365 subscription.

Windows 365

The most recent Windows operating systems are Windows 10 and 11. You might be familiar with Windows. Windows 365 is not quite an operating system and is not set up on your computer like Windows. You may build and manage PCs remotely using Windows 365, a business subscription service. Windows 365 securely broadcasts your customized Windows desktop, programs, settings, and material from the cloud to any device, earning it the moniker "cloud PC." You may stream your Windows experience from the Microsoft cloud to any device using a cloud PC, which gives you a virtualized computing environment. Windows transitions from a device-based operating system (OS) to hybrid personalized computing with a Cloud PC.

Microsoft 365 Subscription Options

Microsoft offers various subscriptions to meet your organization's demands because every organization has different requirements. Let's look at some of the more well-known subscription options.

Microsoft 365 Home

To give your personal and family life the same fantastic productivity benefits, Microsoft 365 Home was created. Two plans are available for family and individual use of Microsoft 365 Home.

Microsoft 365 Education

Educational institutions can use Microsoft 365 Education. Academic licenses can be customized to meet the requirements of every institution, including security and productivity solutions for faculty, staff, and students.

> **EXAM TIP:** Microsoft 365 Education allows teachers to foster collaboration and unleash creativity with a single, cost-effective solution.

Microsoft 365 for business

Small and medium-sized businesses are the target audience for Microsoft 365 for business. By lowering costs, enhancing cybersecurity, and enabling workers to work remotely, Microsoft 365 for Business can benefit your company. It contains security and device management features in addition to the complete set of Office 365 productivity tools.

Microsoft 365 Enterprise

Large enterprises can use Microsoft 365 Enterprise. From the office to frontline staff, every person can be connected and empowered by Microsoft 365 Enterprise, increasing efficiency and spurring innovation.

Organizations looking for a productivity solution with strong threat prevention, security, compliance, and analytics features can get enterprise-class services from this company.

EXAM TIP: To learn more about Microsoft 365, enroll in the Microsoft 365 Developer Program. You can use the program's Microsoft 365 E5 developer subscription to build your sandbox and develop solutions. Your production environment has no bearing on this program.

Microsoft 365 tenant

To learn more about Microsoft 365, enroll in the Microsoft 365 Developer Program. You can use the program's Microsoft 365 E5 developer subscription to build your sandbox and develop solutions. Your production environment has no bearing on this program. The program has a 90-day duration and 25 user licenses. You may use Microsoft Graph, the SharePoint Framework, Power Apps, and other tools to create Microsoft Teams apps, Office add-ins for Word, Excel, PowerPoint, Outlook, or SharePoint add-ins.

How to Join the Microsoft 365 developer program?

The following are the ways through which we can access and join Microsoft 365 developer program.

1. Go to the Developer Program or Microsoft 365 Dev Center page to sign in with your Microsoft account. Visit Microsoft Account or tap Sign In or Create Your Account Today if you do not already have one and register for free. Choose to Create a Microsoft account, then proceed as directed.
2. Select Join now and proceed after logging in.

How to Set up and Configure a Microsoft 365 E5 Developer Sandbox Subscription?

1. Select Set up E5 subscription from the Microsoft 365 E5 developer profile page.
2. Choose whether you want a customizable or an instant sandbox, click next, and then follow the instructions.
   - **Instant Sandbox:** Microsoft Teams, SharePoint, Outlook, and Office are already pre-provisioned in the immediate sandbox. You receive pre-installed data and are unable to change the domain name
   - **Configurable Sandbox:** You must add sample data to the configurable sandbox, which is initially empty. The provisioning of this sandbox may take up to two days. Your domain name can be modified
3. Your subscription domain name and expiration date are displayed on your profile page after the subscription.
4. Choose **Go to subscription** and sign in with your user ID On your profile page (for example, username@domain.onmicrosoft.com) and the password that you specified for your developer subscription.
5. Then Use the app launcher to go to the **Microsoft 365 admin center.**
6. Choose **Go to guided setup** on the admin center home page; It will take you to the **Microsoft 365 E5 Developer Setup** page.

Following the exercises below, you can explore the Microsoft 365, Azure Active Directory, and Teams admin centers after setting up and configuring your Microsoft 365 developer membership.

Microsoft 365 Amin Center

You may administer your cloud-based company through the Microsoft 365 admin center. You can add and take away users, change licenses, and reset passwords. For more precise control, use specialized workspaces like Security or Device management.

Two perspectives are available in the Microsoft 365 admin center.

- Simplified view
- Dashboard view

The simplified view aids smaller enterprises in managing their most often tasks. The dashboard view has more intricate settings and duties. A button at the top of the admin area allows you to change between them.

Demo 1-01 Explore the Microsoft 365 Admin Center

1. Log in to the Microsoft 365 admin center using the following link.
https://www.microsoft.com/en-us/microsoft-365/business/office-365-administration

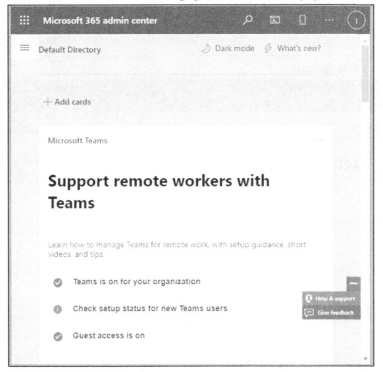

2. Expand Users in the navigation pane of the Microsoft 365 admin center, and then click Active users. See which user accounts are accessible.

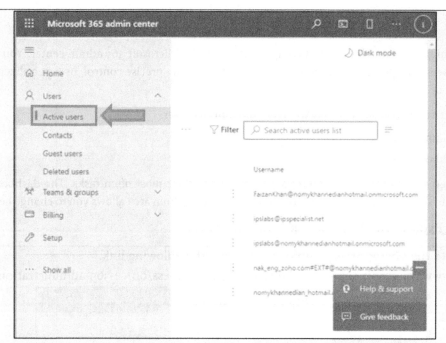

3. A list of users will appear.

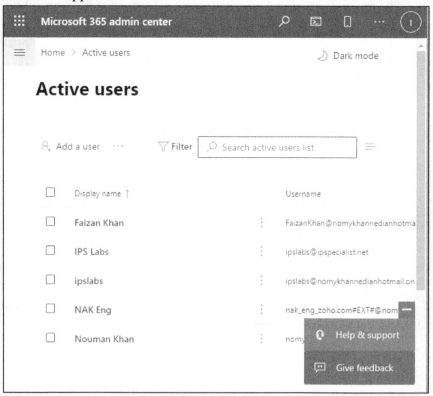

4. Click the user's name at the top of the list to select it. More information about the user account is shown in a blade that opens. By clicking the X in the blade's upper right corner, you can close it.

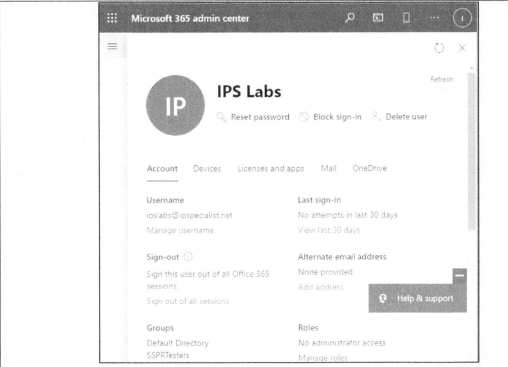

5. Select Active teams & groups after expanding Teams & groups. View the groups and teams that are currently active.

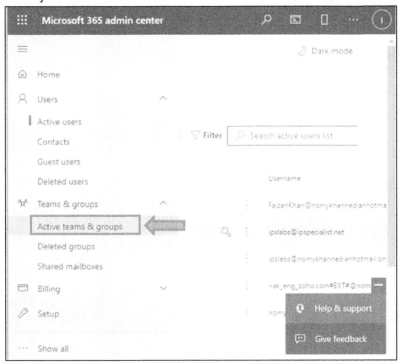

Note: If you do not have any groups yet, create one by choosing Add a group and following the instructions.

6. By clicking on its name, choose the first group on the list.

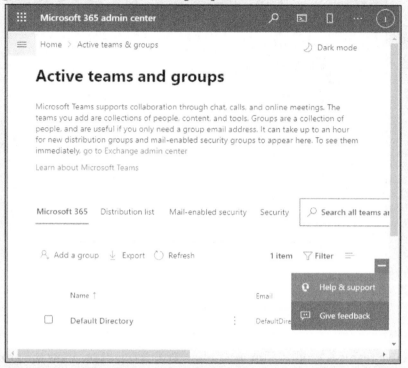

7. Click on the active team or group to view the details.

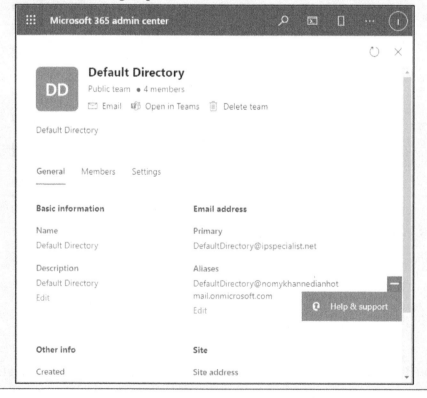

8. Select Licenses after expanding Billing. There should be at least one set of licenses visible. To get more information, including a list of users to whom this license has been assigned, choose the license.

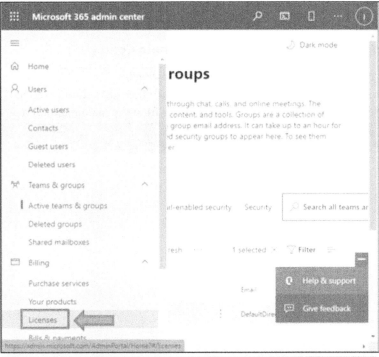

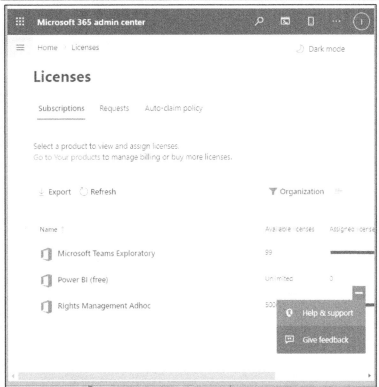

Azure Active Directory Admin Center

Azure Active Directory (Azure AD) is a service for managing identities and access in the cloud. This solution facilitates access to thousands of additional SaaS applications, the Azure portal, and external resources like Microsoft 365 for your staff members.

Demo 1-02 Explore the Azure Active Directory Admin Center

1. Log in to the Microsoft 365 admin center using the following link.
https://www.microsoft.com/en-us/microsoft-365/business/office-365-administration
2. Click on **Azure Active Directory** under Admin centers from the main menu. A new tab will now open.

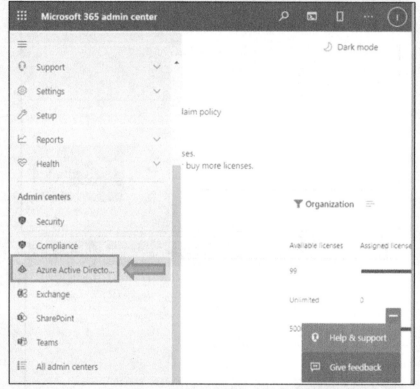

3. Choose Azure Active Directory from the navigation pane on the Dashboard of the Azure Active Directory admin center.

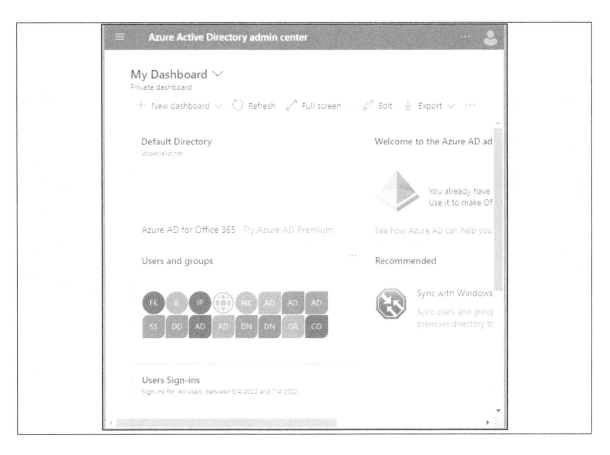

Microsoft Teams Admin Center

The controls in the Microsoft Teams admin center are comparable to those accessible in the Microsoft 365 admin center, such as those for managing users, adding users, deleting users, enabling add-ons, assigning responsibilities, etc.

As an admin, you might need to inspect or update your company has established teams for collaboration, or you might need to take corrective action like giving ownerless teams an owner. Both the Microsoft Teams admin center and the Microsoft Teams PowerShell module let you manage the teams used by your company. The admin center can be accessed at https://admin.microsoft.com. You should make sure that you are allocated one of the following roles if you want to have full administrative powers with these two toolkits:

- Teams Administrator
- Global Administrator

> **Note:** For more information on the admin roles in Teams, visit To manage Teams, utilize the Microsoft Teams admin roles. For more information on managing Teams with PowerShell cmdlets, see the Microsoft Teams cmdlet reference.

Demo 1-03: Explore the Microsoft Teams Admin Center

1.   In the Microsoft 365 admin center, select the Teams admin center under All admin centers. Notice that a new tab opens.

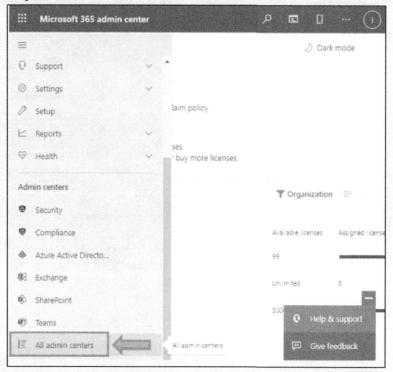

2. Choose any option to view the details.

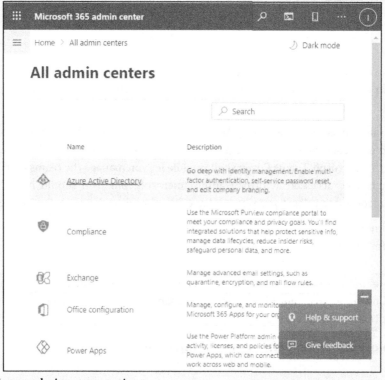

3. Click on the Teams admin center option.

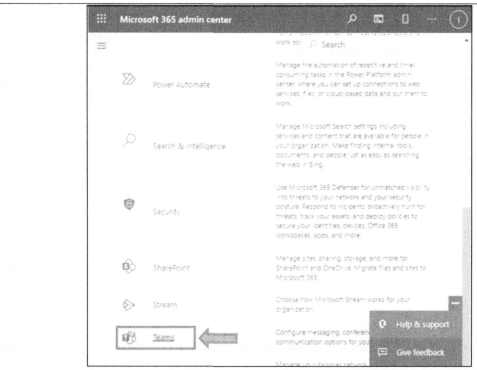

4. In the Teams admin center, you can view the available options in terms of Teams, Manage Teams, Team settings, policies, etc.

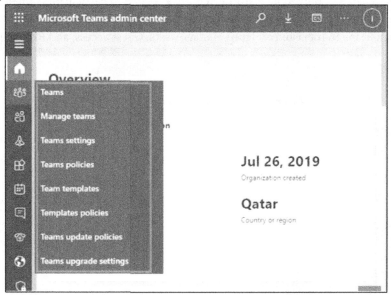

Note: The dashboard shows cards for organization information, deployment status, recent activity, user searches, helpful links, and more.

5. Use the navigation pane on the left to manage settings for Teams, Users, Meetings, Locations, and more.

6. Admins can configure policies for Teams, including Meeting policies, Messaging policies, Updating policies, creating Policy packages, and more.

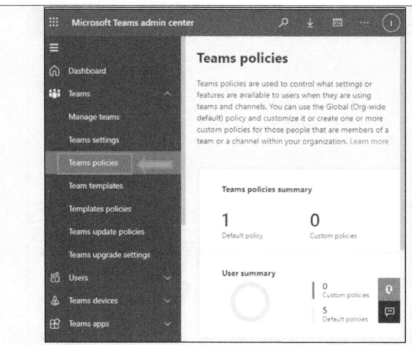

Note: Policies are used across the Microsoft Teams service to ensure the experience end-users receive conforms to the organization's needs.

- A **policy package** is a collection of predefined policies and settings.
- **Meeting policies** control the features that are available to participants in meetings.
- **Messaging policies** control which chat and channel messaging features are available to users.

7. Under **Users,** administrators can configure Manage users, Guest access, and External access settings.

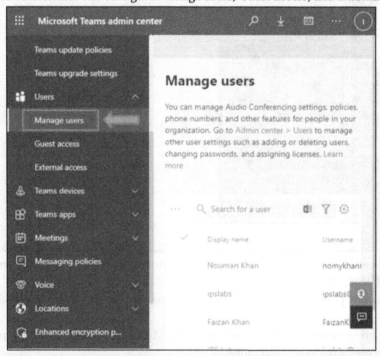

8. **Guest access** lets individuals outside your organization access teams and channels.

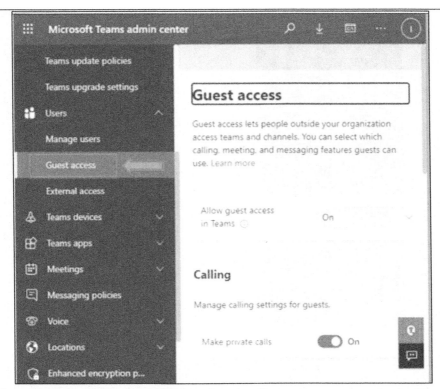

9. **External access,** formerly known as a **federation,** lets Teams users communicate with users outside your organization.

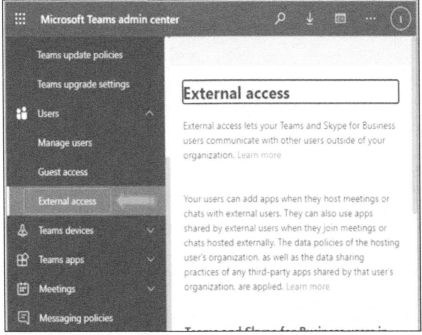

10. The policy package option will give you multiple options to define the packages, manage, and group the package assignment.

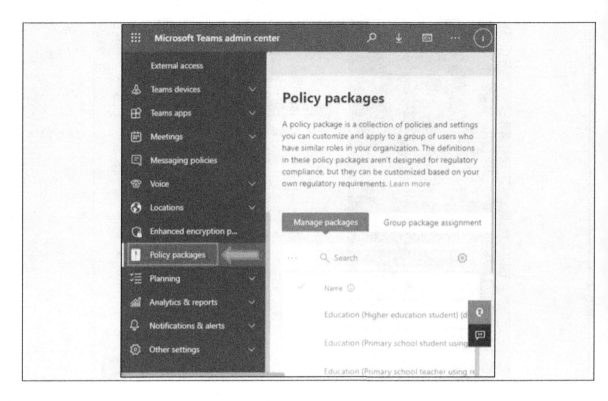

Mind Map

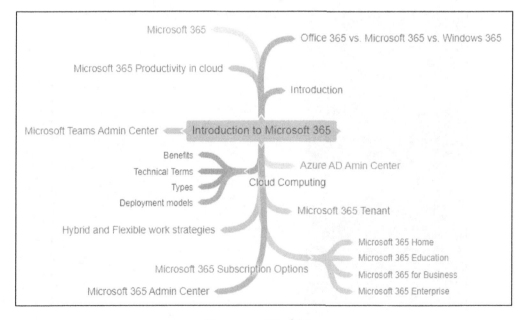

Figure 1-04 Mind Map

Practice Questions

1. What are the most recent operating systems?
A. Windows 10 and 11.
B. Windows 8 and 9
C. Windows 6 and 7
D. None of the above

2. What is a policy package?
A. A collection of user-defined policies and settings
B. A collection of predefined policies and settings
C. A collection of user-defined and predefined policies and settings
D. None of the above

3. What is Microsoft 365?
A. A cloud-based subscription service including   a portfolio of integrated goods like Office applications, Teams, Windows, top-notch security, and more
B. A cloud-based automation and configuration solution
C. Templates that are created with Bicep
D. None of the above

4. What is Microsoft 365 Fundamentals?
A. A managed service for security
B. Teams users communicate with users who are outside of your organization
C. Your gateway and guide to everything Microsoft 365
D. None of the above

5. What is the function of messaging policies?
A. Updates APIs
B. Control which chat and channel messaging features are available to users
C. It lets individuals outside your organization access teams and channels
D. None of the above

6. What is the full form of MFA?
A. Multi-Factor Authentication
B. Multi-Framing Authentication
C. Multi-Factoring Authentication
D. Multiplication of Factor Authentication

7. How can we set up an E5 subscription?
A. Select Groups under Manage
B. Select Set up E5 subscription from the Microsoft 365 E5 developer profile page
C. Choose Azure Active Directory
D. None of the above

8. How many types of options does Microsoft 365 Fundamentals offer?
A. 4
B. 6
C. 3
D. 5

9. What are meeting policies?
A. Control the features that are available to participants in meetings.
B. A collection of predefined policies and settings
C. Controls which chat and channel messaging features are available to users.
D. None of the above

10. How many types of sandboxes are there?
A. 3
B. 2
C. 5
D. 6

11. What is the time duration of the Microsoft 365 Developer Program?
A. 90-day duration
B. 10-day duration
C. 100-day duration
D. None of the above

12. How many licenses does Microsoft 365 Developer Program provide?
A. 30 licenses
B. 25 licenses
C. 21 licenses
D. 20 licenses

13. What settings can be configured by administrators under users?
A. Guest access and External access
B. Guest access
C. External access
D. None of the above

14. What is External access formerly known as _____.

A. Event Hubs
B. Microsoft Teams service
C. Federation
D. Cloud

15. What does Infrastructure-as-a-Service mean?
A. Services on CSP that are updated automatically to provide a stable infrastructure for your applications
B. The layer of services that enable a complete cloud infrastructure for your business

C. Any hardware service provided by CSP, such as Virtual Machines and Virtual Networks

D. Any service on Azure that you can rent and do not have to buy upfront

16. A cloud server is being migrated to Azure. External users can access the web application. To reduce the administrative effort needed to manage the web application, which service would you suggest from the following?

A. IaaS

B. SaaS

C. FaaS

D. PaaS

17. Which of the following offers Microsoft Office 365?

A. SaaS

B. IaaS

C. FaaS

D. PaaS

Chapter 02: Productivity Solutions in Microsoft 365

Introduction

Working wherever and whenever is the meaning of productivity in today's world. Industry-leading tools are conveyed and delivered by Microsoft 365, powered by Artificial Intelligence (AI) that unbridles the creativity and potential embedded inside. Microsoft 365 has been playing a significant role in providing solutions to the problems we face. With the help of Microsoft 365, we can easily get our hands on the versatility of its apps like Word, Excel, PowerPoint, OneNote, and Outlook. Apps like Exchange offer us an intuitive email box with a calendar. Microsoft 365's work management tools help us spend more time on our work and less time managing it. Such tools include Project, Planner, Bookings, and To-Do.

All of these solutions have been combined into a connected platform by Microsoft. Discover how Microsoft 365's productivity tools improve operations, engage users, and enable workers to carry out activities in real-time from almost anywhere.

Core Productivity Tools in Microsoft 365

Microsoft 365 helps us ace productivity through its variety of productivity tools. Below are given the tools that will assist in achieving productivity.

- **All-time collaboration**: Microsoft Teams is an app that helps us connect to the world with its astounding capabilities. Distance is never an obtrusion in MS Teams; you can easily chat, call and collaborate anytime, anywhere
- **Creation of content in real-time**: Microsoft 365 enables teammates, classmates, or family members to give a new perspective to their ideas with apps like Word, Excel, PowerPoint, and OneNote
- **Initiation of a cohesive file-sharing experience:** OneDrive cloud storage helps us share and access files easily anywhere
- **Engaging and informing an organization**: Share files, data, news, knowledge, and resources with your project team, department, and organization through the assistance of SharePoint
- **Staying connected**: You can send, receive, and manage emails with Outlook. Use the built-in calendar to keep a good track of appointments and events happening around you
- **Working smartly with business-class email and calendaring**: Get a customized inbox, an organized way to read and engage with email and an automated event recording on your calendar via Exchange
- **Organizing well-endowed content tasks**: We can organize teamwork using the Planner's easy, collaborative, and visual task management
- **Staying on the right track seamlessly**: Through Project, you can easily organize your projects with the capability of dynamic scheduling depending on the effort required, project length, and allocated team members
- **Simplifying lineups to save time**: Customize appointment data, booking criteria, and service providers to streamline the booking process for you and your clients

Increments in Productivity through Microsoft 365 Apps

Microsoft 365 Tools is a collection of apps that help you stay connected and productive. Create beautiful content, collaborate in real-time, and transform data into insights with Microsoft 365 Apps. Microsoft 365 Apps are offered in two subscriptions: Microsoft 365 Apps for Business and Microsoft 365 Apps for Enterprise. These programs include the Office suite, which includes Word, Excel, PowerPoint, OneNote, Outlook, Teams, Publisher, and Access (Publisher and Access are only available on PC).

Microsoft 365 Apps offers the benefits of the cloud, allowing you to work from anywhere, any time, on any device, and be more productive.

- **Working across multiple devices:** Depending on your package or plan, you can install Microsoft 365 apps on up to five PCs or Macs and five tablets (iPad, Windows, or Android). You may transfer the installation if you change devices. Microsoft 365 mobile applications allow you to view and modify files on the go
- **Working with up-to-date apps:** You do not have to waste time installing updates or wondering when new features will be available because it is all taken care of for you. You and your coworkers will always be working with the most recent features
- **Working inventively through connected experiences:** To assist you in completing tasks more quickly and producing great content, connected experiences assess your material and make recommendations to help you better your job. For example, obtain design advice from PowerPoint Designer, editing and proofreading suggestions from Word Editor, and automated bibliography updates from Word Researcher

> **EXAM TIP:** Connected experiences assess your material and make recommendations to help you better your job.

Features of connected experiences:

- Use built-in intelligence capabilities like Microsoft Editor and Researcher to produce impressive documents and enhance your writing skills
- Excel may assist you in simplifying complex data and creating simple spreadsheets and visuals
- With sophisticated tools like Presenter Coach and PowerPoint Designer, PowerPoint can help you produce professional presentations that stand out effortlessly
- Outlook allows you to manage your email, calendar, tasks, and contacts all in one location
- OneNote may assist you with your note-taking requirements by arranging your notes into tabs and subsections, resulting in a single digital notebook

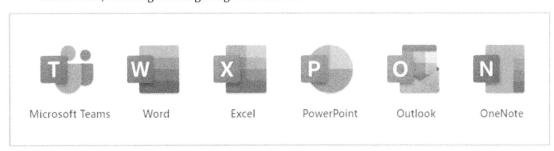

Figure 2-01: Microsoft 365 Apps

Work Management Tools in Microsoft 365

Your team is not productive if it is always managing tasks. To concentrate on producing high-quality work on schedule, you and your team need an effective procedure for managing work. Through a suite of specifically designed tools that add structure to all the components that go into producing high-quality business results, such as tasks, status updates, schedules, and projects, Microsoft 365 streamlines job management. Your team will have more time to work together on the actual project if the work process is handled more effectively.

Work management solutions from Microsoft 365 enable your employees to work the way they want, providing companies with the outcomes they want. The Project, Planner, Bookings, and To Do are among the job management tools provided. Each tool is built with unique characteristics to allow you to select the ideal tool to assist you in managing your specific sort of job.

Note: Project, Planner, Bookings, and To Do are among the job management tools provided in Microsoft 365.

Microsoft Project

Project is a strong project management application intended for more complicated work initiatives. Microsoft's current cloud-based work and project management option is Project for the Web. Project for the Web offers easy, robust work management tools that can be tailored to most needs and roles. Take on little undertakings as well as huge efforts. Regardless of team size, project managers and team members may utilize Project for the Web to plan and manage work involving dynamic scheduling, subtasks, and/or dependent tasks.

Note: Microsoft's latest cloud-based work and project management option is Project for the Web.

Features of Microsoft Project:

- Launch a project quickly and assign tasks and timelines while keeping team members and management on the same page
- The smart scheduling engine will automatically update the timetable, saving you time and effort
- Use simple views like grid views, Kanban-style task boards, and timeline Gantt charts
- Integrate with Teams to improve project collaboration
- Create visually attractive interactive dashboards with Power BI to see every part of the project at a glance
- Because Project is developed on the Power Platform, it is extensible to other platform apps and data

Figure 2-02 Microsoft Project

Microsoft Planner

The Planner is an easy-to-use, collaborative task management application that allows users to plan, organize, and accomplish task-based activities. Planner allows teams to schedule their work straightforwardly and visually. The Planner is a web-based application accessible from anywhere and has a mobile app for iOS and Android.

Features of Microsoft Planner

- Create a strategy to add structure to task-based teamwork and arrange the activities in your project
- Use task cards to assign and manage tasks on a Kanban board, and then add those tasks to buckets
- Due dates, status, priority, checklists, labels, and file attachments are all shown and can be accessed through task cards
- Keep track of deadlines by receiving alerts
- With vivid visual signals and built-in status reporting, you can keep track of your team's progress
- To summarize the state of your overall plan and particular tasks, use visualizations such as the task board, charts page, and a timetable view

Integrate with Teams by adding a "Tasks by Planner" tab, assign tasks with @mentions in Word, Excel, and PowerPoint, and add your plans to your Outlook calendar.

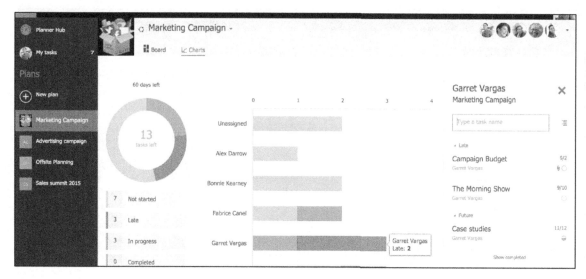

Figure 2-03 Microsoft Planner

Microsoft Bookings

Bookings is an appointment scheduling and management system accessible over the internet. Bookings makes it easier to schedule and manage appointments. It features a web-based booking calendar, interacts with Outlook to optimize your staff's schedule, and allows your clients to book at a time that works best for them.

> EXAM TIP: Microsoft Bookings features a web-based booking calendar and interacts with Outlook to optimize any schedule.

Features of Microsoft Bookings

- Using a web-based business-facing website, you may define appointment kinds and details, manage employee schedules, determine company hours, services, and pricing, and personalize how appointments are books
- Allow extra time between appointments for any pre-or post-appointment activity
- Create a booking page where your customers and clients may independently plan and reschedule appointments
- Share the booking page with a direct link, your Facebook page, or by embedding a link within your website
- With automated appointment notifications through email and SMS, you can ensure that consumers receive correct confirmations and reminders
- View your appointments, access client lists, and contact information, and make manual reservations on the fly with the business-facing mobile app
- Integrate with Microsoft Teams or Skype for Business to manage virtual appointments and Bookings calendars using the Bookings app in Teams

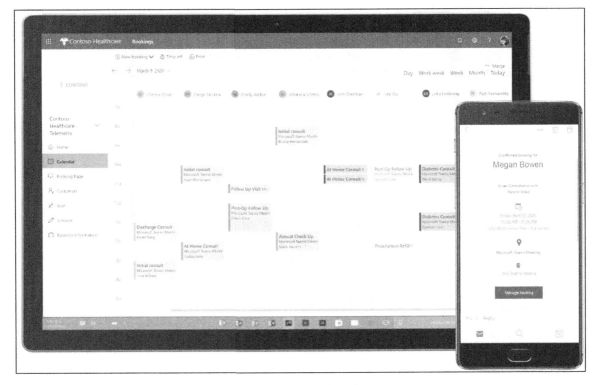

Figure 2-04 Microsoft Bookings

Microsoft To Do

To Do is an intelligent task management program that helps you plan and organize your day. To Do is a better, more personal, and intuitive method for individuals to remain organized and make the most of their days. It works with Outlook and Planner and is powered by Office 365 Exchange Online. To Do is accessible via iOS, Android, Windows, and the web. To Do encourages you to do the most critical tasks you need to get done every day, whether for work, school, or home.

EXAM TIP: Microsoft To Do works with Outlook and Planner and is powered by Office 365 Exchange Online.

Features of Microsoft To Do

- You can easily focus and achieve your most important tasks with a daily Microsoft to do list called "My Day"
- Utilization of smart suggestions to add tasks, upcoming or overdue tasks can be done
- You can get an overview of yesterday's achievements and tasks you could not meet
- The creation of lists for any occasion can be done with the ability to share lists with others
- You can break down more complex tasks into subtasks
- You can effortlessly create a separate list of tasks generated from flagged Outlook emails
- Scheduling of reminders and repeatable tasks can be done
- You can view your assigned tasks from Planner in To Do

Figure 2-05 Microsoft To Do

Business-class email and calendaring with Microsoft Exchange

Microsoft Exchange Online is a cloud-based messaging system that provides the functionality of the Microsoft Exchange Server. It allows users to access email, calendar, contacts, and tasks from PCs, the web, and mobile devices all in one location. It fully interfaces with all other Microsoft 365 workloads, making management simple.

Microsoft corporate email and calendaring assist you in staying on top of your work by providing a clear, uniform perspective of what is important.

> **EXAM TIP:** Microsoft Exchange Online is a cloud-based messaging system that provides the functionality of the Microsoft Exchange Server.

Features of Microsoft Exchange

- **Stay connected**: Microsoft 365 syncs your emails, calendars, and contact information across all of your devices, keeping you in the loop no matter where you are. All you need is an internet connection to stay in touch with ease. If you misplace your phone, you may remotely wipe data to keep your sensitive information safe
- **Customizing your email:** Create your format, integrate graphics, and use your domain name based on where you reside. You may save the emails that you require, including graphics
- **Collaboration:** Create a public folder for shared access to give an easy and effective way for other members of your workgroup or company to collect, organize, and exchange information. Create a shared mailbox where users may view and send email messages as well as share a calendar. Create

distribution groups, which are groupings of two or more receivers in the shared address book. When an email is sent to a distribution list, it is read by all members of the list

- **Sharing your calendar:** You may need to arrange schedules with colleagues from other organizations, friends and family members to collaborate on projects or plan social activities. Administrators may set up several degrees of calendar access in Exchange Online with Microsoft 365 and Office 365 to allow businesses to interact with others and individuals to share their calendars
- **Staying primed and up to date:** By integrating your LinkedIn and Microsoft 365 profiles, you may gain valuable insights about the individuals you work with both inside and outside your business
- **Streamlined administration**: Create new users, recover deleted accounts, and write custom scripts, among other things
- **Stay safe and protected:** Exchange has anti-spam and anti-malware security and anti-spam and anti-malware rules that can be customized. Defenders for Office 365 may be activated to provide an additional defense against sophisticated threats such as phishing, business email compromise, and malware assaults. The defender also protects against spoofing and gives mailbox intelligence to all receivers

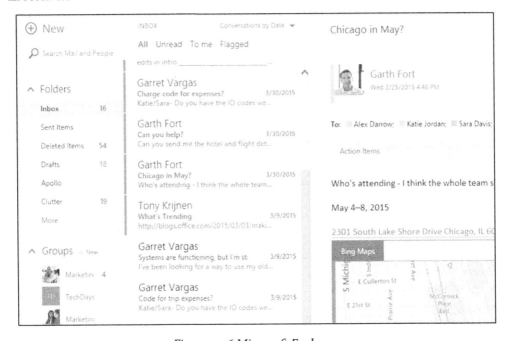

Figure 2-06 Microsoft Exchange

Mind Map

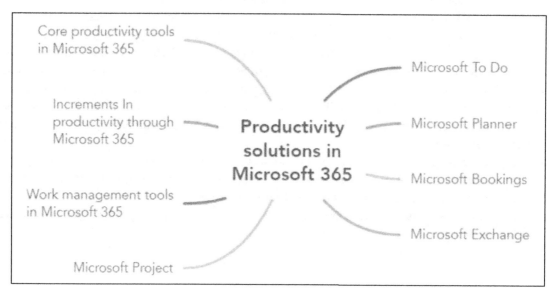

Figure 2-07: Mind Map

Practice Questions

1. What is the function of OneDrive?
   A. Keep a check on the organization's data.
   B. OneDrive cloud storage helps us share and access files easily anywhere.
   C. Both A and B
   D. None of the above

2. Which of the following provides an automated event recording on the calendar?
   A. Microsoft Exchange
   B. Microsoft Planner
   C. Microsoft Project
   D. Microsoft Bookings

3. Which of the following can be used for Dynamic scheduling?
   A. OneDrive
   B. Project
   C. Planner
   D. None of the above

4. Which of the following accesses material and makes recommendations to help you better your job?
   A. Windows
   B. Android
   C. Connected Experiences

D. PowerPoint

5. What do 'connected experiences' use to enhance writing in documents?
   A. Microsoft Editor
   B. Researcher
   C. Excel
   D. Both A and B

6. Which of the following can be used to produce Professional presentations?
   A. Sophisticated tools and PowerPoint Designer
   B. Presenter Coach and PowerPoint Designer
   C. Calendar and tasks
   D. None of the above

7. Which of the following arranges notes and tabs into a single digital notebook?
   A. Presenter Coach
   B. Microsoft Excel
   C. OneNote
   D. PowerPoint

8. Which of the following management tools are provided in Microsoft 365?
   A. Project, Planner, Bookings, and To Do
   B. Microsoft Word and Microsoft Excel
   C. PowerPoint and Planner
   D. None of the above

9. Which of the following is a Project for the Web?
   A. Website
   B. Webpage
   C. Microsoft's cloud-based work and project management
   D. None of the above

10. How can we create interactive dashboards to see every part of our project at a glance?
   A. With PowerBI
   B. With Kanban-Style Task Boards
   C. With Gantt Charts
   D. None of the above options

11. Microsoft Project is developed on _____.
   A. Power Platform
   B. GUI
   C. Smart scheduling engine
   D. Cloud

12. Microsoft Planner is a\an _____ application.
   A. Kanban
   B. Web-based
   C. iOS
   D. Android

13. The web-based booking calendar of Microsoft Bookings interacts with _____.
   A. Outlook
   B. Internet Explorer
   C. Mozilla Firefox
   D. Gmail

14. Microsoft To Do is powered by _____.
   A. Outlook
   B. Planner
   C. Office 365 Exchange Online
   D. All of the above

15. What is Microsoft Exchange Online?
A. Microsoft Exchange Server
B. Cloud-based Messaging System
C. Microsoft 365 Workloads
D. None of the above

Chapter 03: Collaboration Solutions in Microsoft 365

Introduction

People work together more often   in different groups and across multiple locations. They create, share, and collaborate on content to move their teams and organizations forward. Organizations need modern content management and collaboration solutions that are intelligent, secure, and integrated into their daily tools. Microsoft 365 has the tools required for these individuals to connect, collaborate, and get work done swiftly.

Teams provide engaging and inclusive meetings and real-time messaging to connect with colleagues wherever they are. Viva is an employee experience platform that supports organizations in creating a thriving culture with engaged employees and inspiring leaders. SharePoint lets you collaborate, share content and coordinate your work within your organization. OneDrive gives you secure access and file storage from anywhere. Yammer is an enterprise social connection that lets people engage and connect across the organization. Learn how these Microsoft 365 tools unlock new forms of collaboration to help people stay connected and engaged, ensuring fluid communication across organizations.

Collaboration Workloads of Teams

Microsoft Teams is a hub for teamwork. It is an app for people and teams to come together, stay connected, and get things done across work, home, school, and on the go. Teams help you pull together a team and connect with colleagues through real-time messaging and engaging and inclusive meetings. You can use channels to share files and data, manage tasks, and collaborate on documents with people inside and outside your organization. All these features can be done while staying secure and compliant. Make your own Teams by adding notes and websites and integrating them with your team's other apps and processes.

Users can access Teams through their internet browser or by installing Teams on their computer or mobile device. Teams has many features and functionalities to help your users connect and work together to get things done.

Teams and Channels

Teams encourage your users to organize and collaborate across projects and workloads. Get started by creating a **team** and **channel**.

- **Teams** are a group of people, content, and tools surrounding different organizational projects and outcomes. It is designed to bring together a group of people who work closely to get things done. Teams can be formed to be private to only invited users, or public and open to anyone within the company. A team has a limit of up to 10,000 simultaneous members
- **Channels** are assigned sections within a team to keep conversations organized by specific topics, projects, disciplines, or whatever works for your team. It is a place where users can discuss and get hands-on with work. Channels facilitate features like tabs and enable users to access and work on the same content. For instance, users in a team could have a channel with a tab for a specific report they are all contributing to. You share files in a channel (on the Files tab) stored in SharePoint
  - **Standard channels** can be open to all team members
  - **Private channels** are for selected team members

o **Shared channels** can select people both inside and outside the team

Figure 3-01: Teams and Channels

Chat and Instant Messaging

Chat and instant messaging let you work together without cluttering your email and keeping it clear for important messages. Instant messaging is ideal for checking something with a colleague or asking a quick question. You can also have a group discussion to encourage open discussion and promote thoughtful debate.

The following list describes some of the benefits of Teams chat and instant messaging:

- **Instantly connect.** Message a team member one-on-one or the entire team in a group chat
- **Take conversations anywhere.** Record voice messages while you are on the go, and reply to an instant text from your mobile device
- **Keep the team focused.** Manage your conversations, files, and apps in one place to keep the team in sync
- **Reduce email clutter.** Move email threads into quick chats. Share photos and files with one person or the team

Online Meetings

Meetings help teams share status updates, brainstorm ideas, and solve issues. Microsoft Teams is designed to help you have more productive meetings, collaborating through online meetings, webinars, live events, or audio and video conferencing. Microsoft Teams has many features that help your team quickly engage and improve how they work together through meetings.

- **Schedule and join meetings.** Users can join meetings through links, Teams calendar, or call into meetings using their phones. A user's calendar in Teams is connected to their Exchange calendar, so when users schedule a meeting in Outlook, their meeting is automatically visible and accessible from Teams and vice versa. Users can also start meetings whenever they want, without scheduling them
- **Manage different types of meetings.** Meetings, webinars, and live events are all kinds of meetings, but webinars and live events provide extra control for the organizer over the conversation and participants. Webinars provide two-way interaction, while live events offer a managed Q&A

experience. Teams can detect what is said in a meeting and present real-time captions with the speaker's attribution

- o **Meetings** in Teams include audio, video, and screen sharing for up to 1,000 people. View-only capabilities are for participants over 1,000 up to 20,000
- o **Webinars** are dynamic, hosted presentations or events that audiences remotely attend using a phone, tablet, or computer. Up to 1,000   participants have fully interactive capabilities
- o **Live events** engage and communicate with employees and customers with immersive video broadcasts and interactive discussions using Microsoft Stream, Microsoft Teams, or Yammer. Host live events with up to 20,000 participants
- **Audio conferencing.** Users can call into meetings from their phones. Calling or dialing into meetings is helpful for users on the road or when internet connectivity is limited. Audio conferencing allows up to 1000 phone attendees
- **Record and publish with Microsoft Stream.** Users can capture audio, video, and content by recording the meeting to share with people who could not attend and for future reference. Users can upload meeting recordings and notes in the meeting thread and publish the recordings to Microsoft Stream for archiving and wider usage. The stream can automatically transcript your recorded meetings through Artificial Intelligence (AI) powered translation
  - o **Microsoft Stream** is an enterprise video suite where people in your organization can upload, view, and share videos. You can watch your organization's trending and most popular videos. Video files for the stream are stored in SharePoint and can be accessed through Teams or Yammer integration
- **Custom backgrounds.** Users can blur their backgrounds or use custom backgrounds during meetings to avoid distractions, set the tone, and ensure privacy
- **Screen sharing and content sharing.** Users can share individual screens, windows, and files during a meeting. They can also use whiteboards to sketch ideas and share notes

Microsoft Teams Phone

Stay linked with voice and video calling using **Microsoft Teams Phone** on your computer, tablet, mobile device, or desk phone. Teams phone provides a secure, integrated calling program that unifies classic and modern calling features. You can start a call from chat, contact card, Outlook, or the Calls app, to save time and reduce costs. Teams phone has updated cloud calling features like voicemail transcription and group call pickup to elevate your experience beyond traditional calls. Your calls, voicemail, and call history move with you no matter where you decide to work. Transition calls from your home Wi-Fi to your cellular service while on the go, and then to your office Wi-Fi when you arrive, all from one number using Teams phone.

Figure 3-02: Microsoft Teams Phone

Extend Teams by Using Collaborative Apps

A **collaborative app** is a solution integrated or built into Teams that enables employees to work better, using the tools they already know. Microsoft Teams is an extensible platform that allows you to create custom applications.

> **EXAM TIP:** You can form apps for an individual, your team, your organization, or all Microsoft Teams users everywhere.

Some of the ways that you can use Teams using collaborative apps are:

- **Power BI** in Teams can empower your organization to collaborate with data to improve outcomes
- **Power Apps** can help you build apps to add directly to Teams by creating a tab
- **Power Automate** can help you automate tasks and processes all within Teams
- **Dynamics 365** and Teams integration can provide high-level details of your customers to ensure you have helpful context and can be prepared in customer meetings
- **Power Virtual Agents** allows you to create chatbots that can be integrated into Teams
- **Integrate with third-party partners and services** for more capabilities within Teams, like ServiceNow or Salesforce. Integration with third parties can be done through incoming and outgoing webhooks and connectors

Security and Compliance

Teams are built on Microsoft 365 groups, Microsoft Graph, and the same enterprise-level security, compliance, and manageability as the rest of Microsoft 365 and Office 365.

Core Employee Experience Capabilities in Microsoft Viva

Viva is an EXP (Employee Experience Platform) that empowers people and teams to be their best from anywhere. Viva brings communications, insights, knowledge, learning, and resources within everyday work and collaboration flow. Viva includes four modules – Viva Connections, Viva Insights, Viva Topics, and Viva Learning.

Viva Connections

Viva Connections was formed to keep everyone in the workforce connected. Today, Microsoft 365 has many capabilities for employee communications and engagement. We have SharePoint, Yammer, Teams, and Stream. Viva Connections brings all of these capabilities into a company-branded app in Teams. It is a gateway to the employee experience, with personalized news, communications, tasks, people, and resources. It offers a single curated employee destination that can be configured for specific roles like frontline workers. Leaders can discuss and engage their employees, and employees can easily access the tools and resources they need from one place.

Viva Connections offers added functionality through three primary components described in the following list:

- **Dashboard.** The dashboard is your employee's digital toolset. It brings together the tools and resources your employees need, enabling quick and easy access whether they are in the office or the field. The dashboard uses dynamic cards that employees can interact with to complete simple tasks such as time-off requests or review health checks
- **Feed.** The feed posts update to the right people at the right time with powerful targeting and scheduling capabilities. It is closely integrated with Yammer, SharePoint news, and stream to display a personalized and relevant feed based on post-level targeting of the group's employees
- **Resources.** The resource's experience enables a way to navigate across platforms. It provides users with a familiar navigation structure from the SharePoint app bar and allows them to open sites, pages, news, and more

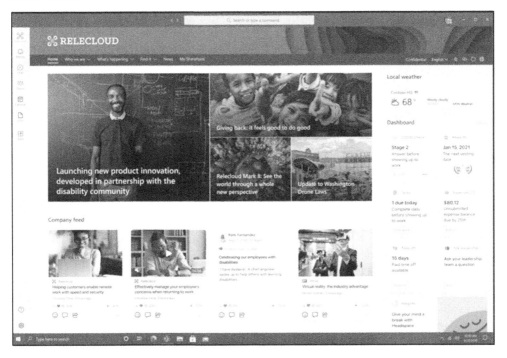

Figure 3-03: Viva Connections

Viva Insights

Viva Insights provides privacy-protected insights and actionable recommendations that help everyone in the organization work smarter and achieve balance. Viva Insights is accessed in Microsoft Teams. It uses quantitative and qualitative data to empower individuals, managers, and leaders to improve organizational productivity and wellbeing.

- **Individuals** - These insights provide personal insights that only you can see. The insights will help you identify opportunities to change how you might work so you can do your best work. Get actionable recommendations, such as recharging with a quick mental break, protecting time for focused work, and mindfully disconnecting after hours to help you improve your wellbeing and boost productivity
- **Managers** - These insights give managers much-needed visibility into work patterns that might lead to burnout and stress. These include regular after-hours work, meeting overload, or too little focus time. Viva Insights can provide managers with recommendations like encouraging their team to turn off notifications and set calendar boundaries and daily priorities to focus on what matters most to help foster a healthy and successful work environment. Viva Insights in Microsoft Workplace Analytics also has advanced analysis tools and templates for customized, deep-diving into data shown to managers
- **Organizations** - These insights can help company leaders address complex challenges and respond to change by shedding light on organizational work patterns and trends. Leaders can see how their work culture affects their organizational resiliency and boosts employee engagement. Viva Insights can provide recommendations on the outcomes page to see opportunities where a change could improve both employee experience and business outcomes. Viva Insights in Microsoft Workplace Analytics also has advanced analysis tools and templates for customized, deep-diving into data that is shown to leaders

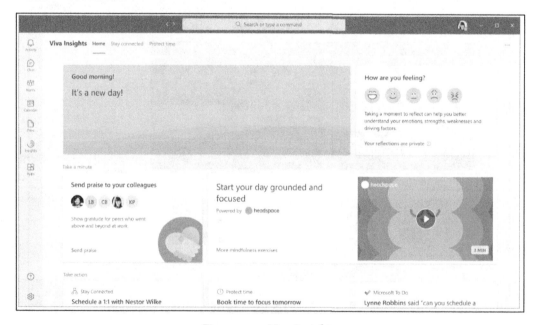

Figure 3-04: Viva Insights

Viva Topics

Viva Topics focuses on knowledge and expertise. It uses Artificial Intelligence (AI) to identify knowledge and experts and organizes them into shared topics. Viva Topics helps address many companies' critical business issues: providing users with information when needed. For example, new employees need to learn a lot of information quickly and encounter terms they know nothing about when reading company information. Viva Topics brings knowledge to your users in the Microsoft 365 apps they use daily.

AI automatically forms a topic page for each topic. The topic page gives you more details, including definitions, relevant people, and resources across Microsoft 365, and external sources like ServiceNow. These topic pages surface as topic cards in apps like Office, SharePoint, and Microsoft Teams. When employees select a card, a topic page appears with documents, videos, and related people.

The topics are displayed to users through:

- Topics highlighted on SharePoint pages
- Topic answers in search results
- Search in office applications
- Topic center homepage

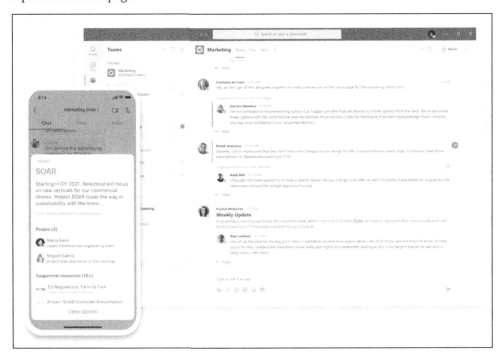

Figure 3-05: Viva Topics

Viva Learning

Viva Learning is a learning hub in Microsoft Teams that lets you seamlessly integrate learning and building skills into your day. In Viva Learning, your team can discover, share, advise, and learn from your organization's and your partners' content libraries.

Viva Learning allows employees to quickly discover informal and formal learning in the workflow. It takes content from LinkedIn Learning, Microsoft Learn, third-party training, and your internal content in one place. Along with AI providing aggregation and recommendations, it allows managers to assign, track, and report on training within and across multiple teams.

There are three main views in the Viva Learning app:

- **Home** - Discover new content and trending content, and browse learning content libraries
- **My Learning** - Access your recommendations and assignments, bookmarked, recently viewed, and completed courses
- **Manage** - Track the progress of recommendations that you made

Figure 3-06: Viva Learning

Features of SharePoint and OneDrive Promote Collaboration

When it comes to filing storage, you want your work to be accessible and secure. You want to be able to work with co-authors, and share files, both inside and outside your organization. **SharePoint** and **OneDrive** enable you to access, share, and collaborate on your files from anywhere.

SharePoint

SharePoint, the intelligent intranet, can help you transform employee communications and digital experiences. It is a rich collaboration tool for creating websites, publishing content, and storing files.

The intranet is at the core of many organizations, where employees can stay informed on company news and information, collaborate on content, and connect with colleagues. SharePoint provides three main types of sites to help you create your intranet and foster communication and collaboration across your teams and organization:

- **Team sites** are collaboration sites to connect you and your team to share content and resources. Team sites provide file storage and sharing, co-authoring of documents, managing lists of

information, and workflow integration with Power Automate and file libraries. It can also be integrated with Microsoft Teams

- **Communication sites** are designed to broadcast information to other teams or an entire organization. These sites are perfect for sharing company news, announcements, events, internal cross-company campaigns, status updates, and product launches. Use communication sites to engage and inform broad audiences
- **Hub sites** are used to organize families of team sites and communication sites together. It provides a connection point and central portal for these groups of related teams or communication sites. Hub sites make it easier for users to discover related content, such as news and other site activities

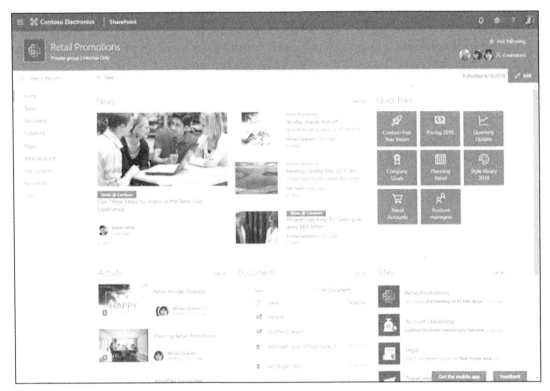

Figure 3-07: SharePoint

OneDrive

OneDrive is the underlying technology that powers the collaborative files experience across Microsoft 365. OneDrive is a cloud-based service that enables you to access, share, and collaborate on files from anywhere. OneDrive lets users view files within a browser, share and find content, and sync that content so they can access it offline. You can work with others inside or outside your organization and terminate sharing whenever you want. OneDrive also empowers your organization to control, secure, and retain content when necessary.

The following list describes how OneDrive empowers you and your team to collaborate in real-time to deliver the right results:

- **Access files from all your devices.** Access and store your personal and shared files on all your devices, containing phone, Mac, and PC, as well as in a browser

- **Manage files on the go.** Users can create, view, edit, and share files on the go with the OneDrive mobile app. They can easily capture whiteboards and scan work receipts, business cards, and other paper documents for safekeeping
- **Seamless collaboration with files.** Document co-authoring capabilities are available across all devices, helping you maintain a single working version of any file. View @mentions, comments, and activity on the details pane of your files when working with a team
- **Share inside or outside your organization.** Securely share files with users inside or outside your organization using their email addresses, even if they do not have a Microsoft account. Work in real-time through the web, mobile, and desktop versions of OneDrive
- **Quickly find files that matter most.** Finding content in your OneDrive is simplified through the intelligence of the Microsoft Graph application programming interface. This feature simplifies finding what is important by providing file recommendations based on your relationship with other people, how you received various files, and when you last accessed them
- **Protect your files with enterprise-grade security.** OneDrive has many security and compliance features, enabling you to meet some of the strictest compliance requirements

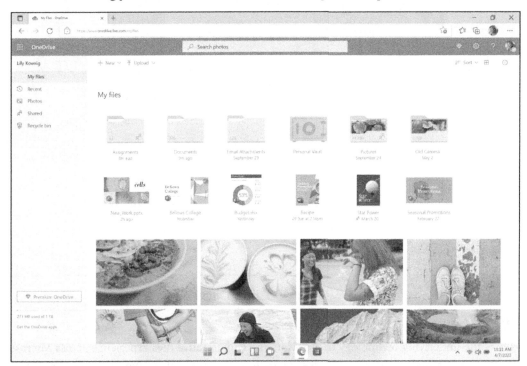

Figure 3-08: OneDrive

Yammer Helps Communities Connect and Grow

Yammer is an enterprise social network internal to an organization. Yammer enables leaders and coworkers to connect and engage from anywhere to share ideas, co-create culture, align on strategy, and innovate. It was designed to help you connect with people you might not work with directly across your organization, and Yammer helps facilitate community collaboration and idea-sharing for your organization. Access Yammer through your browser, or you can install Yammer on your desktop or mobile device.

Yammer supports both internal and external networks to help users communicate and collaborate. An **internal network** is restricted to users inside the organization, while an **external network** is open to users outside the organization's domain. Users in external networks must be invited. External networks are considered extensions of and are always associated with a single internal network. Your organization can have more than one Yammer network.

The following list describes how Yammer helps connect leaders and employees to build communities, share knowledge, and engage everyone:

Leader Engagement

- Align people toward a shared vision and objectives to drive organizational change
- Foster two-way dialogue between employees and leaders with a leadership community
- Broadcast company meetings with live events and real-time Q&A
- Communicate at scale with a site for leaders to share news, events, blogs, and polls

Modernize employee communication

- Keep everyone informed and engaged across web and mobile
- Share news and announcements that reach users as interactive discussions in Microsoft Teams and Outlook
- Target specific communities or reach your entire organization using the All Company Community
- Pin and feature meaningful conversations and send important announcements to ensure the delivery of critical information
- Create compelling communications with rich text, GIFs, photos, and videos

Knowledge Sharing

- Share knowledge, best practices, ideas, and feedback across the organization
- Use questions and answers to gain solutions, highlight the best answers, and upvote replies
- Call in experts with @mentions
- Extend the power of experts with FAQ bots that can auto-respond to common questions
- Follow topics across conversations and communities with tags

Engage your employees

- Ensure that every voice within the organization is heard
- Provide communities for employees to connect, share, and build relationships
- Find and join recommended communities around shared interests
- Designate official communities where employees can find what they need and join the discussion
- Empower employees to express and represent themselves with inclusive reactions

Powering communities in Microsoft 365

- Engage in fully interactive discussions without leaving your Outlook inbox
- Bring the power of communities to SharePoint with the Yammer conversations web part
- Embed a Yammer community on any HTML page
- Collaborate on Office files and Excel documents within Yammer
- In-line video playing and auto-transcription with Microsoft Stream
- Instantly translate messages in 60+ languages

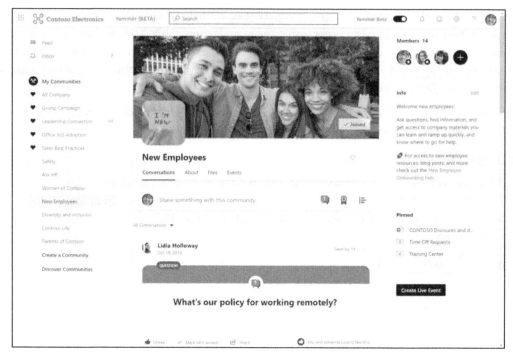

Figure 3-09: Powering communities in Microsoft 365

Mind Map

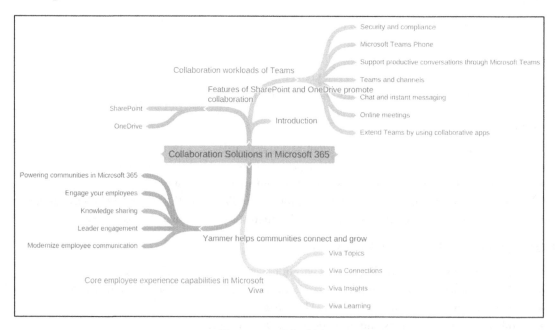

Figure 3-10: Mind Map

Practice Questions

1. You are managing a project with people working in different locations. You encourage more frequent and informal communication via online meetings and chat to improve collaboration and teamwork. Which Microsoft product is most suitable?
   A. SharePoint
   B. Teams
   C. OneDrive
   D. None of the above

2. Microsoft Viva includes which four modules?
   A. Viva Connections, Viva Insights, Viva Topics, and Viva Learning
   B. Viva Connections, Viva Insights, Viva Topics, and Viva Resources
   C. Viva Communications, Viva Insights, Viva Topics, and Viva Learning
   D. All of the above

3. You have recently been asked to manage a project that includes people inside and outside your organization. You have to share files with everyone on the project. Which Microsoft product is most suitable?
   A. Outlook
   B. Yammer
   C. OneDrive
   D. None of the above

4. Which types of sites can you create in SharePoint to foster communication and collaboration across your team and organization?
   A. Team sites, Channel sites, and Hub sites
   B. Team sites, Communication sites, and Hub sites
   C. Team sites, Communication sites, and Group sites
   D. None of the above

5. Your organization is launching an important new product. You want to host a significant online event to announce to your industry. You will have several people speaking plus videos. Which combination of Microsoft products should you use to host the event?
   A. PowerPoint, SharePoint, and Stream
   B. Teams, SharePoint, and Stream
   C. Yammer, Teams, and Stream
   D. None of the above

6. Power _____ in Teams can empower your organization to collaborate with data to deliver improved outcomes.
   A. BI
   B. Apps
   C. Automate
   D. All of the above

7. Viva Connections offers added functionality through _____ primary components.
   A. One
   B. Two
   C. Three
   D. Four

8. Yammer supports _____ network/s to help users communicate and collaborate.
   A. Internal
   B. External
   C. Both of the above
   D. None of the above

9. An _____ network is restricted to users inside the organization.
   A. Internal
   B. External
   C. Both of the above
   D. None of the above

10. An _____ network is open to users outside the organization's domain.
   A. Internal
   B. External
   C. Both of the above
   D. None of the above

Chapter 04: Endpoint Modernization, Management Concepts, and Deployment Options in Microsoft 365

Introduction

As organizations move more of their workload to the cloud, they can now have employees work from any location and device. Microsoft has built comprehensive cloud computer management solutions as a cloud provider and Operating System (OS) provider. These solutions provide IT departments with remote computer configurations and simplified management tools.

Microsoft Endpoint Manager helps you deploy and manage your organization's devices and Microsoft 365 Apps while delivering a better end-user experience. Windows-as-a-service is a way to simplify the lives of IT pros and maintain a consistent Windows experience for its users through more frequent updates. Windows 365, the new Cloud PC, securely streams your personalized Windows experience to any device, including all your apps, content, and settings. Azure Virtual Desktop, a Virtual Desktop Infrastructure (VDI) solution, allows you to quickly deploy virtual desktops and apps to enable secure remote work. These solutions allow you to meet security and productivity needs while providing a streamlined user experience in a changing workforce.

Endpoint Management Capabilities of Microsoft 365

In today's workplace, IT departments support different devices configured differently. Your organization might have Android and iOS mobile phones, Windows and macOS PCs, and custom devices your users bring to work. **Microsoft 365** provides the tools and services to enable you to simplify the management of all these devices through **Microsoft Endpoint Manager (MEM).**

MEM is a secure and intelligent management solution that improves productivity and collaboration with the familiar experiences users expect. MEM allows IT to support diverse scenarios for Bringing Your Own Device (BYOD) and corporate-owned devices. MEM helps you solve the device management challenge in today's mobile and remote work environment.

Endpoint Manager mixes services you may know and already be using.

Microsoft Endpoint Manager includes the following service and capabilities:

- **Microsoft Intune.** Intune is a 100% cloud-based MDM (Mobile Device Management) and MAM (Mobile Application Management) provider for your apps and devices. It combines with other services, including Azure Active Directory (Azure AD), mobile threat defenders, ADMX templates, Win32, and custom LOB apps. Create and check compliance, and deploy apps, features, and settings to your devices using the cloud

- **Configuration Manager.** Configuration Manager is an on-premises management way to operate your network's desktops, servers, and laptops. You can cloud-enable it to combine with Intune, Azure AD, and other various cloud services. Use Configuration Manager to install apps, software updates, and operating systems, monitor compliance, and act on clients in real time

- **Co-management.** Co-management mixes your existing on-premises Configuration Manager investment with the cloud using Intune and other Microsoft 365 cloud services. You decide whether Configuration Manager or Intune is the management authority for the several different workload groups
- **Desktop Analytics.** Desktop Analytics is a cloud-based service that combines with Configuration Manager. It offers insight and intelligence for you to make more informed conclusions about the update readiness of your Windows clients. The service mixes data from your organization with data aggregated from millions of devices linked to the Microsoft cloud. It offers information on security updates, apps, and devices in your organization and identifies compatibility issues with apps and drivers
- **Windows Autopilot.** It is built to simplify the lifecycle of Windows devices for both IT and end-users, from initial deployment through end-of-life. You can use Autopilot to pre-configure devices and automatically enroll devices in Intune. You can also integrate Autopilot with Configuration Manager and co-management for more complex device configurations.
- **Azure AD.** Endpoint Manager uses Azure AD to identify devices, users, groups, and Multi-Factor Authentication (MFA). Azure AD Premium, which may be an extra cost, has other features to help protect devices, apps, and data, including dynamic groups, auto-enrollment, and conditional access
- **Endpoint Manager admin center.** This admin center is a one-stop website to create policies and manage your devices. It plugs in key device management services, including groups, security, conditional access, and reporting. This admin center also shows devices managed by Configuration Manager and Intune.

Compare Capabilities of Windows 365 and Azure Virtual Desktop.

Windows 365 and **Azure Virtual Desktop** services are virtual desktop solutions, also known as Desktop-as-a-Service. Now explore some of the different capabilities of each.

Windows 365

Windows 365 is a cloud-based service that automatically creates a new type of Windows virtual machine, known as **Cloud PCs,** for your end-users. Securely stream the full Windows experience, including apps, data, and settings, from the Microsoft cloud to any personal or corporate device. Windows 365 provides the productivity, security, and collaboration benefits of Microsoft 365. Windows 365 is optimized for simplicity with predictable per-user pricing.

Windows 365 has the following capabilities:

- Personalized Windows 365 Cloud PCs are available across devices
- Install your apps, data, content, and settings from the Microsoft cloud to any device and pick up where you left off
- Simple to deploy and operate from a single console
- Uses a local profile that is stored directly on the cloud PC
- Easily set up Cloud PCs based on your requirements and securely support changing workforce needs and new business scenarios
- Native integration across Azure Active Directory, Microsoft Defender, Microsoft 365 applications, and Microsoft Endpoint Manager

- Windows 365 is provisioned for you once a license is assigned to you
- Dedicated to a single user

Windows 365 is available in two subscription offerings:

- **Windows 365 Business** is explicitly done for smaller organizations (up to 300 seats) who want ready-to-use Cloud PCs with simple management options
- **Windows 365 Enterprise** is for larger organizations that want unlimited seats for creating Cloud PCs. It includes options to create custom Cloud PCs based on your created device images, more management options, and full integration with Microsoft Endpoint Manager

Figure 4-01: Windows 365

Azure Virtual Desktop

Azure Virtual Desktop (AVD) is a modern and secure desktop and app virtualization solution on Azure. AVD allows users to connect to a Windows desktop running in the cloud, and it is the only solution that delivers multi-session on Windows. AVD optimizes Microsoft 365 Apps for Enterprise, simplifies management with Citrix and VMware, and supports Remote Desktop Service environments. AVD is optimized for flexibility with flexible consumption-based pricing.

Azure Virtual Desktop has the following capabilities:

- Set up a multi-session Windows Client deployment with scalability that delivers a full Windows experience
- Present Microsoft 365 Apps for Enterprise and optimize it to run in multi-user virtual scenarios
- Provide Windows 7 virtual desktops with free Extended Security Updates
- Bring your existing Remote Desktop Services (RDS) and Windows Server desktops and apps to any computer
- Virtualize both desktops and apps
- Manage desktops and apps from different Windows and Windows Server operating systems with a unified management experience
- Uses FSLogix profile container technology
- Dedicated to a single user or used by multiple users

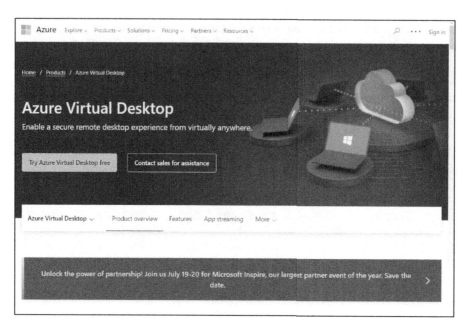

Figure 4-02: Azure Virtual Desktop

Microsoft Office 365 ProPlus

Office ProPlus is a part of Microsoft Office included with our Microsoft 365 license. Like other versions of Microsoft Office, it consists of Access, Excel, OneDrive, OneNote, Outlook, PowerPoint, Publisher, and Skype for Business, Teams, and Word. It is a complete version of the application suite, with the same features and functionality as other versions. Although Office ProPlus is related to other versions of Microsoft Office, there are also differences, which are contained below:

- **For Personal Use:** Unlike other versions of Office on campus, Office ProPlus is supposed to be installed on your systems only (e.g., your home PC or iPad)

- **Licensing:** The licensing model for Office ProPlus is like a subscription - if you remove your subscription, you lose functionality. Suppose you do not connect to the internet after 30 days. In that case, Office ProPlus will go into reduced functionality mode (once you link to the internet again and your status is verified, all features and functionality will be retrieved)

- **Installation & Deployment:** Thanks to Microsoft's "Click-to-Run" technology, you can install Office ProPlus in minutes. You can install this yourself - on your home computer - without the need for additional media or license keys

Deployment and Release Models for Windows-as-a-Service (WaaS)

Windows client is a comprehensive desktop operating system that allows you to work efficiently and securely. It is essential to keep the desktop operating system up to date because it helps devices run efficiently and stay protected. The WaaS model is designed to simplify life for users and IT professionals, and WaaS maintains a consistent and current Windows client experience for users.

Release Types

With Windows client, there are two release types:

- **Feature updates** add new functionality and are released twice a year. Because these updates are more frequent, they are smaller. There are many benefits:
  - There is less disruption and effort to apply new features
  - Users are more productive with early access to new Windows features and take less time to adapt to more minor changes
  - The workload and cost impact of updating Windows is reduced
- **Quality updates** provide security and reliability fixes. These updates are issued monthly as **non-security releases** or **combined security + non-security releases.** Non-security releases allow IT admins to do an early validation of content. In addition, a cumulative update is released, which includes all previous updates. There are a couple of benefits, including:
  - Identified security issues are fixed and deployed quickly, helping to keep devices secure
  - Everyone receives security fixes regularly, keeping all devices aligned

Servicing Channels

Servicing channels are the first way to direct users into deployment groups for feature and quality updates. There are three servicing channels, and each chain channel provides different levels of flexibility when these updates are delivered to client computers.

- **Windows Insider Program** lets organizations test and provide feedback on features shipped in the next update. These features will be delivered during the development cycle. This process will allow organizations to see exactly what Microsoft is developing and start testing as soon as possible. Microsoft recommends that all organizations enroll at least a few devices in this program
- **General Availability Channel** offers new functionality with feature update releases annually. Organizations can choose when to deploy updates. This model is ideal for pilot deployments and testing of feature updates, and it is also ideal for users such as developers who have to work with the latest features
- **A long-term servicing channel** is designed for specialist devices that do not run Office apps, such as medical equipment or ATMs. This channel receives new features every two or three years

Deployment Rings

Deployment rings are a deployment method that separates devices into a deployment timeline, and Microsoft has found that a ring-based deployment works well. Each "ring" contains a group of users or devices that receive a particular update.

A common ring structure utilizes three deployment groups:

- **Preview** is for planning and development
  - The goal of the preview ring is to explain the update's new features
- **Limited** is for pilot and validation
  - The goal of the limited ring is to validate the update on representative devices across the network
- **Broad** is for wide deployment

- o Once the devices in the limited ring have had a sufficient stabilization period, it is time for broad deployment across the network

Deployment Methods for Windows

To successfully deploy Windows in your organization, it is important to understand how it can be deployed. There are three types of deployment categories or methods:

- **Modern deployment methods** embrace traditional on-premises and cloud services to deliver a streamlined, cost-effective deployment experience. These methods are recommended and are supported by existing tools such as Microsoft Deployment Toolkit (MDT) and Microsoft Endpoint Configuration Manager
- **Dynamic deployment methods** let you configure applications and settings for specific use cases without having to deploy a new custom organization image to the device
- **Traditional deployment methods** use existing tools to install operating system images

Modern Deployment Methods

- **Windows Autopilot** allows IT professionals to customize the Out-Of-Box Experience (OOBE) to deploy pre-configured apps and settings for your organization
- **The in-place upgrade** provides a simple, automated process that uses the Windows setup process to upgrade from an earlier version. This process automatically migrates existing data, settings, drivers, and applications. In-place upgrade requires the least IT effort because no complex deployment infrastructure is needed.

Dynamic Deployment Methods

- **Subscription activation** uses a subscription to switch from one edition of Windows to another when a licensed user signs into a device. For example, you can switch from Windows 10 Pro to Windows 10 Enterprise
- **Azure Active Directory (Azure AD) joined with automatic Mobile Device Management (MDM) enrollment** automatically joins the device to Azure AD and is configured by MDM. The organization member must provide their work or school user ID and password
- **Provisioning package configuration** uses the Windows Imaging and Configuration Designer (ICD) tool. This tool creates provisioning packages containing all the configurations, settings, and apps that can be applied to devices

Traditional deployment methods

- **A new computer,** or bare metal, is when you deploy a new device or wipe an existing one with a fresh image
- **Computer refresh,** also called wipe-and-load, is when you redeploy a device by saving the user state, wiping the disk, then restoring the user state
- **Computer replacement** is when you replace an existing device with a new one. You replace the device by saving the user state on the old device and restoring it to the new one

Manage Windows-as-a-Service

In **Configuration Manager,** you can see the state of WaaS in your environment. You can create service plans to form deployment rings and ensure that Windows systems are up to date when new versions are released.

Identify deployment and servicing methods for Microsoft 365 Apps

Microsoft 365 Apps can be installed individually by users on their devices. But it is often beneficial to manage updates and deploy a customized selection of apps to users' devices to ensure that all users have the apps they need. There are four methods to perform larger-scale deployments of Microsoft 365 Apps in the following list:

- **Install from a local source with Configuration Manager.** Operate your deployment with Configuration Manager, and download and install Office from distribution points on your link
- **Install from the cloud with the Office Deployment Tool (ODT).** Manage your deployment with the ODT and use the **Office Customization Tool** to create a configuration file in the cloud that specifies the Microsoft 365 apps that are installed
- **Install from a local source with the Office Deployment Tool (ODT).** Manage your deployment with the ODT, and download and deploy Office from a local source on your network
- **Self-install from the cloud.** Manage your deployment from the Office portal and have your users install Office on their client devices directly from the portal

EXAM TIP: After you deploy Microsoft 365 Apps, Microsoft strongly recommends keeping them updated as new features and updates are released.

Types of Updates Channels for Microsoft 365 Apps

One of the advantages of Microsoft 365 Apps is that Microsoft offers new and updated features for Office apps regularly. For example, adding improved translation capabilities to Word or supporting 3D animations in PowerPoint. Microsoft provides options called update channels that allow you to control how often your organization gets these new feature updates.

As needed, Microsoft also provides each update channel with two other types of updates that are updated on the 2nd Tuesday of every individual month:

- **Security updates,** such as updates that help keep Office protected from potential malicious attacks
- **Non-security updates (quality updates),** such as updates that provide stability or performance improvements for Office

Here are the three primary update channels for Microsoft 365 Apps:

- **Current Channel** receive feature updates at least once a month, but there is no set schedule of when the updates are released. This channel receives security and non-security updates around two or three times a month, including one on the 2nd Tuesday of the month. Microsoft recommends this channel because it provides users with the newest Office features as soon as they are ready
- **Monthly Enterprise Channel** receives feature updates once a month, on the 2nd Tuesday of the month. This monthly update can include feature, security, and non-security updates. Microsoft recommends this channel if you want to provide your users with new Office features once a month on a predictable release schedule
- **Semi-Annual Enterprise Channel** receives feature updates every six months, in January and July, on the 2nd Tuesday of the month. This update can include feature, security, and non-security

updates. Microsoft recommends this channel for those selected devices in your organization where extensive testing is needed before rolling out new Office features

The update channel of Microsoft 365 Apps you deploy to the users in your organization can depend on several factors, such as application compatibility testing and user readiness. Not all users in your organization need to be on the same update channel. For example, you can provide your training department with current channel so they can start learning about the new Office features, while the rest of your organization is on a semi-annual enterprise channel.

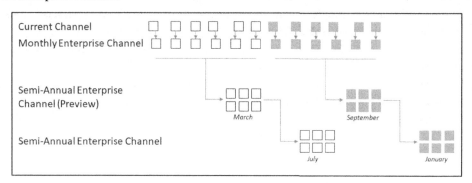

Figure 4-03: Channel Updates

How Updates are Installed for Microsoft 365 Apps

Microsoft 365 Apps regularly check for updates and are downloaded and installed automatically. There are no separate downloads for feature, security, or non-security updates. The updates are cumulative, so the most current update includes all the updates previously released for that update channel. While updates are being downloaded, your users can continue to use Office apps. After they are downloaded, all the updates for that update channel will install simultaneously.

Mind Map

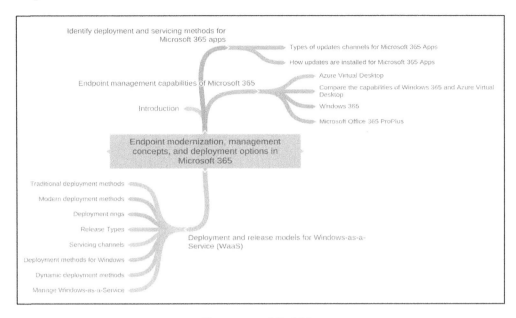

Figure 4-04: Mind Map

Practice Questions

1. Which statement is correct?
   A. Configuration Manager manages both on-premises infrastructure and cloud-based functions
   B. Windows's Autopilot is the new method for infrastructure management for both on-premises and cloud-based scenarios
   C. Configuration Manager manages on-premises infrastructure, and Intune manages cloud-based functions
   D. All of the above

2. What types of services are Windows 365 and Azure Virtual desktop?
   A. Desktop-as-a-Service
   B. On-premises service
   C. Windows-as-a-Service
   D. All of the above

3. What is Windows-as-a-Service?
   A. The ability to run Windows as a virtual desktop
   B. Windows with regular feature updates
   C. Windows mobile
   D. All of the above

4. Which of the following update channels are used if you require frequent feature updates for Microsoft 365 Apps on a predictable release schedule?
   A. Current Channel
   B. Monthly Enterprise Channel
   C. Semi-Annual Enterprise Channel
   D. All of the above

5. Azure Virtual Desktop allows you to quickly deploy virtual _____ to enable secure remote work.
   A. Desktop
   B. Apps
   C. Both of the above
   D. None of the above

6. Windows 365 is available in _____ subscription offerings.
   A. One
   B. Two
   C. Three
   D. Four

7. With Windows client, there are _____ release types.
   A. One
   B. Two
   C. Three
   D. Four

8. A common ring structure uses _____ deployment groups.
   A. One
   B. Two
   C. Three
   D. Four

9. There are _____ types of deployment categories or methods.
   A. One
   B. Two
   C. Three
   D. Four

10. Microsoft provides each update channel with _____ other types of updates that are released on the 2nd Tuesday of every month.
   A. One
   B. Two
   C. Three
   D. Four

Chapter 05: Analytics Capabilities in Microsoft 365

Introduction

Organizations adapting to hybrid work environments focus on encouraging their employees to build better work habits. They want their staff to achieve a balance between productivity and wellbeing. Microsoft Viva Insights gives leaders, managers, and employees privacy-protected insights that help everyone work smarter and thrive. Furthermore, the capabilities of the Microsoft 365 admin center, like the activity reports, can help organizations understand how people are adopting Microsoft 365 products and services. These analytic tools gather data and use Artificial Intelligence (AI) to provide actionable insights that help individuals and organizations do their best work.

Capabilities of Viva Insights

Viva Insights provides privacy-protected insights and actionable recommendations that help everyone in the organization work smarter and achieve balance. Individuals can receive personal insights visible only to them to help identify opportunities to change their habits to do their best work. Insights make it easy for managers to understand current team norms and act to help their groups strike a balance between productivity and wellbeing. Organizational insights for business leaders provide broad visibility across the organization, helping them understand where a change in organizational norms could improve employee experience and business outcomes.

Personal Insights

Individuals can gain valuable insights to improve work patterns through actionable recommendations from the personalized **Viva Insights app in Teams**. For example, prepare for the day with a briefing email, protect time for focused work, and mindfully disconnect after-hours. Now, let's dive deeper into what Viva Insights can do for you:

- **Personal wellbeing** - Through this experience, you can access this home page to tap into moments of self-reflection, gratitude, and breathing breaks. You can set reminders to self-reflect, view self-reflection history, send praise to express appreciation to your colleagues, or do a guided meditation
- **Stay connected** - This experience intelligently surfaces prior communications that might require follow-up. AI-based task suggestions and meeting assistance make it seamless to schedule 1:1s to catch up with important people in your network
- **Protect time** - This experience makes it easy to schedule focus time to work uninterrupted during the day before it fills up with meetings. You can set your working hours and manage reminders for a virtual commute to mindfully wrap up the workday. Also, set quiet time to silence mobile notifications from Teams and Outlook after-hours
- **Viva Insights in Outlook add-in** - Shows you insights within Microsoft Outlook about preparing for upcoming meetings, gaining focus time, maintaining your work relationships, planning time away from work, and improving your overall work-life balance
- **Daily briefing** - The daily briefing email from Viva automatically appears in your inbox near the start of the day. The email provides recommendations of documents for you to review before the

day's meetings. It also provides commitments from previous emails that you may want to follow up on

- **Effective meetings** - Meeting organizers can view personalized insights and suggestions to help improve their meeting habits and feedback for their meetings. You will be able to create and share meeting plans to help build shared team meeting norms

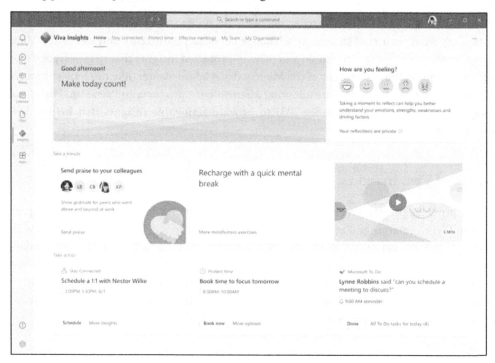

Figure 5-01: Personal Insights

Manager Insights

Manager Insights can provide insight to foster a healthy and prosperous team. Understand the work patterns that can lead to burnout and stress for your teams, such as regular after-hours work, meeting overload, or too little focus time. The **Viva Insights App in Teams** makes it easy for managers to understand current team norms and take action to create positive change.

- **Nudges** - Intelligent nudges or reminders help you stay connected with your team
  - Keep up with managerial demands like scheduling 1:1s and responding to requests in emails and document mentions
  - Recognize strengths and accomplishments through 'Send Praise' to increase engagement and morale
- **Reflective Insights** - Insights that can help influence your team culture
  - Identify unique work patterns and behaviors that may be impacting team stress and feelings of burnout
  - In Outlook, gain insights through the briefing and digest emails
- **Action Plans** - Create action plans to help you foster positive team norms
  - Prioritize team wellbeing by promoting healthy norms and boundaries, like setting shared, recurring 'No meeting' days or quiet hours for focused, uninterrupted work

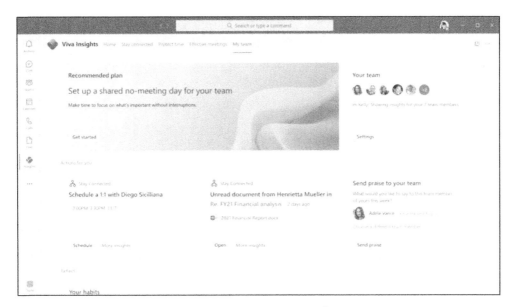

Figure 5-02: Manager Insights

Organizational Insights

Viva Insights provide organizational views to senior business leaders, CEOs, business unit leaders, and other department heads. These experiences in the **Viva Insights App in Teams** show leaders an aggregated view of work and collaboration patterns across their organizations. Leaders can see how people protect personal time, stay connected, manage focus time, and prioritize manager coaching. Now, let's explore how the visual insights under the **My organization** tab can help your organization:

- **Organizational resilience.** Enable work-life balance, provide 1:1 support, connect across boundaries, and provide cohesion within teams
- **Employee engagement.** Promote coaching and development, protect employee capacity, and drive employee empowerment and cohesion within teams
- **Improve agility.** Organize better meetings and connect across boundaries
- **Foster innovation.** Plan focus without interruption for your employees
- **Effective managers.** Optimize manager meetings, protect manager capacity, promote coaching and development, empower employees, and foster connectivity
- **Operational effectiveness.** Free up capacity, improve meeting quality, keep employees engaged, and protect time to get work done
- **Accelerate change.** Learn about how your employees can drive change within your workforce
- **Transform meeting culture.** Optimize meeting hours, examine recurring meetings and promote healthy meeting habits
- **Increase customer focus.** Optimize time with customers and promote coaching and development

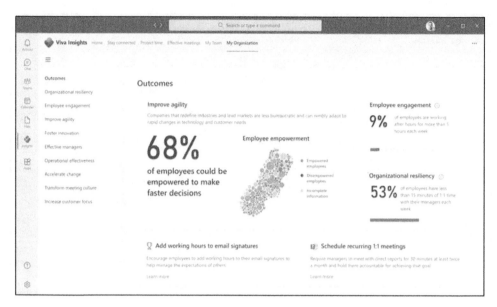

Figure 5-03: Organizational Insights

Capabilities of the Microsoft 365 Admin Center and Microsoft 365 User Portal

Microsoft 365 Admin Center

The **Microsoft 365 Admin Center** is designed for IT professionals and administrators to manage the organization's Microsoft 365 subscription. The admin center allows you to carry out various tasks, like managing users, viewing reports, and much more. Admins can also customize their home page by adding tile cards that point to apps, SharePoint sites, external sites, and more. This customization feature makes it easy for admins to find the relevant sites, apps, and resources to do their job.

The following list defines some of the main tasks that are done in the admin center:

- Manage users by adding, deleting, or restoring users
- Manage licenses by adding and removing their license
- Manage a Microsoft 365 group by creating a group, deleting a group, and editing the name or description
- Manage the bill
- View or create service requests
- Manage global settings for apps
- View activity reports
- View service health

Microsoft 365 User Portal

The **Microsoft 365 user portal** allows users to access their email, calendar, and documents through Microsoft 365 apps like Office, Teams, Outlook, and more. Users can sign in with their email account and password through www.office.com. Only the apps that the user has licenses for will appear. The portal allows for quick and easy viewing and editing of files saved online through OneDrive.

Figure 5-04: Microsoft 365 User Portal

Reports Available in the Microsoft 365 Admin Center and Other Admin Centers

Reports in the Microsoft 365 Admin Center

Gather insights on security and see how employees use Microsoft 365 products and services through the available reports in the **Microsoft 365 Admin Center.** You need to have admin permissions to be able to view these types of reports. To access the admin center, go to admin.microsoft.com and sign in with your admin account. Alternatively, you can access the Microsoft 365 admin mobile app.

The following list describes the two types of reports available in the admin center:

- **Productivity score** - The score in this report measures the work done in your organization compared to other organizations like yours. It provides metrics, insights, and recommended actions you can take to help your organization use Microsoft 365 products and services efficiently
- **Usage** - View these reports by time period and Microsoft 365 product or service to understand how people in your organization are using the products and services. You can drill down into each product report to get more detailed insights into the activities within each product. For example, view the number of files stored within OneDrive and SharePoint or Exchange's email and mailbox activity

---

EXAM TIP: You can also use Power BI with Microsoft 365 usage analytics to gain insight into your organization's workflow.

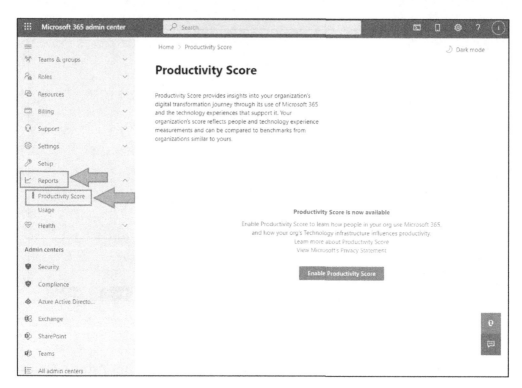

Figure 5-05: Productivity Score

Reports in other admin centers

The **Microsoft 365 Admin Center** also gives you access to other admin centers for specific products and services, such as Exchange, Teams, and more. To access the other admin centers, go to admin.microsoft.com and sign in with your admin account. Once logged in, select **Show** in the navigation menu to find the other admin centers.

Each specialist admin center gives you more options for that area, including reports. The following list describes some of the other admin centers and the reports available:

- **Azure Active Directory** - The reports available provide a comprehensive view of activity in your environment. View activity reports, which include audit logs and sign-ins
- **Endpoint Manager** - Microsoft Intune reporting allows you to proactively monitor the health and activity of endpoints across your organization. You can view reports about device compliance, device health, and device trends. In addition, you can create custom reports to obtain more specific data
- **Exchange** - View email flow reports within your organization and mailbox migration batches created for your organization
- **Security & Compliance** - View reports about security trends and track   the protection of your identities, data, devices, apps, and infrastructure. Also, view a collective security score that includes your organization's security posture and how to improve it. These monitoring features allow your compliance and security admin to focus on high-priority issues like security attacks or increased suspicious activity
- **SharePoint** - The reports available are about data access governance, and these reports help you maintain the security and compliance of your data in SharePoint. View reports on sharing links to

identify potential oversharing and reports on sensitivity labels applied to files to monitor sensitive content

- **Teams** - User activity and device usage reports are available to gain insights into your organization's Microsoft Teams activity. Your organization can use these reports to better understand usage patterns, like how users use Teams and their devices to connect to Teams. These reports can help organizations decide where to prioritize training and communication efforts

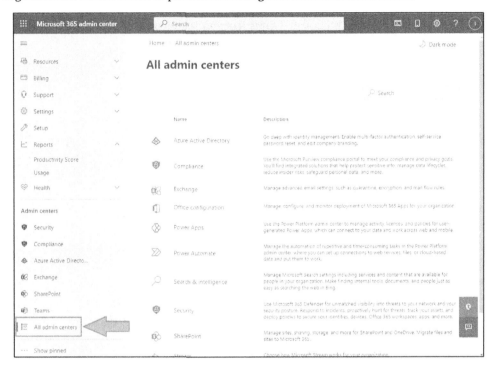

Figure 5-06: All Admin Centers

Mind Map

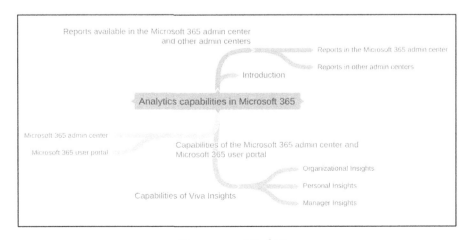

Figure 5-07: Mind Map

Practice Questions

1. What are Viva Insights?
   A. A tool that provides data-driven, privacy-protected insights and recommendations to improve productivity and wellbeing
   B. A tool that brings together relevant news, conversations, and resources in the daily applications and devices you use
   C. A centralized learning hub in Microsoft Teams lets you seamlessly integrate learning and building skills into your day
   D. None of the above

2. Viva Insights provides insights into which three areas?
   A. Personal, Teammates, and Organizations
   B. Personal, Managers, and Organizations
   C. Managers, Frontline Workers, and Organizations
   D. All of the above

3. Which reports are available in the Microsoft 365 admin center?
   A. Productivity Score and Security Score
   B. Usage and Device Health
   C. Productivity Score and Usage
   D. All of the above options

4. Which admin center can you view activity reports of audit logs and sign-ins?
   A. Exchange Admin Center
   B. Azure Active Directory Admin Center
   C. Endpoint Manager Admin center
   D. None of the above

5. There are _____ types of reports available in the admin center.
   A. One
   B. Two
   C. Three
   D. Four

Chapter 06: Security and Compliance Concepts

Introduction

Security and compliance have become dominant concerns as more business data is accessed from locations outside the traditional corporate network. In addition, organizations must ensure they comply with industry and regulatory requirements to ensure the protection and privacy of data.

This chapter introduces some critical security and compliance concepts. You will learn about shared responsibility, defense-in-depth, and Zero Trust models. You will be introduced to encryption and hashing as ways to protect data. Lastly, you will learn about concepts that relate to compliance.

Shared Responsibility Model

The *shared responsibility model* defines which security tasks are managed by the cloud provider and which are managed by you, the customer. The responsibilities differ depending on where the workload is hosted:

- Software as a Service (SaaS)
- Platform as a Service (PaaS)
- Infrastructure as a Service (IaaS)
- On-premises data center

The following diagram defines areas of responsibility between customer and cloud provider, as per the location of data.

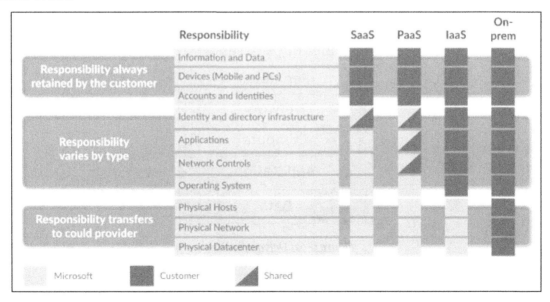

Figure 6-01: Shared Responsibility Model

- **Infrastructure as a Service (IaaS)**. With IaaS, you are using the cloud provider's computing infrastructure. The cloud customer is not responsible for the physical components, such as computers, the network, or the data center's physical security

- **Platform as a Service (PaaS)**. PaaS offers an environment for building, testing, and deploying software applications. With PaaS, the cloud provider operates the hardware and operating systems, and the customer is accountable for applications and data
- **Software as a Service (SaaS)**. It is usually licensed through a monthly or annual subscription, and SaaS requires the minimum amount of management by the cloud customer

Defense in Depth

Each layer offers protection so that if one layer is breached, a subsequent layer will stop an attacker from getting unauthorized access to data.

Example layers of security might include:

- **Physical** security limits the view of a data center to only allowed personnel
- **Identity & Access** layer ensures that identities are safe, that access is allowed only when necessary, and that changes are tracked.
- **Perimeter** security of your corporate network consists of Distributed Denial of Service (DDoS) protection to filter large-scale attacks before they can form a denial of service for end-users
- **Network** security, such as network segmentation and access controls, limits the link between resources
- **Compute** layer focuses on ensuring that your compute resources are secure and that you have the necessary controls in place to minimize security issues.
- **Application** layer security ensures applications are secure and free of security vulnerabilities
- **Data** layer security contains controls to manage access to business and customer data and encryption to secure data

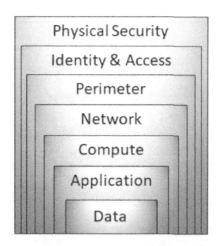

Figure 6-02: Defense in Depth

Confidentiality, Integrity, Availability (CIA)

All the different mechanisms (technologies, processes, and training) are key to a cybersecurity strategy, whose goals are ensuring confidentiality, integrity, and availability, often called CIA.

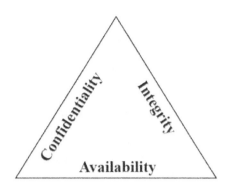

Figure 6-03: Confidentiality, Integrity, Availability

- **Confidentiality** defines the need to keep sensitive data confidential, such as customer information, passwords, or financial data
- **Integrity** defines as keeping data or messages correct. Integrity is the confidence that data has not been tampered with or modified
- **Availability** is making data available to those who need it when needed

While the goals of a cybersecurity strategy are to preserve the confidentiality, integrity, and availability of systems, networks, applications, and data, it is the goal of cybercriminals to disrupt these goals. Microsoft's portfolio includes the solutions and technologies to enable organizations to deliver on the goals of the CIA triad.

Zero Trust Model

Introduction

"Trust no one, verify everything" is a principle upon which Zero Trust Methodology operates. It believes that nothing is worth our trust, even the resources behind the firewalls of a corporate network. The way the attackers get their hands-on conventional access controls proves that traditional security strategies are no longer satisfactory and, hence, have been marked as inadequate to serve all types of security needs. Multifactor authentication should be used to provide appropriate scrutiny for the networks and data to validate the user. Another way to shield all networks is by limiting the access to data of corporate networks.

Principles of Zero Trust Model

The Zero Trust Model works on three principles that perfectly show how the security is actually carried through. These three principles are jotted down below:

Verify Explicitly

Verification and authentication of these data points are necessary: user identity, location, device, service or workload, data classification, and anomalies.

Least Privileged Access

To protect data effectively, you must limit user access through ingenious tactics, such as risk-based adaptive policies, data protection to safeguard data and productivity, and Just-In-Time and Just-Enough Access (JIT/JEA).

Assume Breach

Division of access should be conducted amongst the user, devices, and application. Analytics promote security and detect threats, while encryption protects all the data.

Six Foundational Pillars of Zero Trust Model

To provide end-to-end security, six elements that act as the foundational pillars of a Zero Trust Model work together to secure grounds.

Identities

This includes the identities of users, services, or devices. Proper and strong authentication is required when any identity tries to access anything.

Devices

Monitoring devices to be in the service of safeguarding and complying is the most crucial aspect of security. Devices create large attack grounds when the data flow from devices to workloads and the cloud; hence, their security should be the goal.

Applications

This pillar defines how data is consumed; it includes discovering all applications being used, sometimes called Shadow IT. Moreover, this pillar also includes managing permissions and access.

Data

Data should be classified, labeled, and encrypted according to its attributes. Security efforts are solely about protecting data and ensuring it remains safe when it leaves devices, applications, infrastructure, and networks that the organization has in control.

Infrastructure

We work on the version, configuration, and JIT access to improve security. The usage of telemetry to detect attacks and anomalies is also witnessed. This allows us to automatically block risky and suspicious behavior and take protective actions against them.

Networks

Networks should be segmented, which includes in-network micro-segmentation. Adding to the list, real-time threat protection, end-to-end encryption, monitoring, and analytics are effectively used.

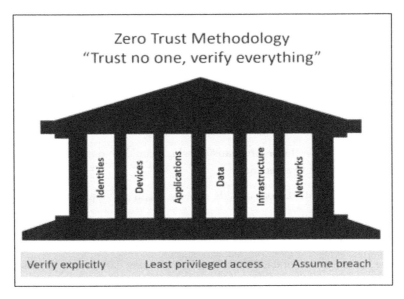

Figure 6-04: Zero Trust Methodology

A security strategy that employs the three principles of the Zero Trust model across the six foundational pillars helps companies deliver and enforce security across their organization.

Encryption and Hashing

Single key can encode data, but a single key cannot be used to decrypt encrypted data. To decrypt, you need a paired key. Asymmetric encryption is used to access sites on the internet using the HTTPS protocol and electronic data signing solutions.

Symmetric and Asymmetric Encryption

Symmetric encryption uses a unique key that must be shared between the persons who need to receive the message.

Asymmetric encryption uses a pair of public keys and a private key to encrypt and decode messages as they are exchanged.

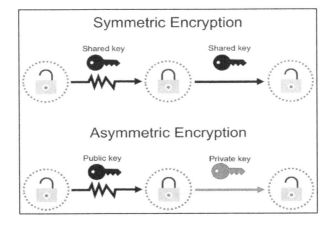

Figure 6-05: Encryption

99

Encryption for Data at Rest

Data at rest is the data that is stored on a physical device, such as a server.

If an attacker receives a hard drive with encrypted data and does not have a view of the encryption keys, he will be unable to view the data.

Encryption for Data in Transit

Several different layers can handle the secure transfer, which could be done by encrypting the data at the application layer before sending it to a network.

Encrypting data in transit prevents it from outside observers and provides a mechanism to transmit data while limiting the risk of exposure.

Encryption for Data in Use

An everyday use case for encryption of data in use involves securing data in non-persistent storage, such as RAM or CPU caches. This can be achieved through technologies that create an enclave (a secured lockbox) that protects and keeps data encrypted while the CPU processes the data.

Hashing

Hashing utilizes an algorithm to convert text to a *unique* fixed-length value called a hash. The same hash value is produced each time the exact text is hashed using the same algorithm.

> **EXAM TIP:** Hashing differs from encryption in that it does not use keys, and the hashed value is not subsequently decrypted back to the original.

Hashing is used to store passwords. When a user writes their password, the same algorithm that formed the stored hash forms a hash of the entered password. This is combined with the stored hashed version of the password. If they match, the user has written their password correctly. Hashing algorithms are also known to hackers. To remove this risk, passwords are often "salted." This refers to adding a fixed-length random value to the input of hash functions to create unique hashes for the same input.

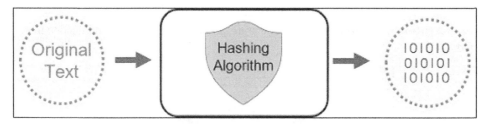

Figure 6-06: Hashing

Compliance Concepts

Data has become more critical than ever. Organizations, institutions, and entire societies generate and rely on data to function daily. The sheer scale of data generated and the increasing reliance on it means that the privacy and protection of that data have become pivotal. As organizations and institutions move their data to service provider clouds, with data centers worldwide, additional considerations come into play.

Government agencies and industry groups have issued regulations to help protect and govern the use of data. Listed below are some essential concepts and terms that relate to data compliance.

- **Data residency** - When it comes to compliance, data residency regulations govern the physical locations where data can be stored and how and when it can be transferred, processed, or accessed internationally. These regulations can differ significantly depending on the jurisdiction
- **Data sovereignty** - Means that data, particularly personal data, is subject to the rules of the country/region in which it is physically collected, held, or processed. This can add a layer of complexity regarding compliance because the same data can be collected in one location, stored in another, and processed in another, subjecting it to laws from different countries/regions
- **Data privacy** - Providing notice and transparency about collecting, processing, using, and sharing personal data are fundamental principles of privacy laws and regulations. Privacy laws, previously referenced PII (personally identifiable information), have expanded the definition to any data directly linked or indirectly linkable to a person. Organizations are subject to and must operate consistently with many laws, regulations, codes of conduct, industry-specific standards, and compliance standards governing data privacy

In most cases, laws and regulations do not define or prescribe specific technologies organizations must use to protect data. They leave it to an organization to identify compliant technologies, operations, and other appropriate data protection measures.

Microsoft 365 Compliance Center

The Microsoft 365 compliance center combines the tools and data needed to help understand and manage an organization's compliance needs.

The compliance center is available to customers with a Microsoft 365 SKU with one of the following roles:

- Global Administrator
- Compliance Administrator
- Compliance Data Administrator

When an admin signs into the Microsoft 365 compliance center, the card section on the home page shows briefly how your organization is doing with data compliance and what solutions are accessible for your organization. Admins can customize the card section by moving cards around or adding/removing cards displayed on the home screen.

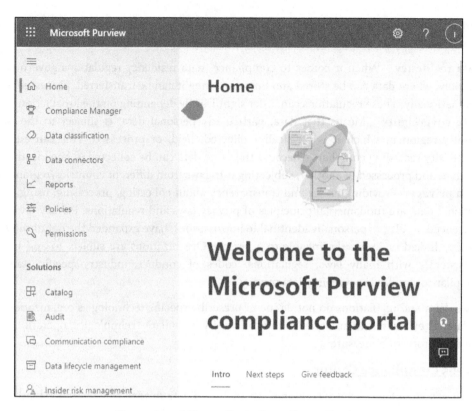

Figure 6-07: Microsoft 365 Compliance Center

The default compliance center homepage has several cards, including:

- **Compliance Manager Card:** This card leads you to the Compliance Manager solution. It calculates a risk-based compliance score that measures progress toward completing recommended actions to reduce risks associated with data protection and regulatory standards. It also provides workflow capabilities and built-in control mapping to help you efficiently carry out improvement actions

Figure 6-08: Compliance Manager

- **Solution Catalog Card**: It connects to groups of integrated solutions to help you manage end-to-end compliance scenarios. Solutions areas involved are:
  - **Information Protection & Governance** - These solutions help organizations classify, protect, and retain your data where it lives and wherever it goes. Data loss prevention, information governance, information protection, and records management are also included
  - **Privacy** - It builds a more privacy-resilient workplace. Privacy management gives actionable insights into your organization's data to help you spot issues and reduce risks
  - **Insider Risk Management** - These solutions help organizations identify, analyze, and remediate internal risks before they cause harm. These include communication compliance, information barriers, and insider risk management
  - **Discovery & Respond** - These solutions help organizations quickly find, investigate, and respond to relevant data. These include audits, data subject requests, and eDiscovery

Figure 6-09: Discovery & Respond

- **Active Alerts Card**: It includes a summary of the most active alerts and a link where admins can view more detailed information, such as alert severity, status, category, etc.

Figure 6-10: Active Alerts

Navigation

You can access alerts, reports, policies, and all the solutions included in the solutions catalog. There is access to data connectors that you can use to import non-Microsoft data to Microsoft 365, so your compliance solutions can cover it. The **Customize navigation** control allows customization of items that appear in the navigation pane.

Figure 6-11: Navigation

Compliance Manager

Microsoft Compliance Manager is a Microsoft 365 compliance center feature that helps admins manage an organization's compliance requirements with greater ease and convenience. It can help organizations throughout their compliance journey, from taking inventory of data protection risks to managing the complexities of implementing controls, staying current with regulations and certifications, and reporting to auditors.

Compliance Manager helps simplify compliance and lower risk by offering:

- Prebuilt assessments based on joint regional and industry regulations and standards

- Workflow capabilities that enable admins to efficiently complete risk assessments for the organization
- Some actions will also be managed for the organization by Microsoft, and Admins will get implementation details and audit results for those actions
- A compliance score is a calculation that helps an organization understand its overall compliance posture by measuring how it is progressing with improvement actions

The Compliance Manager dashboard shows the current compliance score, helps admins see what needs attention, and guides them to key improvement actions.

Figure 6-12(a): Compliance Manager Dashboard

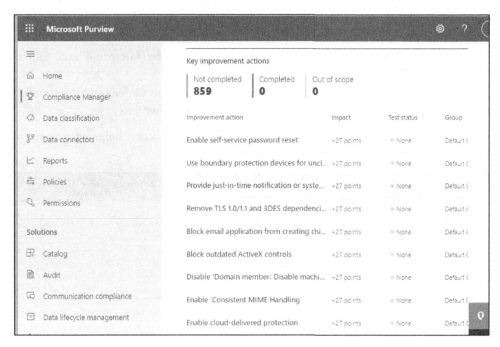

Figure 6-12(b): Compliance Manager Option with Key improvement actions

The Compliance Manager uses several data elements to help manage compliance activities.

Controls

It defines assessing and managing system configuration, organizational process, and people responsible for meeting a specific regulation requirement, standard, or policy.

The Compliance Manager tracks the following types of controls:

- **Microsoft-managed controls**: Switches between Microsoft cloud services, which Microsoft is responsible for applying
- **Your controls**: Sometimes described as customer-managed controls, these are applied and managed by the organization
- **Shared controls**: The organization and Microsoft share the responsibility for implementing these controls

Compliance Manager continuously assesses controls by scanning your Microsoft 365 environment and detecting your system settings, constantly and automatically updating your technical action status.

Assessments

An assessment is a set of controls from a specific regulation, standard, or policy. Completing the actions within an assessment helps meet the requirements of a standard, regulation, or law. For example, an organization may have an assessment that, when completed, helps bring the organization's Microsoft 365 settings in line with ISO 27001 requirements.

An assessment consists of several components, including the in-scope services, controls, and an assessment score that shows progress toward completing the actions needed for compliance.

Templates

Compliance Manager offers templates to help admins quickly make assessments. They can modify these templates to make an assessment optimized for their needs. Admins can also build a custom assessment by creating a template with their controls and actions.

Improvement Actions

Improvement actions help centralize compliance activities. Each improvement action provides recommended guidance to help organizations align with data protection regulations and standards. Admins can also store documentation and notes and record status updates within the improvement action.

Benefits of Compliance Manager

Compliance Manager provides many benefits, including:

- Offering access to a large variety of out-of-the-box assessments and custom assessments to help organizations with their unique compliance requirements
- Mapping regulatory controls against suggested improvement actions
- Helping admins and users prioritize actions that will impact their organizational compliance by associating a score with each action

Uses and Advantages of the Compliance Score

Compliance score determines progress in completing suggested improvement actions within controls. It also helps organizations prioritize actions based on their potential to reduce risk.

EXAM TIP: Admins can get a summary of the compliance score in the Compliance Manager Overview pane.

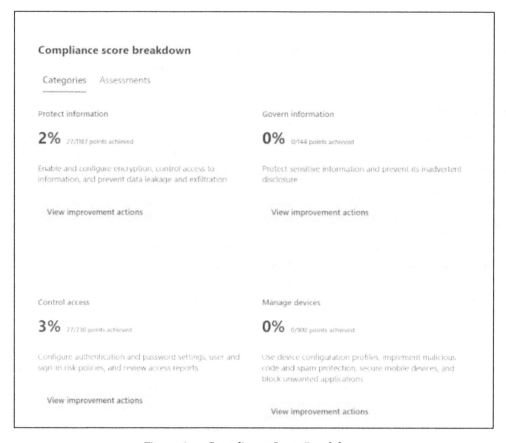

Figure 6-13: Compliance Score Breakdown

How to Understand the Compliance Score

The overall compliance score is estimated using scores that are given to actions. Actions come in two types:

- **Your improved actions**: Actions that the organization is supposed to manage
- **Microsoft actions**: Actions that Microsoft controls for the organization

Actions are categorized as mandatory, discretionary, preventative, detective, or corrective:

- **Mandatory** – These actions should not be bypassed. For example, creating a policy to set password length or expiration requirements
- **Discretionary** – These actions depend on the user's understanding and adherence to a policy. For example, a policy where users must ensure their devices are locked before leaving them

The following are subcategories of actions that can be categorized as mandatory or discretionary:

- **Preventative** actions are designed to handle specific risks, like using encryptions to protect data at rest if there are breaches or attacks
- **Detective** actions monitor systems to detect irregularities that could represent risks or be used to detect breaches or intrusions. Examples of these actions are system access audits or regulatory compliance audits
- **Corrective** actions help admins minimize the adverse effects of security incidents by undertaking corrective measures to reduce their immediate effect or reverse the damage

Organizations accumulate points for every action completed. The compliance score is presented as a percentage representing all the actions completed, compared with the ones outstanding.

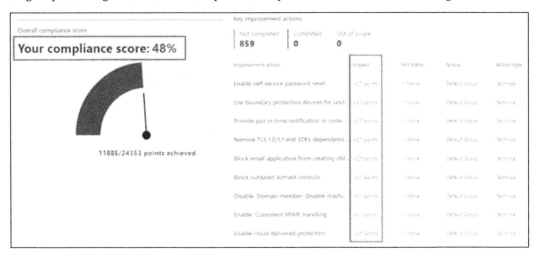

Figure 6-14: Compliance Score Percentage

Compliance Manager and Compliance Score

Compliance Manager is an end-to-end solution in Microsoft 365 compliance center to allow admins to manage and track compliance activities. On the other hand, a compliance score is a calculation of the overall compliance posture across the organization. The compliance score can be accessed through the Compliance Manager.

Compliance Manager allows admins to understand and increase their compliance score to improve the organization's compliance posture, helping it stay in line with compliance requirements.

Mind Map

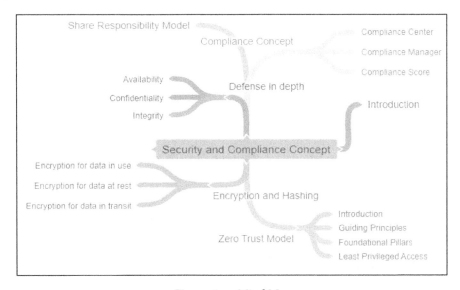

Figure 6-15: Mind Map

Practice Questions

1. An organization has deployed Microsoft 365 applications to all employees. Considering the shared responsibility model, who is responsible for the accounts and identities relating to these employees?
   A. The organization
   B. Microsoft, the SaaS provider
   C. There has shared responsibility between an organization and Microsoft
   D. None of the above

2. What measures might an organization implement as part of the defense-in-depth security methodology?
   A. Locating all its servers in a single physical location
   B. Multifactor authentication for all users
   C. Ensuring there is no segmentation of your corporate network
   D. All of the above

3. An organization's HR wants to ensure that stored employee data is encrypted. Which security mechanism would they use?
   A. Hashing
   B. Encryption in transit
   C. Encryption at rest
   D. All of the above

4. Which of the following best defines the concept of data sovereignty?
   A. Some regulations govern the physical locations where data can be stored and how and when it can be transferred, processed, or accessed internationally
   B. Data, particularly personal data, is subject to the laws and regulations of the country/region in which it is physically consumed, held, or processed
   C. Trust no one; verify everything
   D. All of the above

5. The Zero Trust model has _____ principles.
   A. One
   B. Two
   C. Three
   D. Four

6. The _____ elements are the foundational pillars of the Zero Trust model.
   A. Three
   B. Four
   C. Five
   D. Six

7. There are _____ top-level types of encryption.
   A. One
   B. Two

C. Three

D. Four

8. _____ encryption uses the same key to encrypt and decrypt the data.

A. Symmetric

B. Asymmetric

C. Both of the above

D. None of the above

9. _____ encryption uses a public key and private key pair.

A. Symmetric

B. Asymmetric

C. Both of the above

D. None of the above

10. _____ is used to store passwords.

A. Encryption

B. Hashing

C. Both of the above

D. None of the above

11. A new admin has joined the team and needs to be able to access the Microsoft 365 Compliance Center. Which roles can the admin use to get into the Compliance Center?

A. Compliance Administrator Role

B. Helpdesk Administrator Role

C. User Administrator Role

D. All of the above

12. Your new colleagues on the admin team are unfamiliar with the concept of shared controls in Compliance Manager. How would the concept of shared controls be described?

A. Controls that both external regulators and Microsoft share responsibility for executing

B. Controls that both your organization and external regulators share responsibility for executing

C. Controls that both your organization and Microsoft share responsibility for executing

D. All of the above

13. A customer has requested a presentation on how the Microsoft 365 Compliance Center can help improve their organization's compliance posture. What is the difference between Compliance Manager and score?

A. Compliance Manager is an end-to-end Microsoft 365 Compliance Center solution that allows admins to manage and track compliance activities

B. Compliance Manager is an end-to-end solution in Microsoft 365 Compliance Center to enable admins to manage and track compliance activities. Compliance score is a score the organization receives from regulators for successful compliance.

C. Compliance score calculates the overall compliance stance across the organization

    D. None of the above

14. Compliance _____ is an end-to-end solution in Microsoft 365 compliance center to enable admins to manage and track compliance activities.
    A. Manager
    B. Score
    C. Regulation
    D. None of the above

15. A compliance _____ is a calculation of the overall compliance posture across the organization.
    A. Manager
    B. Score
    C. Regulation
    D. None of the above

Chapter 07: Identity Concepts

Introduction

Identity is how people and things are identified on your corporate network and in the cloud. Knowing who or what is accessing your organization's data and other resources is fundamental to securing your environment.

In this section, you will study critical concepts of authentication and authorization and why identity is essential in securing corporate resources. You will also learn about some identity-related services.

Identity Services

When users use an online service with no privacy criteria, the user requires at least a username (the User ID) and password. Identity services include authentication, authorization, and access management policies.

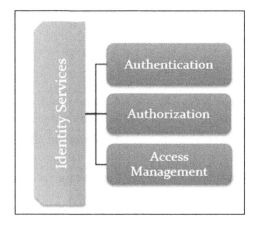

Figure 7-01: Identity Services

Authentication and Authorization

Authentication

Authentication is proving that a person is who they say they are. Anyone purchasing an item with a credit card may be required to show an extra form of identification, proving that they are the person whose name appears on the card. In this example, the user may show a driver's license that is a form of authentication and proves their ID.

You will encounter similar authentication when accessing a computer or device. You may get asked to enter a username and password. The username states who you are, but by itself is not enough to grant you access. When combined with the password, which only that user should know, it allows access to your systems. The username and password are a form of authentication, and authentication is sometimes shortened to AuthN.

Authorization

Once you authenticate a user, you must decide where they can go and what they are allowed to see and touch. This process is called authorization.

Suppose you want to spend the night in a hotel. The first thing you will do is go to reception to start the "authentication process." After the receptionist has verified you, you are given a keycard and can go to your room. Think of the keycard as the authorization process. The keycard will only let you open the doors and elevators you are permitted to access, such as your hotel room.

In cybersecurity terms, authorization determines the level of access or the permissions an authenticated person has to your data and resources. Authorization is sometimes shortened to AuthZ.

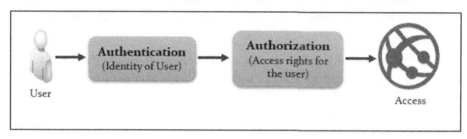

Figure 7-02: Process of Identity Management

Authentication vs. Authorization

Authentication and authorization have very little difference. The summarized table shows the difference between these two entities.

Authentication	Authorization
The first step toward accessing resources	A person can be authorized only when their authentication has been done
A way to verify the customer or user's identity	Authorization allows authenticated users to access files, databases, mail, etc.
Typically, a user can be authenticated using a user ID and password	Controls user access
Factor-based authentication is usually preferred for security purposes	Authorization is the granular part of identity services

Table 7-01: Authentication vs. Authorization

EXAM TIP: Authentication is the process of verifying users using the user ID and password. Authorization is the method of providing the rights to authenticated users.

Access Management

Access management is a critical part of any cloud infrastructure as it ensures the restriction of access to services toward other users. It provides confidentiality, integrity, and availability. This means that access to any online application should be confidential for an unauthorized user and immediately available to authorized users. Access management policies should also be responsible for the following:

- **Authentication and Authorization:** The user must be authenticated first, then authorized for the particular application
- **Faraway from Unauthorized Users:** Access management policies must be designed in such a way that no unauthorized person can access the information.

Identity as the Primary Security Perimeter

Digital collaboration has changed. Your employees and partners now need to collaborate and access organizational resources from anywhere, on any device, and without affecting their productivity.

Enterprise security requires adapting to this new reality. The security perimeter can no longer be performed as the on-premises network, and it now extends to:

- SaaS applications for business-critical workloads that might be formed outside the network
- The personal devices that users are using to let corporate resources (BYOD or bring your device) while working from home
- The unmanaged devices used by users or customers when working with corporate data or collaborating with employees
- Internet of things, referred to as IoT devices, are installed throughout your professional network and inside customer locations

An identity is the set of things that define or characterize someone or something. For example, a person's identity includes the information they use to authenticate themselves, such as their username, password, and authorization level.

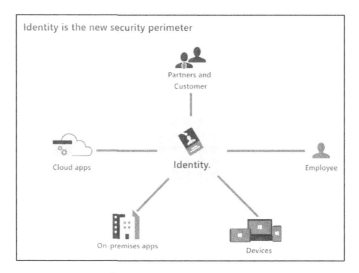

Figure 7-03: Identity as the Primary Security Perimeter

Four Pillars of an Identity Infrastructure

There is a collection of processes, technologies, and policies for managing digital identities and controlling how they are used to access resources. These can be organized into four fundamental pillars that organizations should consider when creating an identity infrastructure.

- **Administration** - The administration is about the formation and management/governance of identities for users, devices, and services
- **Authentication** - The authentication pillar describes the story of how much an IT system needs to know about identity to have sufficient proof that they are who they say they are
- **Authorization** - The authorization pillar lets the incoming identity data define the level of access

- **Auditing** - The auditing pillar tracks who does what, when, where, and how. Auditing contains in-depth reporting, alerts, and governance of identities

---

EXAM TIP: Addressing the four pillars of an identity infrastructure is key to a comprehensive and robust identity and access control solution.

Role of the Identity Provider

With modern authentication, all services are supplied by a central identity provider. Information used to authenticate the user with the server is stored and managed centrally by the identity provider.

Organizations can establish authentication and authorization policies with a central identity provider, monitor user behavior, identify suspicious activities, and reduce malicious attacks.

The server checks the security token through its *trust relationship* with the identity provider. The user or application accesses the required resources on the server by using the security token and the information. In this case, the token and the information it contains is stored and managed by the identity provider, and the centralized identity provider supplies the authentication service.

Single sign-on

Another essential capability of an identity provider and "modern authentication" is the Single Sign-On (SSO) support. With SSO, the end-user logs in once, and that request is used to view multiple applications or resources. When you set up SSO between multiple identity providers, it is called federation.

Multi-Factor Authentication

Multi-Factor Authentication (MFA) provides a layer-based authentication using more than one form of authentication. This means that if attackers compromise one, they will still be unable to get in. MFA is recommended as a default. It is a part of AAD that enables other ways to authenticate users. MFA is needed in organizations that have a large number of users, devices, and resources. Extra security is required for protection and efficient throughput, to avoid any collapse.

How MFA Works

Multi-Factor Authentication (MFA) conducts user authentication in multiple steps. The first step is to verify the user with ID and password. The second step is to send a code on the user's phone for further verification. The third step is biometric verification (optional).

For example, an Azure user wants to log in to the online booking web app. A large number of people are already accessing that web application due to its efficient throughput and fast response. Using MFA, the simplest way to use the application requires the user to put user ID and password for verification. Once a user correctly enters the ID and password, the second step of MFA verification is to confirm the user's credentials from the database by sending a code (a combination of numbers) to the user's phone. When the user gets the code, they are required to put it in the text box to confirm the validity. Once the code is entered, the authentication of the user is complete. Another way to authenticate the user is biometric verification, but this step is only needed for highly advanced security purposes.

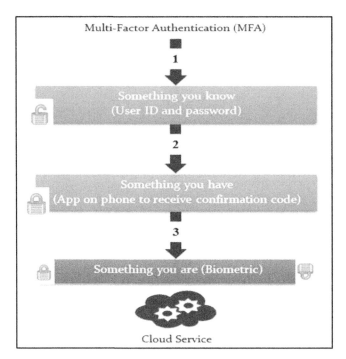

Figure 7-04: Multi-Factor Authentication

EXAM TIP: Multi-Factor Authentication (MFA) provides the combined version of authentication that results in an advanced level of security and protection.

Lab 7-01: Set up MFA for Microsoft 365

Introduction

One of the simplest methods to secure your company is through multifactor authentication, which requires both you and your employees to offer more than one way to sign in to Microsoft 365.

Problem

An organization wants a secure authentication process that protects its resources from un   authorized authorities. How would it be possible?

Solution

By simply enabling the Multi-Factor Authentication option, the organization protects its resources.

1. Log in to your Microsoft Account.

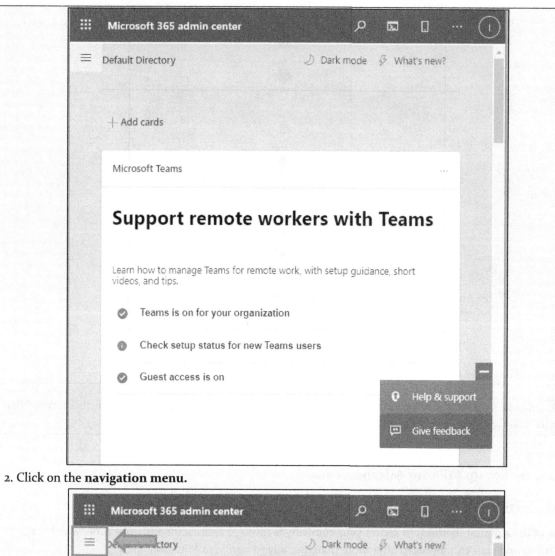

2. Click on the **navigation menu.**

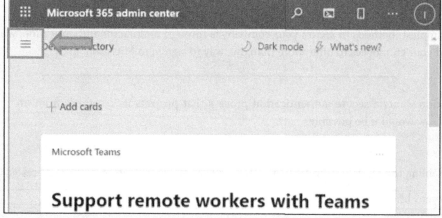

3. Click on **Azure Active Directory** present inside **Admin Center.**

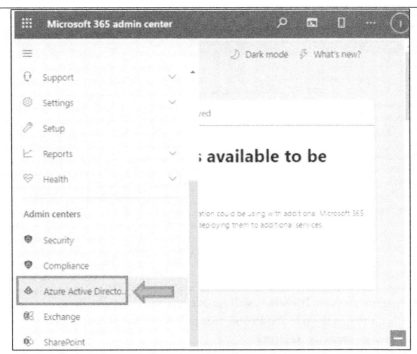

4. The **Dashboard** of **Azure Active Directory admin center** will automatically open and appear as shown below.

Note: Microsoft's identity and access management (IAM) service for businesses is called Azure Active Directory (Azure AD). Azure AD, which powers Office 365, can sync with on-premises Active Directory and use OAuth to authenticate users of other cloud-based services.

5. From the left side given menu, click on Azure Active Directory.

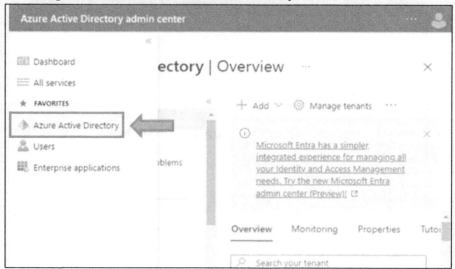

6. The **Overview** page of **Default Directory** will appear.
7. From the left side given menu, go to the **Properties** present inside **Manage** section.
8. Then, click on **Manage security defaults.**

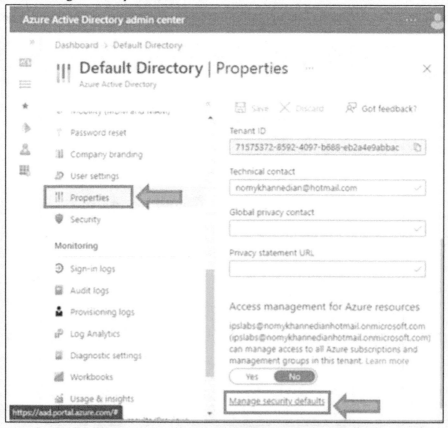

9. Initially, the security default setting is set to **No.** Enable it and click on **Save.**

Note: This default setting with **Yes** enabled provides identity security mechanisms recommended by Microsoft.

Concept of Directory Services and Active Directory

In the view of a computer network, a directory is a hierarchical structure that keeps data about users on the network.

Active Directory

Active Directory (AD) is a group of directory services developed by Microsoft as part of Windows 2000 for on-premises domain-based networks. Active Directory Domain Services (AD DS) is the best-known service of this kind. It stores information about domain members, containing devices and users, verifies their credentials, and describes their view rights.

AD DS is the main component in organizations with on-premises IT infrastructure. AD DS allows organizations to operate multiple on-premises infrastructure components and systems using a single identity per user. AD DS does not, however, natively verify mobile devices, SaaS applications, or line of business apps that require *modern authentication* methods.

The growth of cloud services, SaaS applications, and personal devices being used at work have resulted in the need for modern authentication and the evolution of Active Directory-based identity solutions.

Active Directory (AD) is a directory service created by Microsoft for storing information about users, resources, and other networked objects. Offices, educational institutions, and management departments all employ AD.

- **Limitation of Active Directory:** Active Directory provides information for authentication and authorization, but it has some limitations;
  - **Traditional Use Only:** Active Directory provides directory services for physical access only. It is most commonly used in the on-premises network
  - **Not Permitted for Web Applications:** Active Directory is not applicable to serve its services for web applications
  - **Authentication:** Active Directory provides such directory services for authentication that is not available on Azure

Figure 7-05 shows the conceptual view of the Microsoft Active Directory (AD) services.

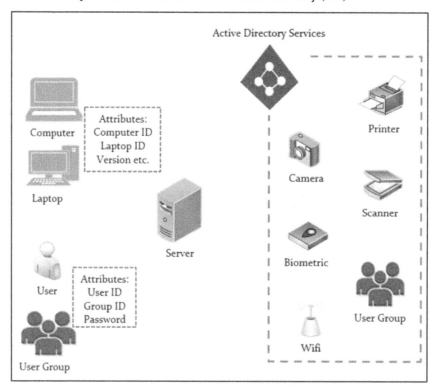

Figure 7-05: Active Directory Services

Azure Active Directory is the next formation of identity and access management solutions. It offers organizations an Identity as a Service (IDaaS) solution for all their apps across the cloud and on-premises. It focuses on Azure AD, Microsoft's cloud-based identity provider.

Concept of Federation

Federation allows the access of services across organizational or domain boundaries by establishing trust relationships between the respective domain's identity providers. With federation, users are not required to maintain a different username and password when viewing resources in other domains.

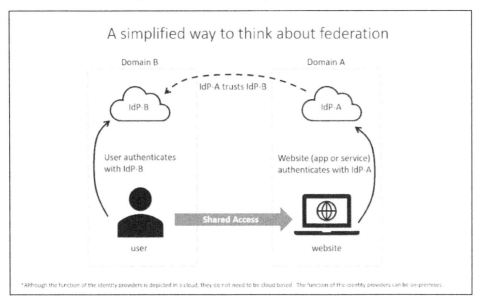

Figure 7-06: Concept of Federation

The modified way to think about this federation scenario is as follows:

- The website, in domain A, uses the authentication services of Identity Provider A (IdP-A)
- The user, in domain B, authenticates with Identity Provider B (IdP-B)
- IdP-A has a trust relationship contained with IdP-B
- When the user, who wants to access the website, provides their credentials to the website, the website trusts the user and allows access. This access is permitted because of the trust between the two identity providers

With federation, trust is not always bidirectional. Although IdP-A may trust IdP-B and let the user in domain B view the website in domain A, the opposite is invalid unless that trust relationship is configured.

In this case, Twitter is an identity provider, and the third-party site might be using a separate identity provider, such as Azure AD. There is a strong relationship between Azure AD and Twitter.

Conditional Access

By establishing conditions that must be satisfied before allowing access to a piece of material, conditional access safeguards controlled content in a system. If-then clauses are the most basic form of conditional access restrictions. The completion of an activity is required for users to access a resource.

Conditional Access Policies

Conditional Access policies might provide you greater control if your company needs more precise sign-in security requirements. With conditional access, you can design rules that respond to sign-in events and demand further steps before allowing a user access to a service or application.

Customers who have purchased Azure AD Premium P1 or licenses that contain it, such as Microsoft 365 Business Premium and Microsoft 365 E3, are eligible for Conditional Access. Create a Conditional Access policy for additional details.

Through the Azure AD Premium P2 license or licenses that contain it, such as Microsoft 365 E5, risk-based conditional access is allowed.

Mind Map

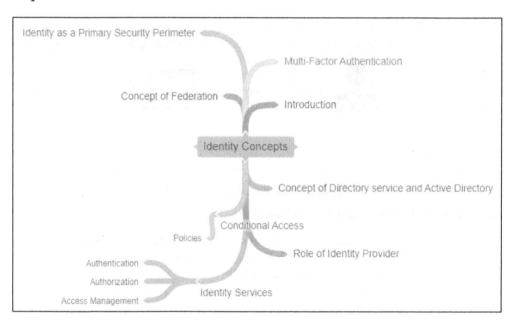

Figure 7-07: Mind Map

Practice Questions

1. What is the benefit of single sign-on?
   A. A central identity provider can be used
   B. The user signs in once and can access many applications or resources
   C. Passwords always expire after 72 days
   D. None of the above

2. Which relationship allows federated services to access resources?
   A. Claim relationship
   B. Shared access relationship
   C. Trust relationship
   D. All of the above

3. Authentication is the process of doing what?
    A. Verifying that a user or device is who they say they are
    B. The process of tracking user behavior
    C. Enabling federated services
    D. All of the above

4. Identity infrastructure can be organized into _____ fundamental pillars.
    A. One
    B. Two
    C. Three
    D. Four

5. The _____ pillar tells the story of how much an IT system needs to know about identity.
    A. Administration
    B. Authentication
    C. Authorization
    D. Auditing

6. The _____ pillar is about processing the incoming identity data.
    A. Administration
    B. Authentication
    C. Authorization
    D. Auditing

7. The _____ pillar tracks who does what, when, where, and how.
    A. Administration
    B. Authentication
    C. Authorization
    D. Auditing

8. _____ is the process of proving that a person is who they say they are.
    A. Authentication
    B. Authorization
    C. Both of the above
    D. None of the above

9. _____ determines the level of access or the permissions an authenticated person has to your data and resources.
    A. Authentication
    B. Authorization
    C. Both of the above
    D. None of the above

10. Federation enables the access of services across _____ or _____ boundaries by establishing trust relationships.

    A. Organizational

    B. Domain

    C. Both of the above

    D. None of the above

Chapter 08: Threat Protection with Microsoft 365 Defender

Introduction

This chapter will teach you how Microsoft 365 Defender can help protect your organization. You will explore each of the different Defender services to understand how they can protect your organization: Identity, Office 365, Endpoint, and cloud apps. You will also explore the capabilities of the Microsoft 365 Defender portal, including Microsoft Secure Score, reports, and incident management.

Microsoft 365 Defender Services

Microsoft 365 Defender is a defense suite that prevents cyberattacks. With Microsoft 365 Defender, you can natively communicate the detection, prevention, investigation, and response to threats across endpoints, identities, emails, and applications.

Microsoft 365 Defender allows administrators to evaluate danger signals from endpoints, applications, emails, and identities to ascertain the breadth and effect of an assault. It sheds more light on how the threat materialized and which systems were impacted. The assault can then be prevented or stopped automatically by Microsoft 365 Defender.

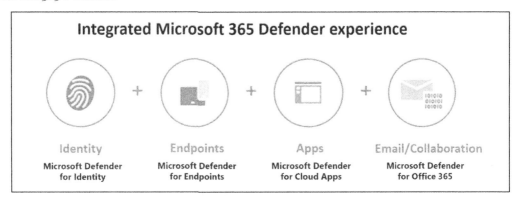

Figure 8-01: Microsoft 365 Defender Services

Microsoft 365 Defender suite prevents:

- **Indicate with Microsoft Defender for Identity and Azure AD Identity Protection** - It utilizes Active Directory signals to identify, define, and investigate advanced threats, compromised identities, and malicious insider actions taking place at your company
- **Endpoints with Microsoft Defender for Endpoint** - It is a single endpoint for preventative protection, post-breach identification, automated investigation, and response
- **Applications with Microsoft Defender for Cloud Apps** - Microsoft Defender for Cloud Apps is a leading cross-SaaS solution that offers deep visibility, strong data controls, and identify threat protection
- **Email and collaboration with Microsoft Defender for Office 365** protects your organization against malicious threats from email messages, links (URLs), and collaboration tools

Use Microsoft Defender to safeguard your organization against sophisticated cyberattacks. It comprises your detection, prevention, investigation, and response to threats across endpoints, identities, emails, and applications.

Microsoft Defender for Office 365

Microsoft Defender for Office 365 protects your organization against malicious threats from email messages, links (URLs), and collaboration tools containing Microsoft Teams, SharePoint Online, OneDrive for Business, and other Office clients.

Microsoft Defender for Office 365 contains these key areas:

- **Threat protection policies**: Describe threat protection policies to set the appropriate level of protection for your organization
- **Reports**: View real-time reports to monitor your organization's Microsoft Defender for Office 365 performance
- **Threat investigation and response capabilities**: Use leading-edge technologies to identify, understand, simulate, and modify threats

Microsoft Defender for Office 365 is accessible in two plans. The plan you choose influences the tools you will see and use. It is important to select the best plan to meet your organization's needs.

Microsoft Defender for Office 365 Plan 1

This plan offers configuration, protection, and identification tools for your Office 365 suite:

- **Safe Attachments**: Verifies email attachments for harmful content
- **Safe Links**: A safe link remains accessible but stops harmful links
- **Safe Attachments for SharePoint, OneDrive, and Microsoft Teams**: Prevents your organization when users collaborate and share files by defining and blocking malicious files in team sites and document libraries
- **Anti-phishing protection**: Recognize attempts so that internal or custom domains can be impersonated
- **Real-time detections**: A real-time report lets you detect and analyze recent threats

Microsoft Defender for Office 365 Plan 2

This plan contains all the core features of Plan 1 and provides automation, investigation, remediation, and simulation tools to help prevent your Office 365 suite:

- **Threat Trackers**: Offer the latest intelligence on prevailing cybersecurity issues, allowing an organization to take countermeasures before an actual threat
- **Threat Explorer**: A real-time report that lets you detect and analyze new threats
- **Automated Investigation and Response (AIR)**: This contains a set of security playbooks that can be formed automatically, such as when an alert is generated or created
- **Attack Simulator**: This lets you run realistic attack cases in your organization to identify vulnerabilities.
- **Proactively hunt for threats with advanced hunting in Microsoft 365 Defender**: Advanced hunting is a query-based threat hunting tool that lets you explore up to 30 days of raw data

- **Investigate alerts and incidents in Microsoft 365 Defender**: Microsoft Defender for Office 365 P2 customers can view Microsoft 365 Defender integration to efficiently detect, review, and respond to incidents and alerts

Microsoft Defender for Office 365 Availability

If the subscription does not contain Defender for Office 365, you can buy it as an add-on. Use Microsoft 365 Defender for Office 365 to prevent your organization's collaboration tools and messages.

Microsoft Defender for Endpoint

This technology contains endpoint behavioral sensors that gather and prevent signals from the operating system, cloud security analytics that converts signals into insights, detections, and recommendations, and threat intelligence to detect attacker tools & techniques and generate alerts.

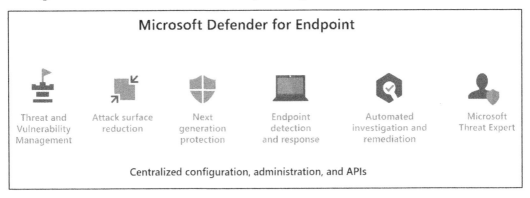

Figure 8-02: Microsoft Defender for Endpoint

Microsoft Defender for Endpoint includes:

- **Attack Surface Reduction:** The capabilities resist attacks and exploitation by ensuring configuration settings are correctly set and exploit mitigation techniques are applied. This set of capabilities also includes network protection and web protection, which regulate access to malicious IP addresses, domains, and URLs, helping prevent apps from accessing dangerous locations
- **Next-Generation Protection**: Brings machine learning, extensive data analysis, in-depth threat resistance research, and the Microsoft cloud infrastructure to identify devices in your enterprise organization
- **Endpoint Detection and Response**: Offers advanced attack detections that are near real-time and actionable
- **Microsoft Threat Experts**: A managed threat hunting ability that offers Security Operation Centers (SOCs) monitoring and analysis tools to ensure critical threats are not missed

Microsoft Defender for Endpoint integrates various components in the Microsoft Defender suite and other Microsoft solutions, including Intune and Microsoft Defender for Cloud.

Microsoft Defender for Cloud Apps

Moving to the cloud enhances flexibility for employees and IT teams. Microsoft Defender for Cloud Apps is a Cloud Access Security Broker (CASB). It is a comprehensive cross-SaaS solution that operates as an intermediary between a cloud user and the provider.

What is a Cloud Access Security Broker?

To facilitate real-time access between your enterprise users and the cloud resources they need, regardless of where they are located or the device they are using, a CASB serves as a gatekeeper. CASBs offer a broad range of capabilities across the following pillars to assist organizations in protecting their environment:

- **Visibility** - Detect cloud services and app use and provide visibility into Shadow IT
- **Threat protection** - Monitor user activities for abnormal behaviors, control access to resources through access controls, and mitigate malware
- **Data security** - Identify, classify and control sensitive information, protecting against malicious actors
- **Compliance** - Assess the compliance of cloud services

These capability areas view the basis of the Defender for Cloud Apps framework described below.

The Defender for Cloud Apps Framework

Microsoft Defender for Cloud Apps is built on a framework that offers the following key points:

- **Monitor and control the use of Shadow IT**: Detect the cloud apps and IaaS and PaaS services used by your organization. Investigate usage patterns, and assess the risk levels and business readiness of more than 25,000 SaaS apps against more than 80 risks
- **Protect against cyber threats and anomalies**: Identify unusual behavior across cloud apps to detect ransomware, and compromised users, analyze high-risk usage, and remove ransomware automatically to limit risks.

Microsoft Defender for Cloud Apps Functionality

Defender for Cloud Apps Security delivers on the framework's components through an extensive list of features and functionality. Listed below are some examples.

Cloud Discovery maps and identifies your cloud environment and your organization's cloud apps. Cloud Discovery utilizes your traffic logs to dynamically discover and view the cloud apps

- **Sanctioned and unsanctioned apps** in your organization using the Cloud apps catalog that includes over 25,000 cloud apps
- Use **App connectors** to integrate Microsoft and non-Microsoft cloud apps with Microsoft Defender for Cloud Apps, extending control and protection
- **Conditional Access** App Control protection provides real-time visibility and control over access and activities within your cloud apps

Figure 8-03: Policies

Note: Visit the https://edxinteractivepage.blob.core.windows.net/edxpages/sc-900/LP03M04-Describe-threat-protection-with-Microsoft-365/index.html. You will learn about the features offered by Microsoft Defender for Cloud Apps in this interactive guide.

Office 365 Cloud App Security

Office 365 Cloud App Security is a part of Microsoft Defender for Cloud Apps that offers enhanced visibility and control for Office 365. Office 365 Cloud App Security consists of threat detection based on user activity logs.

It offers a subset of the core Microsoft Defender for Cloud Apps features. It also provides a reduced subset of the Microsoft Defender for Cloud Apps discovery capabilities.

Use Microsoft Defender for Cloud Apps to intelligently and proactively identify and respond to threats across your organization's Microsoft and non-Microsoft cloud services.

Microsoft Defender for Identity

Microsoft Defender for Identity is a cloud-based security solution. It utilizes your on-premises Active Directory data (called signals) to identify, detect, and investigate advanced threats, compromised identities, and malicious insider actions moved at your organization.

Microsoft Defender for Identity provides security professionals managing hybrid environments functionality to:

- Monitor and profile user behavior and activities
- Protect user identities and reduce the attack surface
- Identify and investigate suspicious activities and advanced attacks across the cyberattack kill chain

Monitor and Profile User Behavior and Activities

Defender for Identity manages and analyzes user activities and information across your network, containing permissions and group membership, forming a baseline for each user. Defender for Identity then describes anomalies with adaptive built-in intelligence.

Protect User Identities and Lower the Attack Surface

Defender for Identity provides insights on identity configurations and suggested security best practices. It offers extra insights into how to improve security posture and policies.

For hybrid environments in which Active Directory Federation Services (AD FS) is present, Defender for Identity protects the AD FS by detecting on-premises attacks and providing visibility into authentication events generated by the AD FS.

Detect Suspicious Activities and Advanced Attacks Across the Cyberattack Kill-Chain

These assets might comprise sensitive accounts, domain administrators, and highly sensitive data. Defender for Identity identifies these advanced threats at the source throughout the entire cyber-attack kill-chain:

- Reconnaissance
- Compromised credentials
- Lateral movements
- Domain dominance

Microsoft Defender Protection

Microsoft's 365 Defender services defend against:

- Endpoints equipped with Defender for Endpoint – Defender for Endpoint is a unified endpoint platform for proactive security, post-breach detection, automated investigation, and response
- Defender's assets - Microsoft Defender Vulnerability Management provides continuous asset visibility, intelligent risk-based assessments, and built-in remediation tools to assist your security and IT teams in prioritizing and addressing important vulnerabilities and misconfigurations throughout your organization
- Email and collaboration with Defender for Office 365 - Defender for Office 365 protects your business from harmful threats from collaboration tools, links (URLs), and email communications
- Defender for Identity – It uses your on-premises Active Directory Domain Services (AD DS) signals to identify, detect, and look into advanced threats, compromised identities, and malicious insider actions targeted at your company.

- Identity protection with Azure Active Directory (Azure AD) and Defender for Identity - Azure AD Identity Protection automates identifying and correcting identity-based hazards in your cloud-based Azure AD

Microsoft 365 Defender portal

Microsoft 365 Defender natively coordinates detection, prevention, investigation, and response across endpoints, identities, emails, and applications to provide integrated protection against sophisticated attacks. The Microsoft 365 Defender portal combines this functionality into a central place designed to meet security

teams' needs and emphasizes quick access to information and more straightforward layouts. You can view your organization's security health through the Microsoft 365 Defender portal.

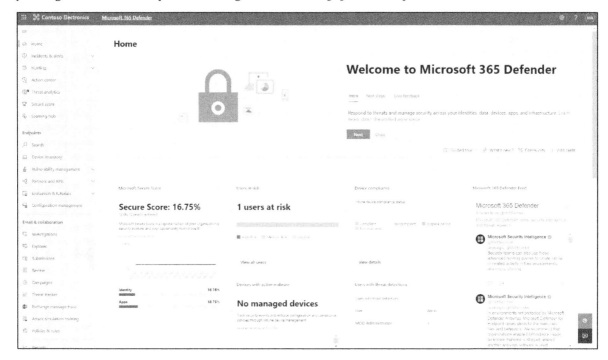

Figure 8-04: Microsoft 365 Defender Portal

The Microsoft 365 Defender portal lets admins tailor the navigation pane to meet daily operational requirements. Admins can customize the navigation pane to view or hide functions and services based on specific preferences.

The left navigation pane provides security professionals easy access to the email and collaboration capabilities of Microsoft Defender for Office 365 and the capabilities of Microsoft Defender for Endpoint, described in the previous sections. Below, it describes a few other capabilities accessible from the left navigation bar in the Microsoft 365 Defender portal.

Incidents and Alerts

Individual alerts offer valuable clues about a completed or ongoing attack, and Microsoft 365 Defender automatically aggregates these alerts. The grouping of these related alerts forms an incident, and the incident provides a comprehensive view and context of an attack.

The incidents queue is a central location that lists each incident by severity. Choosing an incident name displays a summary of the incident and offers access to tabs with additional information, including:

- All the alerts related to the incident
- All the users that have been detected to be part of or related to the incident
- All the mailboxes that have been detected to be part of or related to the incident
- The alerts in the incident that triggered all the automated investigations
- All the supporting evidence and response

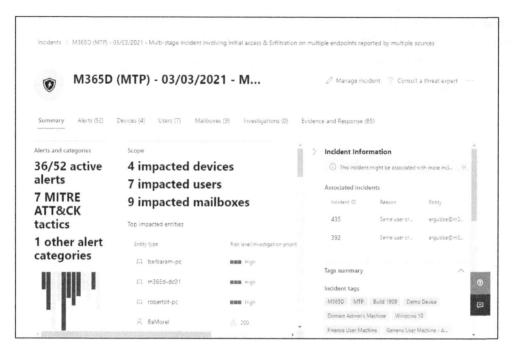

Figure 8-05: Incidents and Alerts

Hunting

Advanced hunting is a query-based threat hunting option that lets security professionals explore up to 30 days of raw data. Advanced hunting queries enable security professionals to proactively search for threats, malware, and malicious activity across your endpoints, Office 365 mailboxes, and more. Threat-hunting queries can be used to build custom detection rules. These rules automatically check for and respond to suspected breach activity, misconfigured machines, and other findings.

Threat Analytics

Threat analytics is our in-product threat intelligence solution from expert Microsoft security researchers. It is designed to assist security teams in tracking and responding to emerging threats. The threat analytics dashboard highlights the most relevant reports to your organization. It includes the latest threats, high-impact threats (threats with the most active alerts affecting your organization), and high-exposure threats.

Selecting a specific threat from the dashboard provides a threat analytics report with more detailed information, including detailed analyst reports, impacted assets, mitigations, and much more.

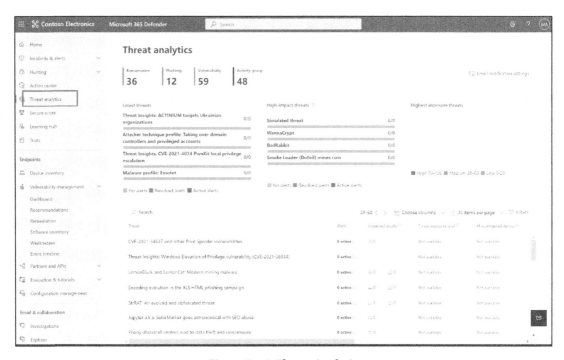

Figure 8-06: Threat Analytics

Secure Score

An indicator of a company's security posture is the Microsoft Secure Score, one of the features in the Microsoft 365 Defender site. Your protection will be better with the score. The security of an organization's Microsoft 365 identities, apps, and devices can be monitored and improved via a single dashboard through the Microsoft 365 Defender site.

Using Secure Score, enterprises can:

- Provide an update on their security posture
- Strengthen their security posture by offering discoverability, visibility, direction, and control
- Identify benchmarks and important performance indicators (KPIs)

Microsoft Teams, Azure Active Directory, Microsoft Defender for Endpoint, Microsoft Defender for Identity, Microsoft Secure Score, and Microsoft 365 (including Exchange Online) are currently supported.

Figure 8-07 displays an organization's Secure Score, a score breakdown by points, and the improvement actions that can boost the organization's score. Finally, it indicates how well the organization's Secure Score compares to similar organizations.

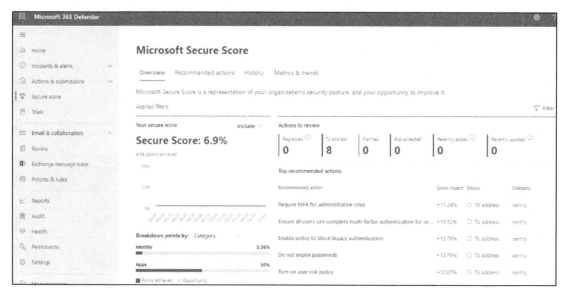

Figure 8-07: Secure Score

To explore Microsoft Secure Score, select the interactive guide below and follow the prompts on the screen.

Alternatively, navigate to https://edxinteractivepage.blob.core.windows.net/edxpages/sc-900/LP03M04-Describe-threat-protection-with-Microsoft-365/index.html

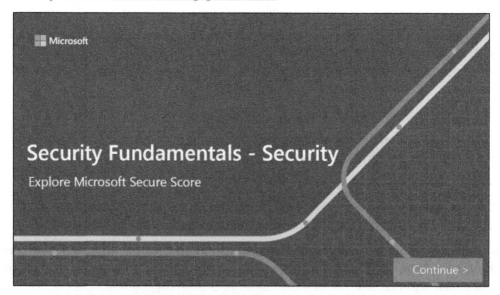

Figure 8-08: Security Fundamentals

Differences between secure Score in Microsoft 365 Defender and Microsoft Defender for Cloud

There are   secure scores for Microsoft 365 Defender and Microsoft Defender for Cloud, but they are subtly different. Secure Score in Microsoft Defender for Cloud measures the security posture of your Azure subscriptions.

> **EXAM TIP:** A secure score in the Microsoft 365 Defender portal measures the organization's security posture across your apps, devices, and identities.

Learning hub

The Microsoft 365 Defender portal contains a learning hub that bubbles up official guidance from resources, for example, the Microsoft security blog, the Microsoft security community on YouTube, and the official documentation at docs.microsoft.com.

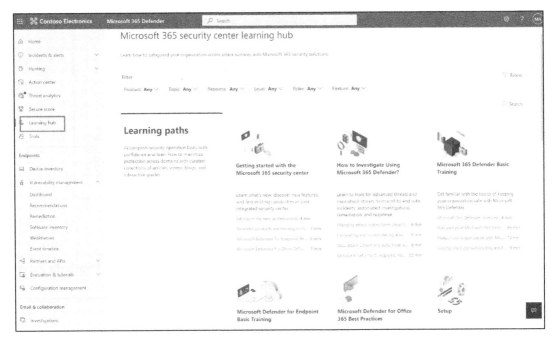

Figure 8-09: Learning Hub

Reports

The Microsoft 365 Defender portal contains a **Reports** section that includes a general security report, reports related to endpoints, and reports related to email and collaboration.

Figure 8-10: Security Reports and Dashboards

Security Report

The general **security report** allows admins to see information about security trends and track the protection status of your identities, data, devices, apps, and infrastructure.

By default, cards are categorized by the following categories:

- **Identities** - user accounts and credentials
- **Data** - email and document contents
- **Devices** - computers, mobile phones, and other devices
- **Apps** - programs and connected online services

The cards are grouped by category (only two of the four categories are displayed in Figure 8-11).

Figure 8-11: Security Report

You can also group cards by topic, which will reorganize the cards and group them into the following areas:

- **Risk** - Cards highlighting entities, such as accounts and devices, that could be at risk
- **Detection trends** - Cards highlighting new threat detections, anomalies, and policy violations
- **Configuration and health** - Cards dealing with the configuration and deployment of security controls, comprising device onboarding states to management services

Endpoint Reports

The endpoints section on the reports page contains a **threat protection report**, a **device health and compliance report**, and a **vulnerable devices report**.

The **threat protection report** offers high-level information about alerts created in your organization. The report contains trending information displaying the detection sources, categories, severities, statuses, classifications, and determinations of alerts across time.

The report's dashboard is organized into two sections:

- **Alert trends** - By default, the alert trends display alert information from the past 30 days ending in the latest full day
- **Alert summary** - The alert summary takes alert information scoped to the current day

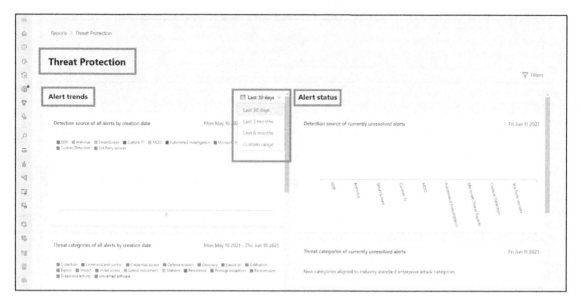

Figure 8-12: Endpoint Reports

- The device health and compliance report enables admins to monitor the health state, antivirus status, operating system platforms, and Windows 10 versions for devices in your organization

This report's dashboard is also organized into two sections:

- **Device trends** - By default, the device trends display device information from the 30 days ending in the latest full day. By adjusting the period, you can fine-tune the reporting period to understand your organization's trends better
- **Device summary** - The device summary displays device information scoped to the current day

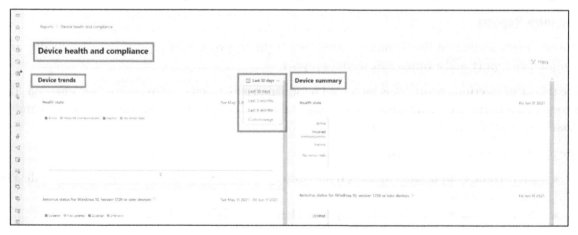

Figure 8-13: Report's Dashboard

- The **vulnerable devices report** allows admins to view information about the vulnerable devices in your organization, involving their exposure to vulnerabilities by severity level, exploitability, age, and more

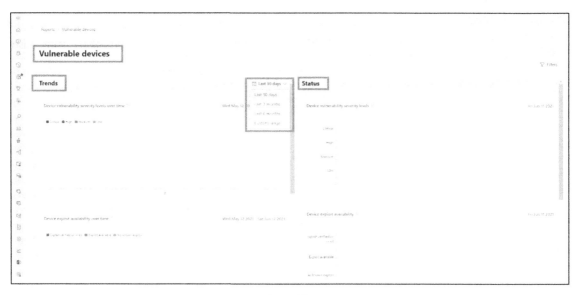

Figure 8-14: Vulnerable Devices Report

Email and Collaboration Reports

The **email and collaboration reports** allow admins to review Microsoft suggested actions to help enhance email and collaboration security.

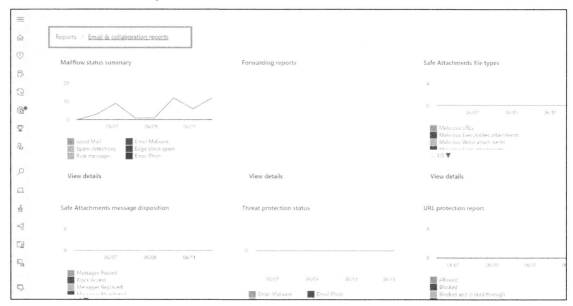

Figure 8-15: Email and Collaboration Reports

Incidents Capabilities

Incidents are a group of correlated alerts made when a suspicious event is found. Alerts are created from different devices, users, and mailbox entities. They can come from many different domains. Microsoft 365 Defender automatically aggregates these alerts.

Permissions & roles

View to Microsoft 365 Defender is configured with Azure Active Directory global roles or by using custom roles.

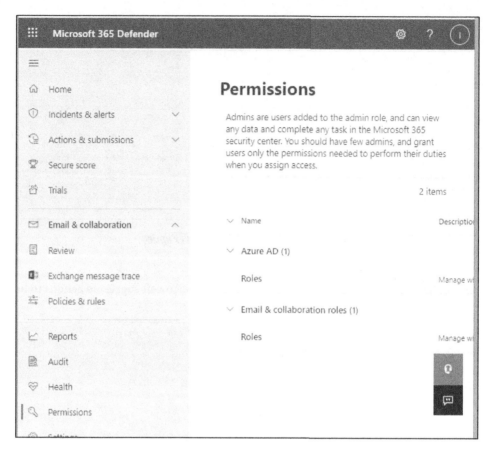

Figure 8-16: Permissions

Incident Management

Managing incidents is critical in safeguarding that threats are covered and addressed. In Microsoft 365 Defender, you can control incidents on devices, users' accounts, and mailboxes.

Incidents are automatically given a name based on an alert. When you examine cases where you want to move alerts from one incident to another, you can also do so from the Alerts tab. You will make a larger or smaller incident that includes all relevant alerts.

Mind Map

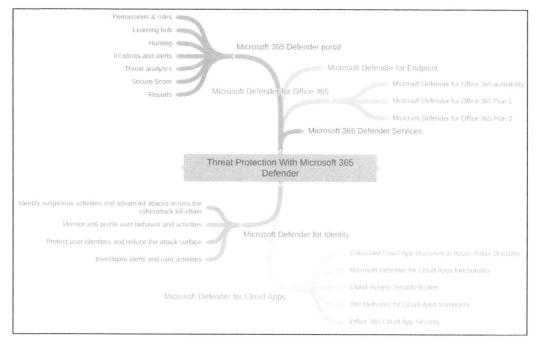

Figure 8-17: Mind Map

Practice Questions

1. A lead admin for a company is looking to prevent harmful threats posed by email messages, links (URLs), and collaboration tools. Which solution from the following best suits this purpose?
   A. Microsoft Defender for Office 365
   B. Microsoft Defender for Endpoint
   C. Microsoft Defender for Identity
   D. All of the above

2. A Cloud Access Security Broker (CASB) protects 4 areas/pillars: visibility to detect all cloud services, data security, threat protection, and compliance. These pillars view the basis of the Cloud App Security framework upon which Microsoft Defender for Cloud Apps is built. Which pillar is accountable for identifying and controlling sensitive information?
   A. Threat protection
   B. Compliance
   C. Data Security
   D. All of the above

3. Which of the following is a cloud-based security solution that identifies, detects, and helps identify advanced threats, compromised identities, and harmful insider actions moved at your organization?
   A. Microsoft Defender for Office 365
   B. Microsoft Defender for Identity

C. Microsoft Defender for Cloud Apps

D. All of the above

4. Admins in the organization use the Microsoft 365 Defender portal daily. They want to understand the organization's current security posture quickly. Which option in the Microsoft 365 Defender portal will they use?

A. Reports

B. Secure Score

C. Policies

D. All of the above

5. Microsoft Defender for Office 365 is available in _____ plans.

A. One

B. Two

C. Three

D. Four

Chapter 09: Describe the Security Capabilities of Microsoft Sentinel

Introduction

Every organization, whatever its size, is vulnerable to security threats and attacks. In this chapter, you will learn about the different security defenses that are available to defend your company's digital estate.

Define the Concepts of SIEM and SOAR

Security information event management (SIEM) and security orchestration automated response (SOAR) offer security insights and security automation that can enhance an organization's threat visibility and response.

What is Security Information and Event Management (SIEM)?

A SIEM system is a tool that a group uses to gather data from across the whole estate, including infrastructure, software, and resources. It does analysis, looks for correlations or anomalies, and creates alerts and incidents.

What is Security Orchestration Automated Response (SOAR)?

A SOAR system gets alerts from many sources, such as a SIEM system. The SOAR system then causes action-driven automated workflows and processes to run security tasks that mitigate the issue.

To offer a comprehensive approach to security, an organization wants to use a solution that embraces or combines both SIEM and SOAR functionality.

Microsoft Sentinel offers integrated Threat Management

Effective management of an organization's network security perimeter needs the right combination of tools and systems. Microsoft Sentinel is a SIEM/SOAR solution that carries intelligent security analytics and threat intelligence across the enterprise.

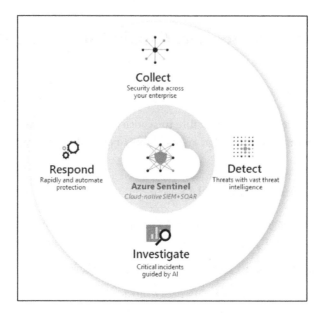

Figure 9-01: Azure Sentinel

This diagram shows the end-to-end functionality of Microsoft Sentinel.

- **Collect** data at the cloud scale
- **Detect** uncovered threats and minimize false positives
- **Investigate** threats with artificial intelligence (AI) and hunt suspicious activities at scale
- **Respond** to incidents rapidly

Microsoft Sentinel helps allow end-to-end security operations in a modern Security Operations Center (SOC). Listed below are some of the key features of Microsoft Sentinel:

Connect Sentinel to your data

To onboard Microsoft Sentinel, you first want to link to your security sources. You can link your data sources using community-built data connectors listed in the Microsoft Sentinel GitHub repository or by following generic deployment procedures for how to connect your data source to Microsoft Sentinel.

Manage incidents in Microsoft Sentinel

Incident management allows you to manage the lifecycle of the incident. View all related alerts that are aggregated into an incident. You can also triage and investigate. Review all related entities in the incident and additional contextual information meaningful to the triage process. Investigate the alerts and related entities to understand the scope of the breach. Trigger playbooks on the alerts grouped in the incident to resolve the threat detected by the alert.

Security automation and orchestration

Microsoft Sentinel mixes with Azure Logic Apps, so you can create automated workflows, or playbooks, in response to events. A security playbook is a collection of procedures that can help SOC engineers and analysts of all tiers to automate and simplify tasks and orchestrate a response.

Investigation

You select an entity on the interactive graph to ask specific questions, then drill down into that entity and its networks to get to the reason for the threat.

Hunting

Use Microsoft Sentinel's hunting search-and-query tools, based on the MITRE framework (a global database of adversary tactics and techniques), to actively search for security threats across your organization's data sources before an alert is triggered.

While hunting, you can bookmark interesting events. Bookmarking events enables you to return to them later, share them with others, and group them with other correlating events to create a compelling incident for investigation.

Notebooks

Microsoft Sentinel supports Jupyter Notebooks. You can use Jupyter Notebooks in Microsoft Sentinel to spread the scope of what you can do with Microsoft Sentinel data.

Understand Sentinel costs

Microsoft Sentinel offers intelligent security analytics across your enterprise. The data for this analysis is kept in an Azure Monitor Log Analytics workspace. There are two types to pay for the Microsoft Sentinel service:

- **Capacity Reservations**: With Capacity Reservations, you are billed a fixed fee based on the selected tier, enabling a predictable total cost for Microsoft Sentinel.
- **Pay-As-You-Go**: With Pay-As-You-Go pricing, you are billed per gigabyte (GB) for the volume of data ingested for analysis in Microsoft Sentinel and stored in the Azure Monitor Log Analytics workspace.

Mind Map

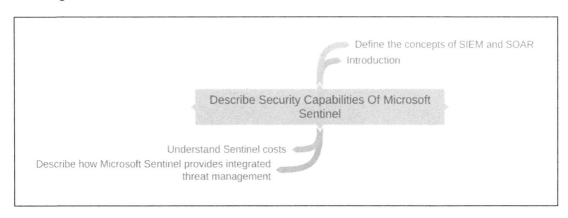

Figure 9-02: Mind Map

Practice Questions

1. As an admin, it is significant to influence your team to start using Microsoft Sentinel. You have put together a presentation. What are the four security operation areas of Microsoft Sentinel that progress in this area?
A. Collect, Detect, Investigate, and Redirect.
B. Collect, Detect, Investigate, and Respond.
C. Collect, Detect, Investigate, and Repair.

2. Your estate has many different data sources where data is kept. Which tool must be used with Microsoft Sentinel to rapidly gain insights across your data as soon as a data source is linked?
A. Azure Monitor Workbooks.
B. Playbooks.
C. Microsoft 365 Defender.

3. A _____ system takes alerts from many sources.
A. SIEM
B. SOAR
C. Both of the above

Chapter 10: Describe The Compliance Management Capabilities In Microsoft Purview

Introduction

Organizations must stay in line with compliance-related legal, regulatory, and privacy standards to protect their customers, partners, and themselves. Microsoft 365 provides tools and capabilities to enable organizations to manage compliance.

The Microsoft Purview compliance portal is the portal for organizations to manage their compliance needs using integrated solutions for information protection, information governance, insider risk management, auditing, and more.

In this chapter, you will learn about the Microsoft Purview compliance portal. You will learn about Compliance Manager and compliance score, which can help organizations manage, simplify, and improve compliance across their organization.

Describe the Microsoft Purview Compliance Portal

The compliance portal is accessible to customers with the following roles:

- Global administrator
- Compliance administrator
- Compliance data administrator

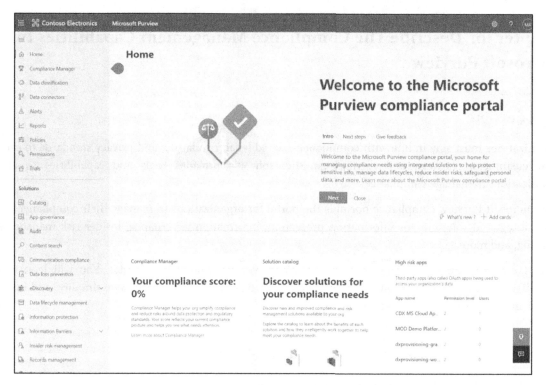

Figure 10-01: Microsoft Purview

The default compliance portal home page contains several cards, including:

- The **Compliance Manager** card. It calculates a risk-based compliance score that calculates progress toward finishing recommended actions to decrease risks related to data protection and regulatory standards. The Compliance Manager solution also offers workflow capabilities and built-in control mapping to help you proficiently carry out development actions.

Figure 10-02: Compliance Score

- The **Solution catalog** card links to collections of integrated solutions to help you manage end-to-end compliance scenarios. Solutions areas included:

  o **Information protection & governance**. These solutions help organizations classify, protect, and retain your data where it lives and wherever it goes. Included are data lifecycle management, data loss prevention, information protection, and records management.

  o **Privacy**. Build a more privacy-resilient workplace. Privacy management gives actionable insights into your organization's data to help you spot issues and reduce risks.

  o **Insider risk management**. Included are communication compliance, information barriers, and insider risk management.

  o **Discovery & response**. These solutions help organizations quickly find, investigate, and respond with relevant data. Included are Audits, data subject requests, and eDiscovery.

Figure 10-03: Compliance Needs

- The **Active Alerts** card includes a summary of the most active alerts and a link where admins can view more detailed information, such as alert severity, status, category, and more.

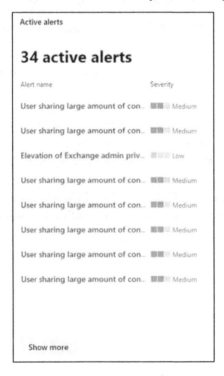

Figure 10-04: Active Alerts

Navigation

You can access alerts, reports, policies, and all the solutions that are included in the solutions catalog. There is access to data connectors that you can use to import non-Microsoft data to Microsoft 365 so it can be covered by your compliance solutions. The **Customize navigation** control allows customization of the items that appear in the navigation pane.

Figure 10-05: Navigation

Describe Compliance Manager

Your entire compliance score is shown on the Compliance Manager dashboard. Your progress towards executing suggested improvement initiatives while staying within controls is tracked by this score. You can learn more about your compliance posture by looking at your score. It can also assist you in setting priorities for actions depending on how well they might lower risk.

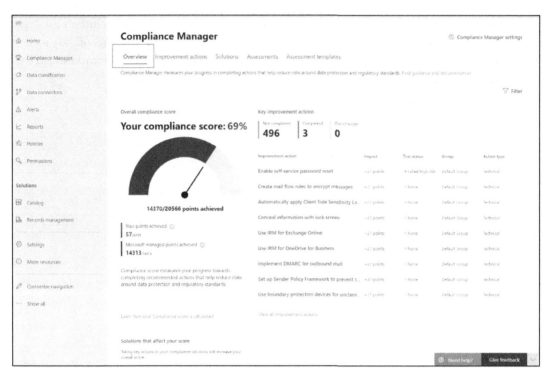

Figure 10-06: Compliance Manager

Controls

Control is a condition of a regulation, standard, or policy. It describes how to assess and manage system configuration, organizational process, and people responsible for meeting a specific condition of a regulation, standard, or policy.

Assessments

Completing the actions within an assessment helps to meet the requirements of a standard, regulation, or law. For example, an organization may have an assessment that, when completed, helps to bring the organization's Microsoft 365 settings in line with ISO 27001 requirements.

An assessment consists of several components, including the services that are in scope, the controls, and an assessment score that shows progress toward completing the actions needed for compliance.

Templates

Compliance Manager provides templates to help admins quickly create assessments. Admins can also build a custom assessment by creating a template with their controls and actions.

Improvement actions

Improvement actions help centralize compliance activities. Each improvement action provides recommended guidance that is intended to help organizations to align with data protection regulations and standards. It can be allocated to users in the organization to do implementation and testing work.

Benefits of Compliance Manager

Compliance Manager provides many benefits, including:

- Translating complicated regulations, standards, company policies, or other control frameworks into simple language.
- Providing access to a large variety of out-of-the-box assessments and custom assessments to help organizations with their unique compliance needs.
- Mapping regulatory controls against recommended improvement actions.
- Providing step-by-step guidance on how to implement the solutions to meet regulatory requirements.
- Helping admins and users to prioritize actions that will have the highest impact on their organizational compliance by associating a score with each action.

Advantages of Cmpliance Score

Admins can get a failure of the compliance score in the Compliance Manager overview pane.

Figure 10-07: Compliance Score Breakdown

How to understand the compliance score

The overall compliance score is designed using scores that are assigned to actions. Actions come in two types:

- **Your improved actions**: actions that the organization is expected to manage
- **Microsoft actions**: actions that Microsoft manages for the organization

Actions are categorized as mandatory, discretionary, preventative, detective, or corrective:

- **Mandatory** – these actions should not be bypassed
- **Discretionary** – these actions depend on the users understanding and adherence to a policy

The following are subcategories of actions that can be classified as mandatory or discretionary:

- Preventative actions are designed to handle specific risks, like using encryption to protect data at rest if there are breaches or attacks
- Detective actions actively monitor systems to identify irregularities that could represent risks or that can be used to detect breaches or intrusions
- Corrective actions help admins to minimize the adverse effects of security incidents by undertaking corrective measures to reduce their immediate effect or possibly even reverse the damage

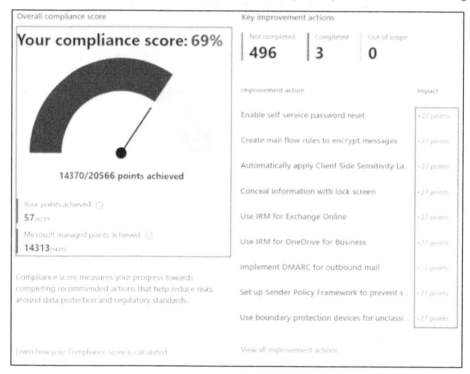

Figure 10-08: Compliance Score

What is the difference between Compliance Manager and a compliance score?

Compliance Manager is a solution in the Microsoft Purview compliance portal to let admins manage and track compliance activities. The compliance score is a calculation of the compliance posture across the organization. It is accessible through Compliance Manager.

Compliance Manager gives admins the ability to understand and increase their score, so they can progress the organization's compliance position and help it to stay in line with compliance requirements.

Mind Map

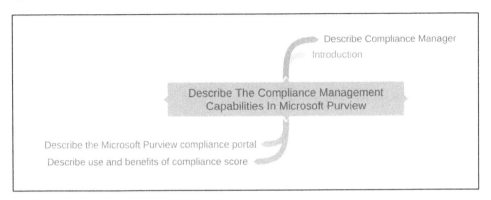

Figure 10-09: Mind Map

Practice Questions

1. A new admin has joined the team and wants to be able to view the Microsoft Purview compliance portal. Which of the roles could the admin use to view the compliance portal?
A. Compliance Administrator role
B. Helpdesk Administrator role
C. User Administrator role

2. Your employees on the team are uninformed about the idea of shared controls in Compliance Manager. How would the idea of shared controls be explained?
A. Regulates that both external regulators and Microsoft share responsibility for applying.
B. Regulates both your organization and external regulators share responsibility for applying.
C. Regulates that both your organization and Microsoft share responsibility for applying.

3. A customer has demanded a document on the Microsoft Purview compliance portal. The presentation will want to cover Compliance Manager and compliance score. What is the change between Compliance Manager and the compliance score?
A. Compliance Manager is an end-to-end solution in the Microsoft Purview compliance portal to allow admins to manage and track compliance activities. The compliance score is a calculation of the compliance posture across the organization.
B. Compliance Manager is a solution in the Microsoft Purview compliance portal to let admins manage and track compliance activities. The compliance score is a score the organization gets from regulators for successful compliance.
C. Compliance Manager is the regulator who will achieve your compliance activities. The compliance score is a calculation of the compliance posture across the organization.

Chapter 11: Service Trust Portal and Privacy at Microsoft

Introduction

Organizations all across the world are very concerned about data protection and compliance. Thanks to the Service Trust Portal launch, those striving to support or safeguard users' right to privacy in Microsoft's online environment may now rest comfortably.

Microsoft Cloud services are built on trust, security, and compliance. The Microsoft Service Trust Portal offers numerous content, tools, and resources about Microsoft security, privacy, and compliance practices.

Microsoft also helps organizations meet their privacy requirements with Microsoft Priva. Priva helps organizations protect personal data and build a privacy-resilient workplace.

In this chapter, you will study Service Trust Portal and its resources, including audit reports, security assessments, and compliance guides that enable organizations to manage compliance. You will learn about Microsoft's commitment to privacy and its privacy principles. Lastly, you will learn about Microsoft Priva, which helps organizations meet their privacy goals.

Trust Center

Trust Center is a shortcut to knowing everything that Microsoft does to ensure you do not lose trust in Microsoft. With this, you have a link to learn about security, privacy, GDPR, data location, compliance, and more.

The Trust Center demonstrates how Microsoft implements and supports security, privacy, compliance, and transparency in all of its cloud products and services and the company's guiding principles for preserving data integrity in the cloud. The Microsoft Trusted Cloud Initiative's Trust Center is a key component that offers materials and assistance to the legal and compliance sector.

The Trust Center gives you:

- Comprehensive details on the capabilities, offerings, rules, and practices used by Microsoft cloud solutions in terms of security, privacy, and compliance
- Additional sources for every subject
- Links to forthcoming events and the security, privacy, and compliance blogs

For additional employees in your company who might be involved in compliance, security, and privacy, the Trust Center is a valuable resource. These individuals consist of business managers, privacy and risk officers, and legal compliance teams

Service Trust Portal (STP)

The Service Trust Portal, often known as STP, is a tool included in Microsoft Office 365 that offers existing and potential users a variety of information on how the tech giant maintains privacy, compliance, and security.

Microsoft publishes information on this platform that businesses need to do due diligence on and assess all of Microsoft's cloud services. Microsoft introduced this service to make its users' assessments more transparent, better understood, and simpler.

What is contained in the STP?

A lot of helpful data has been compiled from all of the Microsoft cloud services and is available in the Microsoft Service Trust Portal (STP). Additionally, it includes the information and tools that enterprises require for everything related to security, compliance, and privacy.

From the main menu, you access multiple services as shown in the following figure:

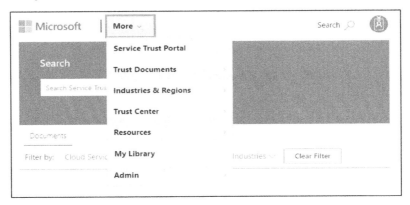

Figure 11-01: Service Trust Portal

- **Service Trust Portal** – This link provides a quick way to get back to the home page for the Service Trust Portal
- **Compliance Manager** – This link currently directs users to Compliance Manager in the Microsoft Purview compliance portal. Users are encouraged to use the Microsoft Purview compliance portal to access Compliance Manager and other compliance management capabilities in Microsoft 365
- **Trust Documents** – Trust Documents provides a wealth of security implementation and design information to make it easier for organizations to meet regulatory compliance objectives by understanding how Microsoft Cloud services keep customer data secure
- **Audit Reports** - Lists independent audit and assessment reports on Microsoft's Cloud services. These reports provide information about Microsoft Cloud service's compliance with data protection standards and regulatory requirements
- **Data Protection** – It consists of a wealth of resources such as audited controls, white papers, FAQs, penetration tests, risk assessment tools, and compliance guides
- **Azure Stack** – It comprises documents that offer security and compliance solutions and support tailored to the requirements of Azure Stack customers
- **Industries & Regions** – This link provides access to compliance information about Microsoft Cloud services organized by industry and region
- **Industry Solutions** – It directs users to the landing page for the Financial Services industry. This includes information such as compliance offerings, FAQs, and success stories
- **Regional Solutions** – It offers documents on Microsoft Cloud services compliance with the laws of numerous countries/regions. Specific countries/regions include Australia, Canada, the Czech Republic, Denmark, Germany, Poland, Romania, Spain, and the United Kingdom
- **Trust Center** – The option links to the Microsoft Trust Center, which provides more information about privacy, security, and compliance in the Microsoft Cloud
- **Resources** – This option links to Security & Compliance for Office 365, the Microsoft Global Data centers, and Frequently Asked Questions

- **My Library** – This feature lets you save documents so that you can quickly view them on your My Library page
- **More** - This option provides a selection of settings and user privacy settings that are available only to Global Administrators and relate to options associated with Compliance Manager. Admins, however, are encouraged to use the Microsoft Purview compliance portal

Accessing the STP

STP is a free tool accessible to everyone, including users of Microsoft online services who are already subscribers as well as those who are just investigating the cloud-based platform.

You must have a Microsoft cloud services account and be logged in to the platform to access the Microsoft Service Trust Portal or any STP documents.

Log into your account to access the available tools and resources, whether you have a Microsoft account or an Azure Active Directory one. Click "Accept" to proceed after being prompted to accept their Non-Disclosure Agreement for Compliance Materials.

Microsoft's Privacy Principles

Introduction

The development and rising popularity of cloud computing bring up crucial policy issues, such as geographical location, shared data storage, transparency, access, and security. Cloud computing services and their uptake are still constrained by competing legal duties and competing claims of governmental jurisdiction over data usage. Different laws governing data retention, privacy, and other topics are ambiguous and present serious legal difficulties.

Since the introduction of the Microsoft Network in 1994, Microsoft has been addressing privacy concerns relating to cloud computing and online services. Microsoft is still dedicated to keeping its customers' information private. Microsoft is aware that trustworthy privacy measures are crucial to fostering cloud computing's growth and enabling it to realize its full potential. Because of this, Microsoft carefully considered data protection when developing Office 365, working with a specialized team of privacy experts.

Privacy Principles

Microsoft privacy principles and standards provide their staff with a clear framework to ensure that Microsoft manage data responsibly. These guidelines are used to gather and use customer and partner information at Microsoft. Microsoft have made significant investments to create an extensive privacy governance program to put their values and standards into practice. In addition to the hundreds of other employees who help ensure privacy policies, processes, and technologies are used across all of Microsoft's products and services, the company employs many full-time privacy professionals.

Microsoft's international privacy community also works to ensure that their business divisions implement the company's privacy policies, practices, and technology. As part of this community, engineers, marketers, lawyers, and business executives collaborate with privacy champs, leads, and managers to examine Microsoft products and services and offer advice on privacy-related matters.

Microsoft's products and services run on trust. Microsoft's approach to privacy is based on the following six principles:

- **Control**: Microsoft's control over your data is applied by compliance with broadly applicable privacy laws and standards.
- **The Microsoft Online Services Subprocessor List:** This document is accessible as one of the data protection resources in the Service Trust Portal
- **Security**: Protecting the data that is trusted to Microsoft by using strong security and encryption. With state-of-the-art encryption, Microsoft safeguards your data at rest and in transit
- **Strong legal safeguards:** Advocating for the legal protection of privacy as a fundamental human right while adhering to local privacy regulations.
- **No content-based targeting**: Not using email, chat, files, or other personal data to target advertising.
- **Benefits to you**: When Microsoft does gather data, it is used to benefit you, the customer, and to make your experiences better. For example:
  - **Troubleshooting:** Troubleshooting is done in order to prevent, identify, and fix issues that affect service operations
  - **Feature improvement:** Constant enhancement of features, such as enhancing service reliability and data protection
  - **Customized consumer experience:** Data enables more individualized enhancements and superior client interactions.experiences

> **EXAM TIP:** The privacy principles form Microsoft's private foundation and shape how products and services are designed.

Microsoft Priva

Regulations and laws impact people worldwide, setting rules for how organizations keep personal data and giving people rights to operate personal data collected by an organization.

To satisfy legal requirements and win over customers, businesses must adopt a "privacy by default" philosophy. Organizations need a comprehensive solution to handle typical problems like:

- Educating users on proper data handling procedures and how to spot and address problems
- Recognizing the dangers posed by the volume, nature, and sharing of personal data
- Quickly and accurately responding to requests for subject data or subject rights

Your privacy objectives can be met by using Microsoft Priva to overcome these difficulties. The capabilities of Priva are accessible through two solutions: **Priva Subject Rights Requests,** which offers automation and workflow tools for completing data requests, and **Priva Privacy Risk Management,** which provides accessibility into your organization's data and policy templates for lowering risks.

Priva Privacy Risk Management

Microsoft Priva helps you combine the data your organization keeps by automating the data of personal data assets and visualizing essential information. These visualizations can be seen on the overview and data profile pages, currently accessible through the Microsoft Purview compliance portal.

The overview dashboard offers an overview of your organization's data in Microsoft 365.

Figure 11-02: Priva Privacy Risk Management

The data profile page in Priva offers a snapshot view of your organization's personal data stores in Microsoft 365 and where it resides. It also gives a view into the kinds of data you store.

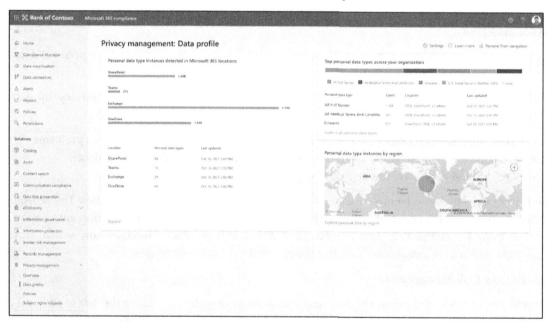

Figure 11-03: Data Profile

Priva assess your organization's data stored in the below Microsoft 365 services within your Microsoft 365 tenant:

- Exchange Online
- SharePoint Online
- OneDrive for Business

- Microsoft Teams

Priva Subject Rights Requests

By specific privacy regulations around the world, individuals (or data subjects) may make requests to review or manage the personal data about themselves that companies have collected. Finding relevant data can be a formidable task for companies that store large amounts of information.

Microsoft Priva can help you handle these inquiries through the Subject Rights Requests solution. It provides workflow, automation, and collaboration capabilities to help you search for subject data, reviews your findings, collects appropriate files, and produces reports.

Mind Map

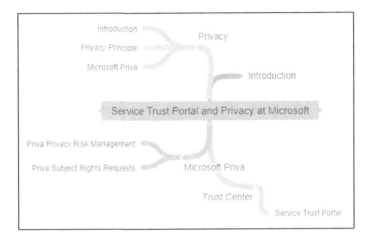

Figure 11-04: Mind Map

Practice Questions

1. When browsing Microsoft compliance documentation in the Service Trust Portal, you have found several documents that are specific to your industry. What is the best way of ensuring you keep up to date with the latest updates?
   A. Save the files to your My Library
   B. Print each document so you can easily refer to them
   C. Download each document
   D. None of the above

2. Microsoft's approach to privacy is built on six principles: Three of the principles are strong legal protections for privacy, no content-based targeting, and benefits to customers from any data we collect. Identify the three other principles part of Microsoft's approach to privacy.
   A. Customer control, transparency, and security
   B. Shared responsibility, transparency, and security
   C. Customer control, transparency, and zero trust
   D. None of the above

3. Microsoft Cloud services are built on a foundation of _____.
   A. Trust
   B. Security
   C. Compliance
   D. All of the above

   4. Microsoft's approach to privacy is built on the _____ principles.
   A. Three
   B. Four
   C. Five
   D. Six

5. Priva's capabilities are available through _____ solutions.
   A. One
   B. Two
   C. Three
   D. Four

Chapter 12: Pricing, Licensing, and Billing Options Available in Microsoft 365

Introduction

Microsoft 365 is available through various licensing models and home, business, enterprise, and subscription plans. These options let you choose the best model and plan for your management and operational needs. By selecting the optimum subscription and license, you can be sure that the functionality you need is in the most cost-effective package.

Explore the Pricing Model for Microsoft Cloud Services

Microsoft offers various licensing programs and channels where you can buy Microsoft 365 products and services. These programs include Microsoft Volume Licensing (VL), Cloud Solution Provider Program (CSP), or Web Direct Programs (MOSP). For example, in Volume Licensing, Microsoft 365 is available for customers through the **Enterprise Agreement (EA)**. If you need a dedicated expert to provide hands-on support, Microsoft has many qualified partners in their **Cloud Solution Provider (CSP) program** who can help.

Cloud Solution Provider Model

The **Cloud Solution Provider (CSP) model** is a Microsoft partner program that provides the expertise and services you need through an expert CSP partner.

Your Microsoft 365 subscription is provided through a CSP partner who can manage your entire subscription and provide billing and technical support. The CSP partner will have admin privileges that will allow them to access your tenant, and they will be able to support, configure and manage licenses and settings directly. The CSP partner can provide extra consultancy and advice to meet security and productivity targets. Furthermore, other Microsoft cloud-based products and services can be added to your subscription, such as Microsoft Azure services and Dynamics 365.

The Cloud Solution Provider (CSP) program provides a pay-as-you-go subscription model with per-user, per-month pricing that lets your business scale up or down from month to month as your needs change.

Enterprise Agreements

The **Microsoft Enterprise Agreement (EA)** is designed for organizations that want to license software and cloud services for a minimum three-year period. The Enterprise Agreement describes the best value to organizations with 500 or more users or devices. One of the benefits of the Enterprise Agreement is that it is manageable, giving you the flexibility to bring cloud services and software licenses inside a single organization-wide agreement. Another benefit is that your organization can get 24x7 technical support, planning services, end-user and technical training, and unique technologies with Software Assurance.

Explore the Billing and Bill Management Options

Microsoft Bill Account

When you register to sample or purchase Microsoft goods, a billing account is generated. You control your account settings, invoices, payment options, and purchases through your billing account. Access to several billing accounts is possible. For instance, you have access to your company's Enterprise Agreement, Microsoft Products & Services Agreement, or Microsoft Customer Agreement, or you directly signed up for Microsoft 365. You would have a different billing account for each of these situations.

The Microsoft 365 admin center now supports the following billing account types:

Microsoft Online Service Program: This billing account is created when you immediately sign up for a Microsoft 365 subscription through the Microsoft Online Services Program.

Microsoft Products & Services Agreement (MPSA) Program: When your company enters an MPSA Volume Licensing agreement to buy software and online services, a billing account called the Microsoft Products & Services Agreement (MPSA) Program is formed.

The Microsoft Customer Agreement: It states that when your company works with a Microsoft agent, an authorized partner, or makes an independent purchase, a billing account is formed.

Your Microsoft business accounts are displayed on the Billing accounts page. Your business automatically has at least one billing account connected to an agreement that was accepted through a direct purchase or as part of a volume licensing agreement.

Billing Account Options

A **billing account** is formed when you sign up to try or buy Microsoft products. You use your billing account to control your account settings, invoices, payment methods, and purchases. The **Microsoft 365 admin center** currently supports the below billing accounts:

- **Microsoft Online Services Program.** This billing account is created when you sign up for a Microsoft 365 subscription directly
- **Microsoft Products & Services Agreement (MPSA) Program:** This billing account is created when your organization signs an MPSA Volume Licensing agreement to purchase software and online services
- **Microsoft Customer Agreement:** This billing account is created when your organization works with a Microsoft representative, an authorized partner, or purchases independently

Bill Management

Microsoft 365 billing is managed from the **Microsoft 365 admin center.** The admin center allows you to manage subscriptions, view billing statements, update payment methods, change your billing frequency, and more. The following list defines in further detail what can be reviewed and modified in the Microsoft 365 admin center:

- Upgrade, renew, reactivate, or cancel subscriptions
- View the number of purchased licenses. Also, see how many of those licenses are assigned to individual users for each service
- View a bill, invoice, and past billing statements

- Modify payment methods like updating, deleting, replacing, and adding other payment types. Payment options can include credit or debit card, bank account, or pay by invoice using a check or Electronic Funds Transfer (EFT)
- Modify your billing frequency to monthly or annual billing
- Buy and manage other services or features. For example, depending on your Microsoft 365 subscription, you can add on Advanced eDiscovery storage, Microsoft Defender for Office 365, Microsoft Teams Calling Plan, and more
- Manage your billing notification emails and invoice attachments, such as the list of email accounts of who should receive automated billing notifications and renewal reminders for the subscription

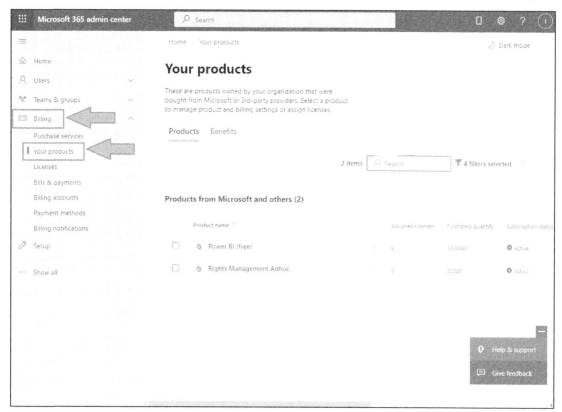

Figure 12-01: Bill Management

Explore the Available Licensing and Management Options

Subscription Plans

The pricing associated with your account depends on the subscription and the number of licensed users. Microsoft 365 offers various subscription plans for home users and organizations and various licensing options to meet your needs. Each service has a specified price that is typically rated on a per-user, per-month basis. The following list describes the subscription plans offered:

- **Microsoft 365 for home** consists of **Microsoft 365 Personal** and **Microsoft 365 Family**. Personal is for a single person with multiple devices, and family is for up to six people
- **Microsoft 365 Education** is for the education department and has two subscription plans for faculty and students that include different features: A1, A3, and A5
- **Microsoft 365 Government** is for government institutions and has two subscription plans with different features: G1, G3, and G5
- **Microsoft 365 Business** is for small to medium-sized organizations with up to 300 employees. It has four subscription tiers that include different features: Apps for Business, Business Basic, Business Standard, and Business Premium
- **Microsoft 365 for frontline workers** is designed to empower and optimize frontline impact. It has three subscription tiers that include different features: F1, F3, and F5
- **Microsoft 365 Enterprise** is for enterprise-sized organizations and has four subscription tiers that include different features: Apps for Enterprise, E3, E5, and F3

Licenses

A **license** allows users to use the features and services included in the subscription plan. Microsoft 365 products and services are available as **User Subscription Licenses (USLs)** and are licensed per-user basis. The following list describes the options available:

- **Full USLs** are for new users without previously paid Microsoft products and services
- **Add-on USLs** are for on-premises software customers who want to add Microsoft 365 cloud products and services
- **From SA, USLs** are for on-premises Software Assurance customers that want to transition to the cloud
- **Step Up USLs** are for customers who want to upgrade their service level

Each user accessing Microsoft 365 products and services must be assigned a USL. Administrators manage licenses in the Microsoft 365 admin center, and they can assign the licenses to individual users or guest accounts.

Types of add-ons

Microsoft 365 business plans have **add-ons** you can purchase for your subscriptions, and add-ons provide more capabilities to enhance your subscription. There are two kinds of add-ons:

- **Traditional add-ons** are connected to a specific subscription; the linked add-on is canceled if you cancel the subscription
- **Standalone add-ons** appear as a separate subscription on the products page within the Microsoft 365 admin center. They have their expiration date and are managed the same way you would manage any other subscription

Group-based Licensing

According to the membership of a group, group-based licensing automatically gives or removes licenses for a user account. Dynamic group membership allows for adding or deleting group members based on user

account attributes like Department or Country. This section provides the examples of adding and removing group members in your test environment for Microsoft 365 for Enterprise.

Group-based Licensing in Azure Active Directory

Licenses are necessary for Microsoft's premium cloud services like Dynamics 365, Enterprise Mobility + Security, and Microsoft 365. Each user who requires access to these services is given a license. Administrators use PowerShell cmdlets and one of the administration portals (Office or Azure) to manage licenses. The foundational technology that allows identity management for all Microsoft cloud services is called Azure Active Directory (Azure AD). Information about the user's license assignment states is stored in Azure AD.

Until now, licenses could only be distributed to specific users, which might be challenging for large-scale management. A complicated PowerShell script must frequently be written by an administrator to add or remove user licenses based on organizational changes, such as users entering or departing the company or a department. This script contacts the cloud service one by one.

Group-based licensing is now a feature of Azure AD to help with these issues. A group may be given access to one or more product licenses. Azure AD makes sure that the licenses are distributed to each group member. Any new members are given the proper licenses as soon as they join the group. Those licenses are taken away when they leave the group. With the help of this licensing management, it is no longer necessary to automate license management using PowerShell to take account of changes in the organizational and departmental structure on an individual user basis.

Licensing Requirements

Each user who gains access to group-based licensing must own one of the following licenses:

- Azure AD Premium P1 and above subscription, whether it is paid or trial
- Microsoft 365 Business Premium, Office 365 Enterprise E3, Office 365 A3, Office 365 GCC G3, Office 365 E3 for GCCH, or Office 365 E3 for DOD and above, whether paid-for or trial version

Required no of License

You must have a license for each individual member of any group to which one has been granted. You do not have to give each group member a license, but you need to have enough licenses to cover everyone. For instance, to comply with the licensing agreement, you must have at least 1,000 licenses if your tenant has 1,000 unique members that are a part of licensed groups.

Features

The key characteristics of group-based licensing are as follows:

- In Azure AD, licenses can be allocated to any security group. Using Azure AD Connect, security groups from on-premises may be synchronized. Additionally, you can automatically build security groups using the Azure AD dynamic group functionality or directly in Azure AD (also known as cloud-only groups)
- The administrator can disable one or more of the product's service plans when a product license is given to a group. This task is typically performed when the company is not yet prepared to begin employing a service that is part of a product. For instance, the administrator might provide a department access to Microsoft 365 while momentarily turning off the Yammer service

- Support is provided for all Microsoft cloud services that demand user-level licensing. All Microsoft 365 products, Enterprise Mobility + Security, and Dynamics 365 are all supported by this service
- Only the Azure portal presently offers group-based licensing. You may continue to manage users and groups using other administration portals, such as the Microsoft 365 admin center. However, if you want to manage licenses at the group level, use the Azure portal
- Changes in group membership that result in license revisions are automatically managed by Azure AD. Usually, licensing changes take effect right away after a membership change
- A user may belong to several groups with different license policies. A user may also possess some licenses that were given to them directly, independently of any groups. All allocated product and service licenses combine to form the user state that is the end outcome. The same license will only be used once if a user is given it from several sources
- Licenses occasionally cannot be given to a user. For instance, there might not be enough licenses available in the tenant, or potentially conflicting services may have been assigned concurrently. Information about users for whom Azure AD was unable to fully process group licenses is available to administrators. Based on that knowledge, they can then take appropriate action

Mind Map

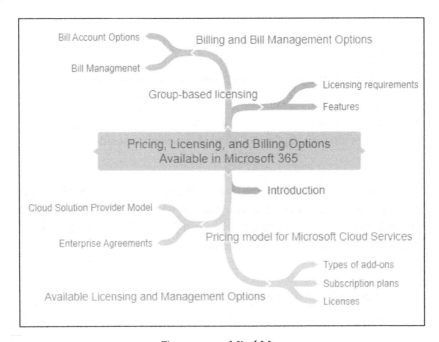

Figure 12-02: Mind Map

Practice Questions

---

1. Who provides your subscription for the Cloud Solution Provider (CSP) model?
   A. A CSP partner provides it
   B. It is provided directly by Microsoft

C. A retail store provides it
D. All of the above

2. Which of the portals below allow modifying the payment method and frequency of a Microsoft 365 subscription?
A. Microsoft 365 Subscription Center
B. Microsoft 365 Security Center
C. Microsoft 365 Admin Center
D. All of the above

3. Which of the following Microsoft 365 subscription plans is appropriate for companies with under 300 employees?
A. Microsoft 365 Enterprise
B. Microsoft 365 Business
C. Microsoft 365 Education
D. All of the above

4. The Enterprise Agreement offers the best value to organizations with _____ or more users or devices.
A. 200
B. 300
C. 400
D. 500

5. There are _____ types of add-ons.
A. One
B. Two
C. Three
D. Four

Chapter 13: Describe Support Offerings for Microsoft 365 Services

Introduction

Support plays an important role in the cloud environment. As we have learned, at least some portion of infrastructure management moves to the cloud provider when we move to the cloud. When something goes wrong, you must get the help you need to keep your applications available. It is also important to understand what level of support is being provided for specific services, particularly services that may be in preview phase and not published officially.

Microsoft is committed to helping you get the best out of your Microsoft 365 services. You can rely on easy-to-access support options with Microsoft 365 to help your organizations remain productive and efficient. Microsoft 365 services guarantee your organization's service level through Service Level Agreements. When you need help using Microsoft 365, create or view an existing support request through the Microsoft 365 admin center. Your organization will also benefit from transparent service health status updates on your Microsoft 356 products or services. Lastly, your organization can use open feedback sharing to help improve products and services based on user experience.

Explore Support Options for Microsoft 365 Services

Administrators and users in your organization might find it challenging to resolve issues independently. Knowing they can receive assistance for Microsoft 365 services whenever they need it through various support options is helpful.

The support option chosen to deal with a particular issue depends on:

- The tool or service where the issue has arisen
- The type of subscription your organization uses
- The kind of support your organization needs

Your organization can get access to support in the following ways:

Support type	Description
Community-based support	Your organization can take advantage of community-based support through the Microsoft 365 Tech Community, where you can collaborate with others, and solve problems. Your organization can also use the Microsoft 365 support forms to ask questions and solve issues with members of Microsoft and the community.
Proactive Support	Your organization can install the Microsoft Support and Recovery Assistant to help identify problems by running tests and offer the best solution for those problems. It can currently fix Office, Microsoft 365, or Outlook problems.
Web chat, email, and phone support	Your organization can submit issues to Microsoft support for technical, billing, and subscription support via email, online web chat, or phone.
Pre-sales support	Your organization is provided with assistance on subscription features, benefits, and your purchasing decision for Microsoft 365 services.
FastTrack	Your organization can connect with expert Microsoft engineers, project managers, and resources to help deploy Microsoft 365 services and resolve issues.
Premier Support for Microsoft 365	Your enterprise organization can receive on-site support, a dedicated technical account manager, and access to advisory services.
Support through a Microsoft Partner	Your organization can get support directly through a certified Microsoft 365 partner. For example, if your organization has purchased a Microsoft 365 subscription through a cloud services provider (CSP), they will receive direct support from the CSP.

Table 13-01: Support Options

Explain Service Level Agreements (SLAs) Concepts

Organizations must know that the products and services are reliable and secure. Microsoft 365 services guarantee the level of service for your organization. The level of service is detailed in a legal agreement referred to as a **Service Level Agreement.** Microsoft details its commitment to provide and maintain agreed service levels for Microsoft 365 services through its **Microsoft Online Services Agreement.**

In addition to the Microsoft Online Service Level Agreement, your organization can also take advantage of the Service Level Agreement with your Cloud Service Provider. The guarantees of service provided for Microsoft 365 services will vary between cloud service providers.

Microsoft's Online Service Level Agreement introduces several concepts:

Concept	Description
Incident	A set of events or single event that results in downtime.
Uptime	The total time your services are functional.
Downtime	The definition of downtime depends on the relevant service. For example, with Microsoft Teams, any period of time where users are unable to initiate online meetings, see presence statuses, or unable to instant message is considered downtime. Your downtime reduces the total time your services are functional (your uptime).
Claim	A claim raises information about an incident. Your organization is responsible for submitting a claim on an incident. The organization should provide the details about the experienced downtime, affected users, and how it was attempted to resolve the incident. Microsoft is responsible for processing the claim.
Service credit	Service credits are submitted by the organization's admin. If the claim is successfully approved by Microsoft, your organization will receive service credits. The service credit will be the percentage of the total monthly fees your organization paid for the month where you experienced downtime.
Service level	The performance metric(s) set forth in the SLA that Microsoft agrees to meet in the delivery of the Services.
Uptime agreement	The uptime agreement is defined by the monthly uptime percentage. This percentage is for a given active tenant in a calendar month and the calculation varies depending on the product or service. For example, the calculation could be as follows: *User Minutes – Downtime / User Minutes x* 100.

Table 13-02: Service Level Agreement

Microsoft is confident in its commitment to service levels. The percentage of service credit your organization can receive is linked to your monthly uptime percentage. For example, if downtime has resulted in a monthly uptime percentage lower than 95 percent, your organization could receive a 100% service credit. The table describes the monthly uptime percentage and corresponding service credit:

Monthly Uptime Percentage Service Credit

< 99.9%	25%
< 99%	50%
<95%	100%

Table 13-03: Uptime Percentage Service Credit

Your organization should always review all Service Level Agreements and ask questions, including the following list:

- If you are using a CSP, how does it determine service levels and whether they are achieved or not?
- Who is responsible for reports? How can your organization access reports?
- Are there any exceptions in the agreement?
- What does the agreement say about both unexpected and scheduled maintenance?
- What does the agreement say about what happens if your infrastructure goes down because of an attack? What about natural disasters and other situations outside of your control?
- Does the agreement cover non-Microsoft service or system failures?
- What are the limits to the cloud service provider's liability in agreement?

Office 365 Support

Microsoft offers a range of plans to help you get the assisted business assistance you need, including pay-per-incident choices and premium care that is available day and night.

Your Microsoft Office 365 subscription includes basic technical help, which you can request via the Microsoft Office 365 online site. You can buy Microsoft Office 365 support plans directly from Microsoft or through volume licensing programs for extra services and quicker response times.

Microsoft 365 Technical Support

Technical support is included with Microsoft 365. However, when purchased alone or as part of a Microsoft 365 service plan, the following restrictions apply to Microsoft 365 subscription support for Microsoft 365 Apps for enterprise or Microsoft 365 Apps for business.

Professional assistance covers most break-fix issues or technical issues you encounter while using Microsoft 365 Apps. A term used in the industry, "break-fix," describes the "effort involved in supporting a technology when it fails in the normal course of its function and needs the assistance of a support organization to be returned to working order."

The following problems are not covered by professional support:

- Customer suggestions regarding product attributes
- Onsite support
- Root cause investigation (investigation of the cause of the issue)
- Ensuring that third-party gear or products integrate properly with Microsoft 365 Apps.
- Data Recovery
- Office Add-ins, Visual Basic for Applications, Microsoft Access, or Publisher developer support includes writing, reviewing, and debugging user-generated code.
- Extensive investigation of performance problems
- Extensive troubleshooting is necessary when a product freezes or crashes

Identify How to Track the Service Health Status

View Health Status of Microsoft 365 Services

An organization must know the health status of the Microsoft 365 services. Your organization's administrators can use the **Microsoft 365 admin center** to view the current **health status** of each of your Microsoft 365 services and tenant. They can also view the history of services affected in the last 30 days and information about current outages or disruptions to services. It is helpful to view the health to find out whether you are dealing with a known issue with a progress solution, so you do not have to spend time troubleshooting or calling support.

To view service health, go to the Microsoft 365 admin center. Select **health** under the left navigation pane, then **Service health.** You can also select the service health card on the home dashboard.

Figure 13-01: Health Status

If your organization is experiencing a service issue, your administrators can report it by going to **Reported Issues,** selecting **Report an issue**, and completing a short form. Administrators can also view specific details about other service issues, like what kind of impact an issue may have on the service, by selecting **Incidents** or **Advisories**.

Figure 13-02: Service Health

Keep track of incidents

Your organization can set up notifications for any new incidents or updates to any active incidents that might affect your organization. Microsoft will provide two different types of notifications:

- **Unplanned downtime** - Where an incident has caused a service to become unresponsive or unavailable
- **Planned maintenance** - Where Microsoft regularly carries out service updates to the software and infrastructure that run services

Microsoft also analyzes unplanned service incidents for you through **Post-Incident Reviews.** Through these reviews, you will receive a preliminary review within the first two days of incident resolution and a final review within five business days. **Final Post-Incident Reviews** will detail the following information:

- How you might have been impacted, and how the user experience was impacted
- A date and time breakdown detailing when an incident started and when it was resolved
- An analysis of the root cause and what actions are to be carried out to prevent the incident in the future

Your organization can keep track of the health status of services in different ways:

Tool	Description
Admin app	Your administrators can use the Admin App to view and stay up to date with the health status of the services on the go.
Microsoft system center	Your administrators can view all service communications from within System Center if your organization has the Office 365 Management Pack.
API	Your organization can use the Office 365 Service Communications API to create or use tools that can connect and monitor the service status for you in real-time.
Continuity and availability	Microsoft services run on highly resilient infrastructures and systems to keep up peak service demand and performance. This infrastructure makes it possible for Microsoft to rapidly recover services from unexpected issues whether they're hardware related issues, software related issues, or even catastrophic issues like natural disasters.

Table 13-04: Track Services

For example, to protect and keep your organization's data available, Microsoft does the following:

- **Data storage redundancy** - Microsoft stores your data through multiple levels of redundancy using data replication and secure data protection capabilities. These capabilities make it possible to ensure rapid availability and recovery of your data
- **Monitoring data** - Your databases are monitored for you, and your data is monitored for packet loss, latencies in queries, and more
- **Preventative measures** - Microsoft regularly carries out checks for database consistency, reviews of error logs, and more

Explore How Organizations Share Feedback on Microsoft 365 Services

There is always room for modification, and Microsoft is committed to improving its services. Your organization's administrators and users often have great insight into how specific elements of products and services can be improved based on their daily experiences. Microsoft encourages idea sharing to improve products and services for everybody.

Microsoft has various channels for you to submit feedback about Microsoft 365 products and services. For example, if you are using feedback from the community feedback web portal, you can submit new feedback directly within the web portal. Community feedback is publicly displayed within different forums. You can

participate in existing feedback by voting or commenting on existing topics. Review your submitted feedback, impact, and status by viewing official responses from the Microsoft product teams.

The following list defines the ways you can communicate directly with Microsoft:

- Feedback
- In-product experiences
- Windows Feedback Hub
- Microsoft Tech Community
- Microsoft Store
- UserVoice forums

Take advantage of these sites to share your thoughts and help improve Microsoft products and services for your organization and other users worldwide.

Mind Map

Figure 13-03: Mind Map

Practice Questions

1. How can your organization receive on-site support from Microsoft?
    A. Community-Based Support
    B. Proactive Support
    C. Premier Support
    D. All of the above

2. Who is responsible for submitting a claim for service credit?
    A. The cloud service provider
    B. Your organization
    C. Microsoft
    D. All of the above

3. Which portals below can you use to view the current health status of your Microsoft 365 services and tenant?
    A. Microsoft 365 Security Center

B. Microsoft 365 Compliance Center

C. Microsoft 365 Admin Center

D. All of the above

4. What is the best place to share ideas about improving a feature for Microsoft 365 products and services?

A. Comment on Microsoft's social media posts

B. Create a support ticket through the Microsoft 365 admin center

C. Create a post in the feedback web portal

D. All of the above

5. Microsoft will provide _____ different types of notifications.

A. One

B. Two

C. Three

D. Four

Chapter 14: Describe the Service Life Cycle in Microsoft 365

Introduction

Every product or service has a lifecycle, including those in Microsoft 365. Microsoft envisions, designs, develops and tests everything internally. Once these features, products, and services are mature enough, they are made available to evaluate and test by users in a preview release. After the tests succeed, the feature, product, or service is released and generally available. Over time, as more product releases occur, older products and services can no longer be supported, and they will reach the end of support. Your organization can stay current on the feature, product, and service updates and releases by using the Microsoft 365 Roadmap.

Service Life Cycle

Microsoft 365 is an evergreen product that is always being improved. Development, testing, and release of new features occur often. In comparison to conventional software, Microsoft 365 has a different life cycle.

Microsoft Lifecycle offers uniform and predictable principles for support throughout a product's life, assisting clients in managing their IT investments and environments while making long-term plans.

Describe Private, Public Preview, and General Availability Releases

A product or service lifecycle typically has three phases:

1. **Private Preview**

2. **Public Preview**

3. **General Availability (GA)**

When a product or a service retires, it reaches the phase **end of support.**

Private preview

In this phase, Microsoft might release a product or service to a limited number of users to test and evaluate new features or functionality. This phase does not include legal support. Typically, users can sign up to be members of a private preview, but the preview release is not made available to the public.

Public preview

In this phase, Microsoft typically releases public previews of products and services before their General Availability (GA) release to receive suggestions from a wide range of users. They are marked as previews and include beta or pre-release features and services. Doing this allows users to explore and test upcoming functionality. Users may also receive some limited support depending on the product or service.

General Availability (GA)

After the public preview is completed, Microsoft releases the product or service. The product or service becomes available to all customers with proper support, known as the **release version.** The products and services in this phase have been through complete development and test lifecycle to ensure stability and

reliability. With Microsoft 365, new features are periodically added to the products and services. It is helpful for IT developers and administrators to be aware of preview features before they have their general availability released. Organizations can then educate users about these new features, ensure products are used optimally and be aware of the change in existing functionality.

End of support

Eventually, older products or retired services can no longer be supported, and they will reach the end of support. Once that happens, the product or service will no longer receive updates or assisted support. Customers are encouraged to shift to the latest version.

Describe the Modern Lifecycle Policy

Microsoft 365 is covered by the **Modern Lifecycle Policy.** The policy includes products and services that are serviced and supported continuously. Products and services managed by the Modern Lifecycle Policy are supported as long as the following criteria are met:

- Customers stay current as per the servicing and system requirements published for the product or service. Staying current means that customers accept and apply all servicing updates for their products and services
- Customers must be licensed to use the product or service
- Microsoft must currently offer support for the product or service

Under the Modern Lifecycle Policy, Microsoft gives a minimum of 12 months' notice before ending support for products. These notifications do not include any free services or preview releases.

Utilize the Microsoft 365 Roadmap Portal to Learn About Upcoming Features

Your organization can plan for the future with the **Microsoft 365 Roadmap**. Microsoft regularly includes updates for its products and services in the Microsoft 365 roadmap. The roadmap is the central location for business decision-makers, IT professionals, and anyone interested in seeing what is coming. It was formed to help you plan, communicate changes, and fully utilize your Microsoft 365 subscription.

The roadmap displays feature cards that include the title, status, release dates, product category, platform, and cloud instance. The roadmap also groups the features into three update phases:

1. **In development**
2. **Rolling out**
3. **Launched**

Figure 14-01: Microsoft 365 Roadmap

The following list describes what the Microsoft 365 Roadmap allows you to do:

- Search by product, keyword, or feature ID
- Filter by product, release phase, cloud instance, platform, or new or updated
- Sort by general availability date or newest to oldest
- Download the current features in development as a CSV file
- View additional information about each update
- Use the RSS feed to be notified of feature updates in real-time
- Share an entire roadmap page or email a single feature

Mind Map

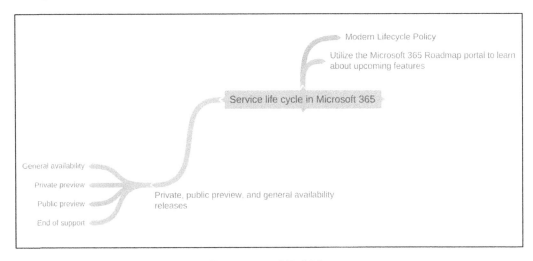

Figure 14-02: Mind Map

Practice Questions

1. Which phase of a product is the release version?
   A. Private Preview
   B. Public Preview
   C. General Availability (GA)
   D. All of the above

2. What is the minimum amount of months Microsoft will give notice before ending support for products under the Modern Lifecycle Policy?
   A. 6 months
   B. 12 months
   C. 24 months
   D. None of the above

3. What three phases does a feature have in the Microsoft 365 Roadmap?
   A. In Development, Launched, Retired
   B. In Development, Rolling Out, Launched
   C. In Development, Testing, Launched
   D. All of the above

4. The roadmap groups the features into _____ update phases.
   A. One
   B. Two
   C. Three
   D. Four

5. A product or service lifecycle typically has _____ phases.
   A. One
   B. Two
   C. Three
   D. Four

Chapter 15: Mobile Device Management

Introduction

This chapter focuses on implementing Mobile Device Management (MDM) in Microsoft 365. Before the introduction of MDM solutions, companies traditionally joined desktop devices to on-premises AD DS and managed them through Group Policies and Configuration Manager. But in today's world, users employ desktops and various devices. Most devices are mobile, and they are used from anywhere. They are often not connected to the company network, and some run non-Windows operating systems. In many cases, joining such devices to an on-premises AD DS is unsuitable or even impossible.

In this chapter, you will learn that Mobile Device Management manages all popular mobile devices without joining them to an on-premises AD DS. To manage a device with MDM, enroll it in your MDM solution. At Microsoft, enroll it in Intune or Basic Mobility and Security. After the device is enrolled in MDM, you can still manage it through group policies and profiles if you want. However, MDM provides more device management features, not available in on-premises AD DS, such as device compliance and Conditional Access.

The following section will examine the two MDM authority solutions included in Microsoft 365 - Microsoft Intune and Basic Mobility and Security. It will also compare the essential features of Microsoft Intune and Basic Mobility and Security. You will learn about the policy settings for mobile devices in each solution.

Device Management Overview

Protecting and securing the data and resources of an organization on devices within that organization is a crucial responsibility of any Administrator. Device management is the task at hand. Users use personal accounts to send and receive email, access websites when dining out and at home, and download apps and games. Students and employees are also among these users. They desire easy access to work and school resources on their devices, such as email and OneNote. In addition to keeping users' access to these resources simple across all of their various devices, it is your responsibility as an administrator to keep them safe.

Organizations may use device management to safeguard their data and resources from various devices.

A business can ensure that only authorized individuals and devices have access to confidential information by using a device management provider. Similar to this, customers who know their smartphone satisfies their organization's security criteria can feel at peace accessing work data from their phone.

Intune by Microsoft is the solution. Mobile device management (MDM) and mobile application management (MAM) are services provided by Intune. Some essential duties of any MDM or MAM solution include:

- Support a variety of mobile environments and safely manage Windows, macOS, Android, iOS, and iPadOS devices
- Check that devices and apps adhere to the security standards set by your company
- Make policies to protect your company's data on both company-owned and personal devices
- Use a single, integrated mobile solution to manage users, groups, devices, apps, and enforcement of these policies

- Control how your staff accesses and shares data to protect the information that belongs to your business

Microsoft Azure, Microsoft 365, and Azure Active Directory (Azure AD) all come with Intune. Controlling who has access and what they can access is made easier by Azure AD.

Microsoft Intune

Microsoft is just one of many companies that utilize Intune to protect confidential information that users access from both company-owned and personal devices. Software update guidelines, installation statuses, and device and app configuration standards are all part of Intune (charts, tables, and reports). These tools support you in securing and managing data access.

People frequently own several devices that run on several platforms. For instance, a worker might use a Surface Pro for work and an Android smartphone or tablet for personal use. People frequently use these various devices to access corporate resources like Microsoft Outlook and SharePoint.

You may manage many devices per person with Intune and the various operating systems that each device runs, including iOS/iPadOS, macOS, Android, and Windows. By device platform, Intune divides policies and settings. Therefore, managing and viewing devices for a certain platform is simple.

A fantastic resource for seeing how Intune addresses typical issues when working with mobile devices is common scenarios. There are scenarios related to:

- Email security using on-premises Exchange
- Safe and secure Microsoft 365 access
- Accessing organizational resources through personal devices

Explore Mobile Device Management (MDM)

An organization should first plan its MDM solution before deploying MDM, enrolling devices in it, and managing device compliance. This section examines the features of effective MDM planning, including the built-in capabilities of mobile device management for Microsoft 365, a comparison of Microsoft's two MDM solutions, policy settings for mobile devices, and controlling email and document access.

Explore Mobile Device Management in Microsoft 365

Mobile Device Management (MDM) is an industry-standard for managing mobile devices, such as smartphones, tablets, laptops, and desktop computers. Before using Microsoft 365 services with your device, you first need to enroll it in MDM.

MDM is implemented by using an MDM authority and MDM clients. Microsoft offers two MDM authority solutions:

- Basic Mobility and Security
- Microsoft Intune

MDM client functionality is comprised as part of the Windows 10 operating system. MDM authority can manage several devices that contain MDM client functionality, such as Android, iOS, and Windows 10. Some device settings can be controlled on all MDM enrolled devices, while other settings are device-specific and can only be configured using device-specific MDM policies.

MDM functionality includes the distribution of applications, data, and configuration settings to devices enrolled in MDM. Windows 10 devices can be enrolled in MDM using any of the following methods:

- Manually
- By using the Settings app
- By submitting a package
- By using Group Policy
- By enrolling into Azure AD, if integration between Azure AD and MDM is configured

MDM authority, such as Intune, offers the following responsibilities:

- **Device Enrollment** - MDM can operate only supported devices enrolled to MDM, for MDM to manage a device. The device can either include MDM client functionality, for example, Windows 10, or you should install a Company Portal app (for example, on Android or iOS devices)
- **Configuring Devices** - Organizations can use profiles and policies to configure devices, control user access, and set device settings to follow company policy. You can also deploy settings that enable devices to access company resources, such as WiFi and VPN profiles
- **Monitoring and Reporting** – In the MDM management tool, you can get notifications about devices that have issues or when an MDM policy is unsuccessful, such as when devices do not follow company requirements. You can also add devices to groups and display a list of enrolled devices. By using Intune, organizations can also configure Windows Autopilot device deployment
- **Application Management** - By using MDM and MAM, an organization can deploy applications, manage their settings, and separate data created by personal and business apps
- **Selective Delete Data** - If a device is misplaced or stolen, or the user is no longer a company employee, you can remove company data stored on the device. You can either wipe all device data or do a selective wipe, which leaves personal user data on the device intact

Devices can be managed by MDM even if they are not members of a domain.

Organizations can manage all important aspects of Windows 10 by using MDM. Each new Windows 10 version includes support for more MDM settings, and since version 1703, you can use many ADMX-backed policies to MDM.

By using MDM, organizations can manage configurations for the following Windows 10 configuration areas:

- Enrollment
- Inventory
- Device configuration and security
- Application management
- Remote assistance
- Unenrollment

The following diagram summarizes all the benefits of using MDM to manage Windows 10 devices.

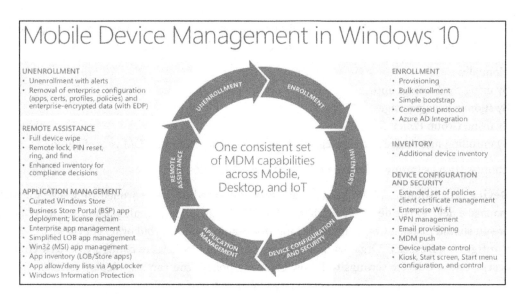

Figure 15-01: Mobile Device Management

The following diagram displays what happens when a user with a new device signs in to an application that offers access control with Basic Mobility and Security.

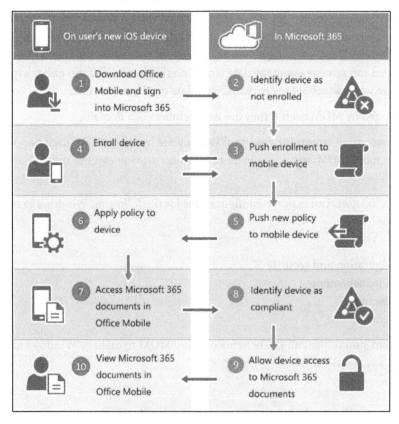

Figure 15-02: Basic Mobility and Security

Explore the Mobile Device Management Services in Microsoft 365

Microsoft 365 includes two Mobile Device Management (MDM) services: Basic Mobility and Security and Microsoft Intune. This section provides a detailed examination of each offer.

Introduction to Basic Mobility and Security

The Basic Mobility and Security service provides a built-in MDM solution within Microsoft 365. This service provides the core device management features available in Microsoft 365. It is hosted by the Intune service and includes a subset of Intune services. Even though it includes some Intune features, it is not an "Intune-lite" solution. The Basic Mobility and Security service provides core MDM functionality within Microsoft 365 for managing devices in your organization.

After Basic Mobility and Security is set up and your users have enrolled, you can manage the devices, block access, or even wipe a device if needed.

Introduction to Microsoft Intune

Microsoft Intune provides the core features within Basic Mobility and Security, plus more advanced device management features. Intune is Microsoft's gold-level standard for MDM solutions. It is not only a cloud-based service; its focus extends beyond Mobile Device Management (MDM) and includes Mobile Application Management (MAM).

- **Device Management** - Intune enables an organization to control how its devices are used, including mobile phones, tablets, and laptops. It also allows people in your organization to use their devices for school or work. Intune helps ensure that organization data stays protected on personal devices and can isolate organizational data from personal data
- **Application Management**

  Many organizations, such as Microsoft, use Intune to secure proprietary data users' access from their company-owned and personal mobile devices. Intune helps organizations secure and monitor data access by including:
    - Device and app configuration policies
    - Software update policies
    - Installation statuses (charts, tables, and reports)

It is common for people to have devices that use different platforms. For example, an employee may use Surface Pro for work and an Android mobile device in their personal life. People can also easily access organizational resources, such as Microsoft Outlook and SharePoint, from each of their devices.

MDM within Microsoft 365 Plans

Basic Mobility & Security is part of the Microsoft 365 plans, while Microsoft Intune is a standalone product with specific Microsoft 365 plans.

Differences in capabilities

While Microsoft Intune and built-in Basic Mobility & Security allow you to manage mobile devices in your organization, there are key differences in capabilities between the two solutions.

The Basic Mobility and Security service provides core MDM functionality and a subset of the functionality provided by Intune. For organizations requiring a more advanced MDM solution, Microsoft Intune provides this same core functionality as Basic Mobility and Security, plus advanced MDM features and MAM.

Examine MDM Policy Settings in Microsoft 365

MDM policies and profiles are groups of settings that control features on mobile devices. Whether related to encryption, passwords, security, email management, or another fundamental issue, policies are the cornerstone of MDM in an organization.

When organizations create policies or profiles, they can only deploy them by assigning them to groups of users, and they cannot assign them directly to individual devices or users. When policies are assigned to groups, the users in those groups get an enrollment message on their devices. When they have completed device enrollment, their devices are restricted by the policies you have set up. The organizations can then monitor policy deployment in the MDM management tool.

Microsoft offers two solutions for managing devices with MDM: Basic Mobility and Security and Microsoft Intune. Both solutions can manage enrolled devices, but they offer different capabilities. Both solutions use Microsoft 365 Endpoint Manager for administering their MDM solutions.

MDM Policy Settings in Basic Mobility and Security

The Basic Mobility and Security service enables organizations to create device policies that help protect their company information on Microsoft 365 from unauthorized access. An organization can apply policies to any mobile device in the company where the user has an applicable Microsoft 365 license and has enrolled the device in Basic Mobility and Security. In Basic Mobility and Security, organizations can manage the following mobile devices settings:

- **Organization-wide device access settings** - Using these settings, an organization can specify whether it wants to allow or block access to Exchange mail for devices not supported by Basic Mobility and Security and which security groups should be excluded from access control.
- **Device security policies** - Organizations can use device security policies to protect their devices from unauthorized access. Device security policies include password settings, encryption settings, managing email profile settings, and other settings that control device features, such as video conferencing and Bluetooth connectivity.

Organizations can create device security policies and apply them to users in Microsoft 365 Endpoint Manager groups. The policies apply to the users; they require users to enroll their devices in Basic Mobility and Security before the device can be used to access Microsoft 365 data. The policies that an organization sets up determine settings for mobile devices, such as how often passwords must be reset or whether data encryption is required.

MDM Policy Settings in Microsoft Intune

Organizations can manage the same settings in Microsoft Intune as in Basic Mobility and Security, along with many other settings. These different device settings that Intune can manage include:

- Device enrollment and restrictions
- Device compliance policies
- Device configuration policies
- Conditional Access
- Software updates including Windows 10 update rings and update policies for iOS
- Apps deployment, app configuration policies, and app protection policies

Policy and Security Configuration

Microsoft 365 includes default MDM policies based on Microsoft's digital security requirements. These policies help ensure that corporate security is maintained while also providing a good user experience. The data on the work devices is more secure when policies manage other users and devices in the same

environment. The following list provides examples of how these policies affect the entire Microsoft 365 experience:

- **Security.** The default policies enforce Microsoft corporate compliance settings on mobile devices, such as password policy and encryption settings
- **Messaging.** The default policies for Exchange align policy settings between Exchange ActiveSync (EAS) and MDM
- **Compliance.** Microsoft took advantage of the default compliance rules for mobile devices built into Configuration Manager. Microsoft then created a configuration baseline for those CIs and targeted the configuration baseline to the collection of mobile devices

An essential benefit of using MDM for managing devices is that organizations can allow access to email and documents only from devices managed by MDM and follow company policy.

Using MDM policies, Microsoft 365

Organizations can define company policy using the Device Security policy in Microsoft 365. They can control access to email, documents, and other cloud apps by using Conditional Access policies. Compliance with company policy is just one criterion that can be evaluated in a Conditional Access policy. Organizations can also evaluate sign-in risk, device type, location, and client apps.

Devices that are not enrolled in MDM cannot have their compliance evaluated. However, organizations can still prevent access to mailboxes, documents, and cloud apps from such devices. If a user tries to access their mailbox from such a device, depending on how the policy is set up, they may experience one of the following outcomes:

- They are removed from accessing Microsoft 365 resources
- They are, redirected to enroll the device in MDM
- The user could have access, but Microsoft 365 would report a policy violation

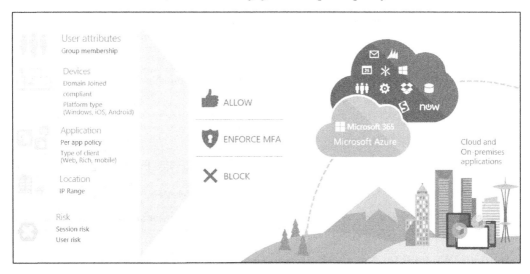

Figure 15-03: MDM Policies

Mind Map

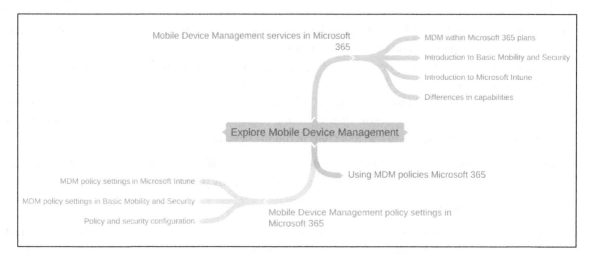

Figure 15-04: Mind Map

Deploy Mobile Device Management

This section examines how to deploy Mobile Device Management in Microsoft 365. Before organizations can start managing devices in Microsoft 365, they must first activate and configure MDM and then enroll their devices. Organizations can activate Microsoft Intune by choosing the MDM authority in Microsoft 365 Endpoint Manager. They must run a link to activate Basic Mobility and Security.

Activate the Mobile Device Management services in Microsoft 365

While Microsoft has two solutions for MDM, Intune and Basic Mobility and Security, they do not have the exact prerequisites. Preparing your MDM environment will be slightly different depending on which solution you want.

- **Essential Mobility and Security** - Start by activating the Mobile Device Management service. Once you activate the MDM service, you must do several other steps to complete the deployment
- **Intune** - Choose the MDM authority before you can start managing devices

Basic Mobility and Security

In Microsoft 365, you activate the Basic Mobility and Security MDM service by running the following link:

https://admin.microsoft.com/EAdmin/Device/IntuneInventory.aspx#

It takes some time for the service to start, after which you will receive an email that explains the next steps for setting up Basic Mobility and Security. These steps include:

1. **Configure domains for Basic Mobility and Security.** If you do not have a domain associated with Microsoft 365 or are not managing Windows devices, you can skip this step. Otherwise, you   need to add DNS records for the domain at your DNS host. This step is complete if you have already added the records to set up your domain with Microsoft 365.

After you add the records, the Microsoft 365 users, who sign in on their Windows device with an email that uses your domain, are redirected to enroll in Basic Mobility and Security.

2. **Configure an Apple Push Notification Service (APNS) certificate for iOS devices.** To operate iOS devices like iPad and iPhones, you must first create an APNS certificate.

3. **Set up multi-factor authentication.** MFA helps secure users sign in to Microsoft 365 for mobile device enrollment by requiring a second form of authentication.

4. **Manage device security policies.** Organizations should create and deploy device security policies to help protect their Microsoft 365 data.

5. **Make sure users enroll their devices.** After you have created and deployed an MDM policy, each licensed Microsoft 365 user in your organization will receive an enrollment message the next time they sign in to Microsoft 365 if the policy applies to their device.

Microsoft Intune

Organizations must configure the MDM authority to set up Microsoft Intune for device management. Device management in Intune is initially disabled, and MDM authority is unknown. Before an organization can start enrolling and managing devices, it must configure the MDM authority by selecting one of three available options:

- **Intune MDM Authority** - This option sets the MDM authority solely to Microsoft Intune. Intune is a cloud-only MDM solution, and it is managed by using a web browser. Microsoft recommends that organizations select this deployment option when using Intune
- **Configuration Manager MDM Authority** - This option is referred to as Hybrid MDM because it assumes the organization uses Configuration Manager for managing on-premises devices. This scenario integrates Intune's MDM capabilities into Configuration Manager in the following manner:
  o   It uses Configuration Manager's on-premises infrastructure to administer content and manage the devices
- **None**. This option indicates that no MDM Authority has been chosen, and Intune can only manage devices if an MDM authority is chosen

If organizations want to enroll and manage iOS devices, they must also add an APNS certificate to Intune. No certificate is needed for enrolling and managing Android and Windows 10 devices.

An organization can use the Configuration Manager console if it wants to change its MDM authority setting. In the past, you had to contact Microsoft Support to make this change, and you also had to unenroll and re-enroll your existing managed devices. However, organizations can now make this change independently, and they no longer need to unenroll and re-enroll their managed devices.

To set up mobile device management with Intune, you must complete the following steps.

1. **Supported configurations.** Need-to-know information before you start. This information includes supported configurations and networking requirements.

2. **Sign in to Intune.** Sign in to your trial subscription or form a new Intune subscription.

3. **Configure a domain name.** Set DNS registration to link your company's domain name with Intune. This setting gives users a familiar domain when connecting to Intune and using resources.

4. **Add users and groups.** Add users and groups, or link Active Directory to sync with Intune. This step is required unless your devices are "useless," such as kiosk devices. Groups of users are used to assign apps, settings, and other resources.

5. **Assign licenses.** Each user or userless device needs an Intune license to connect to the service.

6. **Set the MDM authority.** Groups are used to form apps, settings, and other resources.

7. **Add apps.** Apps can be assigned to groups of users and automatically or optionally installed.

8. **Configure devices.** Set up profiles that operate device settings. Device profiles can preconfigure settings for email, VPN, WiFi, and device features. They can also restrict devices to help protect both devices and data.

9. **Customize Company Portal.** Customize the Intune Company Portal users use to enroll devices and install apps. These settings appear in both the Company Portal app and the Intune Company Portal website.

10. **Enable device enrollment.** Enable Intune management of iOS/iPadOS, Windows, Android, and Mac devices by setting the MDM authority and enabling specific platforms.

11. **Configure app policies.** Supply specific settings based on app protection policies in Microsoft Intune.

Configure Domains for Mobile Device Management

An organization can enable its users to enroll their Windows 10 devices in Mobile Device Management (MDM) using the Autodiscover service. Windows devices (Windows Phone 8.1 and 10 and Windows PCs 8.1 and 10) have a UI built into the operating system to enroll a device for management. The user enters a corporate email address that matches the User Principal Name (UPN) set for user identity. The device tries to auto-discover the enrollment server and start the enrollment process. If the Autodiscover service is not configured, the device enrollment server will not be found. In this case, the device presents a screen for the user to enter the server address.

The Autodiscover service is configured when you create an alias (CNAME resource record type) in the domain DNS zone that automatically redirects enrollment requests to Intune servers.

- **Autodiscover will not be configured if you do not add this CNAME record.** In this case, users can still enroll devices to MDM, but they will have to provide the address of the enrollment server manually
- **Autodiscover will be configured if you add this CNAME record.** With the Autodiscover service enabled, users just have to provide credentials when they want to enroll their devices in MDM

A company using Azure AD Premium can integrate Azure AD with Intune to configure automatic MDM enrollment. This allows Windows 10 devices joined to Azure AD to be automatically enrolled in Intune. In such a scenario, you do not have to add a CNAME record to the domain DNS zone to enable the Autodiscover service. But if your organization is not using Azure AD Premium, or if users manually enroll devices to MDM using the Settings app, you can still benefit from autodiscovery.

The Autodiscover service is simple to set up for your domain because it only requires that you create a CNAME resource record in your external (public) DNS. CNAME records let you hide the implementation details of your network from the clients that connect to it. Used internally in your network, CNAME records enable users to use the simpler URI mail.domain.com instead of host.examplemachinename.domain.com. Creating a CNAME resource record type in the domain DNS zone that automatically redirects enrollment requests to Intune servers is used in multiple scenarios. For example:

- If your company uses the contoso.com DNS domain, you will create a CNAME record that redirects **contoso.com** to **enterpriseenrollment.manage.microsoft.com**

- If your company uses multiple DNS domains or UPN suffixes, you must create one CNAME record for each domain name and point it to **manage.microsoft.com**

Many organizations also want to enable the Autodiscover service for registering devices in Azure AD. In such environments, you would also add an **EnterpriseRegistration** CNAME DNS record that points to **EnterpriseRegistration.windows.net**.

Android and iOS devices are enrolled in MDM using the Company Portal app. The Company Portal app includes information on locating enrollment servers and does not use auto-discover DNS records.

Obtain an Apple Push Notification Service certificate for iOS Devices

Organizations do not need to add certificates to MDM to manage Windows or Android devices with either Intune or Basic Mobility and Security. However, suppose they want to manage Apple-related products such as iPad, iPhone, and Mac devices using MDM. In that case, they need an Apple Push Notification Service (APNS) certificate to communicate securely with those devices.

Apple requires that every MDM use its certificate when communicating on Apple's Push Notification Messaging network. Without the APNS certificate, iOS devices cannot be enrolled or managed. After an organization adds the certificate to Intune or Microsoft 365, its users can enroll their iOS and macOS devices by using the following:

- The Company Portal app
- Apple's bulk enrollment methods, such as the Device Enrollment Program, Apple School Manager, or Apple Configurator

By default, the APNS certificate is valid for one year, and an organization must renew its APNS certificate before it expires. When renewing the certificate, an organization must use the same Apple ID used when it first created the APNS certificate. If your APNS certificate expires, enrollment of new iOS devices will fail, and enrolled iOS devices cannot be managed until the certificate is renewed.

Figure 15-05: Certificate Signing Request

An organization can obtain an APNS certificate and add it to Microsoft Endpoint Manager by completing the following steps:

1. Grant Microsoft permission to send user and device information to Apple.

2. Download the **Intune certificate signing request** required to create an Apple MDM push certificate.

3. Create an Apple MDM push certificate.

4. Enter the Apple ID used to create your Apple MDM push certificate.

5. Browse to your Apple MDM push certificate to upload.

Managing Security Policies for Mobile Device-Managed Devices

Microsoft's two MDM solutions, the Basic Mobility and Security service, and Intune, enable organizations to configure and deploy different types of policies to manage their devices. Security policies can be implemented by configuring the following:

- Device Configuration Profiles
- Device Compliance Policies
- Conditional Access policies

Device security policies include:

- Password Settings
- Encryption Settings
- Settings that control the use of device features, such as a video camera

The following part offers a high-level overview of each of these policies.

Device configuration profiles

Microsoft Intune enables organizations to create and deploy different types of device configuration profiles, including:

- Device Restrictions
- Endpoint Protection
- Microsoft Defender for Endpoint (formerly Microsoft Defender ATP)

A device configuration profile can specify how a specific device setting should be configured. For example, you can configure password settings, lock some device features, and limit access to cloud storage and the app store.

Device compliance policy

A device compliance policy specifies the device configuration that must be met for the device to be compliant, such as using a PIN or device encryption. A device compliance policy is not used for configuring a device. Instead, it defines whether devices are configured in a standard way. Based on that configuration, an organization can treat compliant devices differently from non-compliant ones. For example, you can allow access to Exchange Online only from compliant devices. A device compliance policy includes the following settings:

- Use a password to access devices
- Encryption
- Indicate whether the device is jail-broken or rooted
- Minimum OS version required
- Maximum OS version allowed
- Need the device to be at or under the Mobile Threat Defense level

You can also use device compliance policies to monitor the compliance status of the devices.

Conditional Access policy

Organizations use Conditional Access with Microsoft Intune to control the devices and apps that can connect to their email and company resources. When integrated, you can control access to keep your corporate data secure while giving users an experience that lets them do their best work from any device and location.

Conditional access is an Azure Active Directory capability with an Azure Active Directory Premium license. Through Azure Active Directory, Conditional Access brings signals together to make decisions and enforce organizational policies.

Intune enhances this capability by adding mobile device compliance and mobile app management data to the solution. Standard signals include the following items:

- User or group membership
- IP location information
- Device details, including device compliance or configuration status
- Application details, including using managed apps to access corporate data
- Real-time and calculated risk detection, when you use a mobile threat defense partner

This relationship is shown in the following diagram.

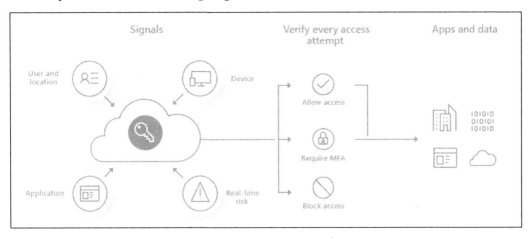

Figure 15-06: Conditional Access Policy

Conditional access also extends its capabilities to Microsoft 365 services. Conditional Access policies enable organizations to control access to company apps and resources, such as Exchange Online or OneDrive for Business - but only if certain conditions are met. Organizations can define conditions such as:

- Location of the device
- Device compliance
- User state
- Application sensitivity

For example, an organization can only allow access to its mail system if a user is authenticated by MFA and is using a compliant device.

Conditional access works with Intune device configuration and compliance policies and with Intune Application protection policies.

- **Device-based Conditional Access** - Intune and Azure Active Directory work together to ensure only managed and compliant devices can access:
  - Emails
  - Microsoft 365 services
  - Software as a service (SaaS) apps
  - On-premises apps

Additionally, you can set a policy in Azure Active Directory to enable only domain-joined computers or mobile devices that have enrolled in Intune to access Microsoft 365 services, including:

- Conditional access based on network access control
- Conditional access based on device risk
- Conditional Access for Windows PCs, including corporate-owned and Bring Your Own Device (BYOD)
- Conditional Access for Exchange on-premises
- **App-based Conditional Access** - Intune app protection policies operate with Conditional Access to help protect an organization's data on its employees' devices. These policies work on devices that are enrolled with Intune and on employee-owned devices that are not enrolled

Security Policy

Organizations can use security policies also to enforce users to enroll their devices in MDM. For example, an organization can only allow access to its company SharePoint portal from compliant devices. Devices can be evaluated for compliance only after they are enrolled in MDM. This requirement means that users must enroll their devices in MDM before their MDM solution can evaluate device compliance.

After a device is enrolled, the company's compliance policy will be downloaded to the device and evaluated. Based on the device's compliance status, the user may not be allowed to access the company portal. After a device is enrolled in MDM, other MDM policies will also be downloaded and applied to the device.

Define a Corporate Device Enrollment Policy

Microsoft Intune and Basic Mobility and Security enable organizations to manage known devices and apps and control access to company data. Using MDM to manage devices requires first enrolling them in Intune or Basic Mobility and Security.

When a device is registered, it is issued an MDM certificate. This certificate is used to communicate with Intune, even if the organization uses Basic Mobility and Security as its MDM solution (remember, Basic Mobility and Security is hosted by the Intune service and includes a subset of Intune services). The certificate is renewed automatically when the device communicates with Intune. If the certificate expires, the device is no longer managed by MDM. If the certification is not renewed, the device is automatically removed from Intune after 180 days.

Intune's default setting allows users to enroll all supported device types. Organizations can optionally configure enrollment restrictions by using the following criteria:

- A maximum number of devices that a user can enroll in
- Device platforms that can be enrolled:
  - Android
  - Android work profile
  - iOS

- o   macOS
- o   Windows
- Required operating system version for Android, iOS, macOS, and Windows devices:
  - o   Minimum version
  - o   Maximum version
- Restrict enrollment of personally owned devices.

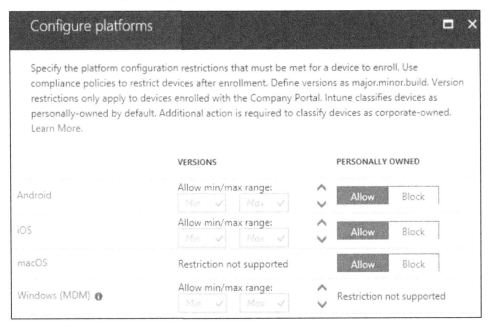

Figure 15-07: Configure Platforms

Mind Map

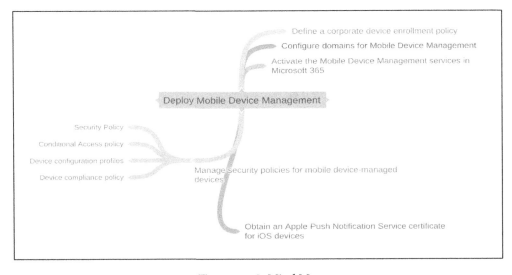

Figure 15-08: Mind Map

Enrolling Devices in Mobile Device Management

Many devices today, such as Android, iOS, and Windows 10 S, cannot be joined to on-premises AD DS. But to manage devices centrally, they must trust the authority that defines configuration settings. In on-premises AD DS environments, such authorities were domain controllers; in today's cloud world, they are MDM authorities. You can manage a device only if it is enrolled in MDM, and an enrolled device means that it trusts the MDM authority, such as Intune or Basic Mobility and Security.

In this section, you will see the benefits of enrolling devices to MDM, how to enroll Windows 10, Android, and iOS devices, and how to create enrollment rules. Since Apple devices have their enrollment mechanism; you will be introduced to enrolling Apple devices using the Apple Device Enrollment Program (DEP).

You cannot require that users enroll their devices to MDM, but you can require that users only access company resources from enrolled devices. Because users access company resources, they must first enroll their devices to access those resources. This section shows you how to configure a security policy with such a requirement while using a Conditional Access policy in Intune to achieve the same goal.

In this section, you will also learn how to manage the enrollment of devices. While users can enroll up to five devices to MDM by themselves, some companies want to provide employees with already enrolled devices. Intune addresses this need by employing Device Enrollment Managers (DEM). This section introduces you to device enrollment managers, who can each enroll up to 1000 devices.

Finally, if your environment requires stronger security, you can configure Azure AD to require Multi-Factor Authentication (MFA) for users enrolling devices to MDM. This section examines how to implement MFA so that users have to prove their identity with another authentication factor before enrolling their devices.

Enroll in Windows 10 and Android devices

When a user enrolls a device to MDM, it creates trust between the device and the MDM authority. Once the device is enrolled, and the trust with MDM authority is established, the organization can then manage the device through MDM

There are several different ways to enroll Windows 10 devices to MDM, based on device type and the device's current state. These methods include:

- Group Policy can automatically enroll devices to MDM if the devices are already joined to the organization's on-premises AD DS
- Windows 10 devices linked to Azure AD can be automatically enrolled to MDM if integration is configured between Azure AD and MDM
- Windows 10 devices can be manually enrolled to MDM by using a Settings app, provisioning packages, or the Company Portal app

Automatic enrollment to MDM only works for Windows 10 devices because only Windows 10 can be joined to an on-premises AD DS and Azure AD. Other devices, such as Android and iOS, can only be manually enrolled to MDM by using the Company Portal app.

The Company Portal app is not included on Android and iOS devices and is available as a free app in the Google Play and Apple app stores. To enroll iOS devices, you must ensure that MDM is configured with a valid Apple Push Notification Service (APNS) certificate. iPhones, iPad, and macOS devices require an APNS certificate for secure communication with MDM, even if MDM is Intune, MDM for Microsoft 365, or a third-party MDM product.

Enrolling iOS Devices using Apple's Device Enrollment Program

Apple DEP is only accessible for devices that an organization purchases through either Apple or authorized resellers to provide to employees.

iOS devices enrolled in DEP do not require manual configuration. Users never have to select MDM links or install the Company Portal app to enroll the device.

If an organization allows users to bring their own devices, they should complete the regular iOS device enrollment in Microsoft Intune.

But if the company provides employees with iOS devices that are part of the Device Enrollment Program, users can enroll those devices in MDM by completing the following steps:

1. Turn on your iOS device.

2. After you select your **Language**, link your device to WiFi.

3. On the **Set-up iOS device** screen, choose whether you want to:

   o   Set up as a new device
   o   Restore from iCloud backup
   o   Restore from iTunes backup

1. Once you have connected to WiFi, the **Configuration** screen will appear and a message will appear.

2. Agree to the **Terms and Conditions** and choose whether you need to send diagnostic information to Apple.

3. Once you finish your enrollment, your device may prompt you to take more action. These steps may include entering your password for email access or setting up a passcode.

Regulating Device Enrollment by Using Enrollment Rules

Organizations must first assign each user an Intune license before they can enroll their devices in Intune. Once users have been assigned an Intune license, organizations can optionally configure enrollment restrictions that users must meet before enrolling a device in   Intune.

Enrollment restrictions

Enrollment restrictions can include the following criteria:

- A maximum number of devices that a user can enroll in. By default, this number is set to five devices per user
- Device platforms that can be enrolled:
   o   Android
   o   iOS
   o   macOS
   o   Windows
- Required operating system version for iOS, Android, Android work profile, and Windows devices
- Minimum version
- Maximum version
- Restrict enrollment of personally owned devices. You can configure this restriction for iOS, Android, Android work profiles, and macOS devices; this restriction is unavailable for Windows devices.

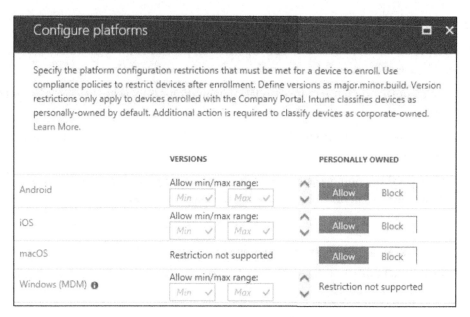

Figure 15-09: Regulate the device

Enrollment options

Organizations can manage device enrollment by configuring the following enrollment options:

- **Terms and conditions** - Organizations can require that users accept the company's terms and conditions before they:
    - Use the Company Portal to register their devices
    - Access resources such as company apps and email
- **Enrollment restrictions** - Organizations can configure the following enrollment restrictions:
    - Identify the device types that can be enrolled
    - Block enrollment of personal devices
    - Restrict the number of devices that each user can enroll
- **Enable Apple device enrollment** - Organizations can control whether Apple devices can be enrolled, and they can only be enrolled in the organization and added an APNS certificate to MDM
- **Corporate identifiers** - Organizations can list International Mobile Equipment Identifier (IMEI) numbers and serial numbers to identify company-owned devices. Intune can complete other management tasks and collect additional information. This data may include the full phone number and an inventory of apps from company-owned devices. Organizations can also prevent the enrollment of devices that are not company-owned
- **Multi-Factor Authentication** - Organizations can require a different verification method when users enroll a device, and verification can be by phone, PIN, or biometric data
- **Device enrollment manager** - The Device Enrollment Manager (DEM) can enroll many devices. A restriction on the number of devices a user can enroll in does not apply to a DEM, and a DEM can enroll in up to 1,000 devices

Examine How Users Enroll Their Devices in Mobile Device Management

Users typically use their devices for personal leisure and work as soon as they obtain their devices. This situation poses two problems for companies:

- Until the devices are enrolled in an MDM solution, the organization does not have control over them, nor can it manage them
- Device enrollment is usually a manual process, and users often forget to do it

As a result, most companies have resorted to making enrollment of personal devices mandatory if users want to use them for work. Organizations also implement rules and policies to help manage these personal devices. For example:

- Users can only access company resources from enrolled devices that follow company policy
- Compliance policies are used to define how devices should be configured
- Conditional Access policies are used to control access to company resources

To control access to company resources, organizations can configure either a Security policy in Microsoft 365 or a Conditional Access policy in Intune. These policies can be configured only to allow access to company resources from enrolled devices.

For example, such a policy is in place, and a user tries to access company resources, such as their Exchange Online mailbox. In that case, the user access will be blocked and redirected to enroll the device first. After the user enrolls the device, they can access their mailbox.

The following diagram displays what happens when a user with a new personal device tries to access Microsoft 365.

Figure 15-10: Device Enrollment

The following section examine how Windows 10, Android, and iOS devices are enrolled in MDM.

Automatic enrollment of Windows 10 devices

Organizations can configure automatic enrollment to MDM for Windows 10 devices only.

- Suppose a Windows 10 device is already joined to an on-premises AD DS synced to Azure AD. In that case, the **Enable automatic MDM enrollment using default Azure AD credentials** Group Policy setting can be configured to enroll devices to MDM
- If Azure AD is integrated with MDM, then any Windows 10 devices that users join to Azure AD are automatically enrolled in MDM

Manual enrollment of Windows 10 devices

Organizations can manually enroll Windows 10 devices in   Intune by using any of the following methods:

- **Settings app** - Use the **Access work or school** option in the **Account** section to manually enroll a Windows 10 device to MDM
- **Provisioning package**   - Use Windows Configuration Designer to create a provisioning package that enrolls devices to MDM. Provisioning packages are typically used for bulk enrollment
- **Company Portal app**   - This app is free in the Microsoft Store and can be installed and used for enrolling devices to MDM

Manual enrollment of Android and iOS devices

Organizations can enroll in Android and iOS devices by using the Company Portal app. To enroll an iOS device, an organization must ensure its MDM is configured with an APNS certificate.

Enrolling Devices Using the Device Enrollment Manager (DEM) Account

In many companies, users enroll company-owned devices in MDM themselves. But there are scenarios where these same organizations prefer to have a device already enrolled when a user receives it, for example, when non-technical users use devices or if multiple users share the same device.

Every user can enroll only a limited number of devices in MDM. This limit does not apply to the DEM. The DEM account is a particular user account used to enroll devices. The features of this account include the following:

- It can be used to enroll up to 1000 devices in MDM
- It enables organizations to use Intune to manage large numbers of mobile devices with a single user account
- An organization can add multiple users to the DEM account to give them special capabilities. Only users that have been assigned an Intune license can be assigned to the DEM account

When a user enrolls a device, they are associated with that device. But when a DEM account enrolls the device, no user is associated with the device, and the device has no assigned user. Suppose an organization plans to bulk enroll many devices at one time. In that case, it can specify the users who will do the bulk enrollment as device enrollment managers on the Intune view in the Azure portal.

Comparing DEM-enrolled devices to user-enrolled devices

Devices that a device enrollment manager enrolls have the following differences when compared to devices that are enrolled individually by users:

- Devices enrolled by a DEM account do not have per-user access. Because devices do not have an assigned user, the device has no email or company data access. VPN configurations, for example, could still be used to provide device apps with access to data
- The DEM account cannot use the Company Portal to unenroll DEM-enrolled devices, and only the Intune administrator can unenroll such devices
- Users cannot use Apple Volume Purchase Program (VPP) apps with user licenses because of per-user Apple ID requirements for app management
- If the DEM account enrolls iOS devices, you cannot use the Apple Configurator, Apple Device Enrollment Program, or Apple School Manager to enroll devices
- A maximum of 10 Android work profile devices may be enrolled per DEM account. This limitation is specific to Android devices and does not apply to legacy Android enrollment
- A device does not need an Intune license to be enrolled by a DEM account

A user must be a Microsoft 365 Global Administrator or an Intune Service Administrator Azure AD role member to complete the tasks related to DEM enrollment.

The DEM account is only used for device enrollment. Removing a DEM account does not affect devices that are already enrolled. When a DEM account is removed:

- Enrolled devices are unaffected and continue to be fully managed
- The removed DEM account credentials remain valid
- The removed DEM account cannot wipe or retire devices
- The removed DEM account can only enroll devices up to the per-user limit configured by the Intune administrator

Examining the Need for Multi-Factor Authentication to Secure Mobile Device Enrollment

By default, a user must authenticate with a username and password to enroll a device in MDM. In an environment where stronger authentication is required, organizations can include multi-factor authentication (MFA). MFA is a two-step verification process that needs that a user passes two or more of the following authentication methods:

- Something they know (typically a password)
- Something they have (a trusted device that is not easily duplicated, like a phone)
- Something they are (biometrics)

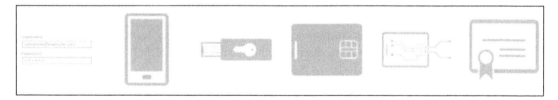

Figure 15-11: Multi-Factor Authentication

For Microsoft 365, Azure Active Directory Multi-Factor Authentication (MFA) helps safeguard access to data and applications. Because MFA is turned off by default, organizations must enable it as an optional step, and MFA can be enabled in the Azure portal or the Microsoft 365 admin portal. It is recommended that organizations turn on MFA for all privileged users, and it is not uncommon for MFA to be turned on for all users.

MFA provides organizations with extra security. It also requires that the user has their trusted device when signing in. Many other settings can be configured for MFA. For example:

- MFA can be required only when a user wants to authenticate from an untrusted network
- MFA can be configured to be valid for just a certain period (for example, one hour). During that time, the second form of authentication is not required, even if a user has to authenticate multiple times

MFA helps secure the sign-in to Microsoft 365 or Intune for mobile device enrollment by requiring a second form of authentication. Users are required to respond to a phone call, text message, or app notification on their trusted mobile device after correctly entering their account password. After a user's devices are enrolled in Intune or Basic Mobility and Security, the user can access resources such as Exchange Online.

Mind Map

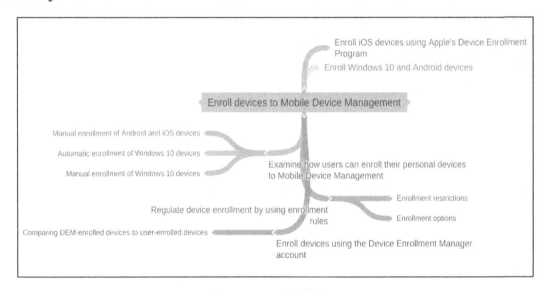

Figure 15-12: Mind Map

Practice Questions

1. As the Enterprise Administrator for Northwind Traders, Allan Deyoung wants to enroll several new Android and iOS devices in MDM. How can Allan enroll these devices in MDM?
    A. Automatically enroll them through Group Policy
    B. Manually enroll them through provisioning packages
    C. Manually enroll them through the Company Portal app
    D. All of the above

2. Contoso has several new users who could not enroll their personal Windows 10 devices in Intune. Which of the following could be the reason why these users could not enroll their devices in Intune?
    A. Contoso did not create an APNS certificate
    B. The users were not assigned an Intune license
    C. Contoso created an enrollment restriction that restricted enrollment of personally owned devices

D. All of the above

3. When a DEM account enrolls a device, which user is associated with the device?
   A. The DEM account is associated with the device
   B. The first user assigned to the DEM account is associated with the device
   C. No user is associated with the device
   D. All of the above

4. As the Enterprise Administrator for Contoso, Holly Dickson used a DEM account to bulk enroll multiple devices to MDM. Holly later attempted to retire some older devices using the DEM account but could not do so. Why could Holly not retire the devices?
   A. Holly needed to assign Retire permissions to the DEM account
   B. The DEM account had not been assigned the Microsoft 365 Global admin role
   C. The DEM account is only used for device enrollment
   D. All of the above

5. As the Enterprise Administrator for Lucerne Publishing, Patti Fernandez wants to ensure that Lucerne's users enroll their devices to MDM. To do so, Patti plans to create a policy that only allows access to company resources from enrolled devices. What type of policy can Patti create to provide this feature?
   A. Security policy in Microsoft 365
   B. Compliance Policy in Intune
   C. Conditional Access policy in Microsoft 365
   D. All of the above

6. Fabrikam plans to purchase several Apple iOS devices for its employees. As the Enterprise Administrator for Fabrikam, Holly Spencer wants to ensure these devices get enrolled and configured to MDM through the Apple Device Enrollment Program (DEP). What is the first thing Holly must do to enable this scenario?
   A. Create a Conditional Access policy in Intune that only allows access to company resources from enrolled devices
   B. Purchase the devices through either Apple or an authorized reseller
   C. Create a Security policy in Microsoft 365 that only allows access to company resources from enrolled devices
   D. All of the above

7. As the Enterprise Administrator for Northwind Traders, Allan Deyoung wants to change Northwind's MDM authority from Configuration Manager MDM Authority to Intune MDM Authority. How should Allan make this change?
   A. Allan should contact Microsoft Support to make this change for Northwind Traders
   B. Unenroll the existing managed devices, make the change through the Intune portal, then re-enroll the devices
   C. Through the Configuration Manager console
   D. None of the above

8. Northwind Traders has several users who use iOS devices. Allan Deyoung, Northwind's Enterprise Administrator, obtained an APNS certificate so that the iOS devices can be enrolled and managed by Northwind's MDM. Allan added the APNS certificate to Intune.

It is now up to Northwind's users to enroll their iOS devices for MDM. How can they enroll their iOS devices in Northwind's MDM?

A. Through the Company Portal app

B. Through the Configuration Manager portal

C. Through the Microsoft 365 Device Enrollment Program

D. All of the above

9. Northwind Traders uses Basic Mobility and Security as its MDM authority. Northwind had several devices whose MDM certificates expired over a year ago, and the certificates were never renewed. What was the effect on the devices?

A. They were automatically removed from Basic Mobility and Security 90 days after certificate expiration

B. They were automatically removed from Intune 180 days after certificate expiration

C. The users could still access Microsoft 365 email and documents, but MDM no longer managed the devices

D. None of the above

10. Fabrikam wants to configure the Autodiscover service to aid its users when they enroll their Windows 10 devices to its MDM authority. What does Fabrikam need to do to configure the Autodiscover service for device enrollment to its MDM authority?

A. Purchase an Azure AD Premium license

B. Add an EnterpriseRegistration CNAME DNS record that points to EnterpriseRegistration.windows.net

C. Create a CNAME record in the external (public) DNS zone that automatically redirects enrollment requests to Intune servers

D. None of the above

11. Contoso wants to use Conditional Access with Microsoft Intune to keep its corporate data secure while giving users an experience that enables them to do their best work from any device and location. What must Contoso do to enable Conditional Access?

A. Purchase an Azure AD Premium license

B. Enable it through the Company Portal app

C. Enable it in Microsoft Defender for Endpoint

D. All of the above

12. Which type of policy should Contoso create to control the devices and apps that can connect to its email and company resources?

A. Device Compliance Policy

B. Security Policy

C. Conditional Access Policy

D. All of the above

13. As the Enterprise Administrator for Northwind Traders, Allan Deyoung wants to implement Microsoft Intune as Northwind's MDM authority. Which of the following rules must Allan consider when planning this implementation?
    A. Only Group Policy can manage Windows 10 devices that are domain members
    B. Only MDM can manage Windows 10 devices that are domain members.
    C. Group Policy and MDM can simultaneously manage Windows 10 devices that are domain members
    D. None of the above

14. Contoso has implemented Microsoft's Basic Mobility and Security service as its MDM solution. As Contoso's Enterprise Administrator, Holly Dickson wants to configure a mobile device setting or policy that specifies whether Contoso allows or blocks access to Exchange mail for devices not supported by Basic Mobility and Security. Which mobile device setting or policy must Holly configure to support this requirement?
    A. Organization-wide device access settings
    B. Device security policies
    C. Device compliance policies
    D. None of the above

15. Which capabilities are provided in both Microsoft Intune and Basic Mobility and Security?
    A. Managed browser
    B. Zero-touch enrollment programs
    C. Remote actions
    D. All of the above

16. As the Enterprise Administrator for Northwind Traders, Allan Deyoung wants to implement Microsoft Intune as Northwind's MDM authority. Allan likes the fact that MDM can only allow access to email and documents from devices managed by MDM and follow company policy. Which of the following items is an MDM policy used in Microsoft 365?
    A. Devices that are not enrolled in MDM cannot be prevented from accessing mailboxes, documents, and cloud apps
    B. Devices that are not enrolled in MDM cannot have their compliance evaluated
    C. If a user tries to access their mailbox from a device that is not enrolled in MDM, the user will not have access
    D. None of the above

17. When organizations create policies or profiles, how can they deploy them?
    A. They must be assigned directly to individual users
    B. They must be assigned directly to individual devices
    C. They must be assigned to groups of users
    D. All of the above

18. Microsoft 365 includes _____ Mobile Device Management (MDM) services.
    A. One
    B. Two
    C. Three

D. Four

19. Intune is Microsoft's gold-level standard for _____ solutions.
   A. MAM
   B. MDM
   C. Both of the above
   D. None of the above

20. Devices can be managed by _____ even if they are not members of a domain.
   A. MAM
   B. MDM
   C. Both of the above
   D. None of the above

21. By using _____, an organization can deploy applications, manage their settings, and separate data.
   A. MAM
   B. MDM
   C. Both of the above
   D. None of the above

22. MDM is implemented by using an MDM _____.
   A. Authority
   B. Clients
   C. Both of the above
   D. None of the above

Chapter 16: Microsoft 365 Apps

Introduction

Microsoft 365 Apps is a part of Office available through many Office 365 (and Microsoft 365) plans. It includes many of the applications you are already familiar with. You can use these applications to link with Office 365 (or Microsoft 365) services.

Microsoft 365 Apps vs. Other versions of Office

Microsoft 365 Apps is quite similar to other versions of Office that you can deploy to your users. Here are some significant points:

- Its system needs are the same as other current versions of Office
- Microsoft 365 Apps is available in 32-bit and 64-bit versions
- When you deploy Microsoft 365 Apps, it is installed on the user's local computer. Users do not have to be linked to the internet all the time to use it

Reasons to choose the 64-bit version

Computers having 64-bit versions of Windows generally have more resources like processing power and memory than their 32-bit predecessors. Also, 64-bit applications can have more memory than 32-bit applications (up to 18.4 million Petabytes). Therefore, if your scenarios contain large files and working with large data sets and your computer has a 64-bit version of Windows, 64-bit is the right choice when:

- **You are supposed to work with complex data sets**, such as enterprise-scale Excel workbooks with complex calculations, many pivot tables, and data links to external databases. The 64-bit version of Office may perform well in these cases
- **You are supposed to work with huge pictures, videos, or animations in PowerPoint**. The 64-bit version of Office may be best suited to handle these complex slide decks
- **You are working with files over 2 GB in Project**, especially if the project has many sub-projects

Reasons to select the 32-bit version.

The below-mentioned computer systems can only install 32-bit Office:

- 64-bit OS with ARM-based processor
- 32-bit OS with an x86 (32-bit) processor
- Less than 4 GB RAM

If you are an IT professional or a developer, you must also review the below-mentioned cases where the 32-bit version of Office is still the best selection for you:

- **You run 32-bit COM Add-ins with no 64-bit alternative**. You can continue to have 32-bit COM add-ins in 32-bit Office on 64-bit Windows. You can also try connecting the COM Add-in vendor and asking for a 64-bit version
- **You have 32-bit controls with no 64-bit alternative**. You can continue to have 32-bit controls in 32-bit Office like Microsoft (Mscomctl.ocx, comctl.ocx) or any existing 3rd-party 32-bit controls

- **Your VBA code uses Declare statements**. Most VBA code does not need to change when used in 64-bit or 32-bit unless you use Declare statements to call
- **WindowsAPI.** WindowsAPI uses 32-bit data types such as long for pointers and handles. In most scenarios, adding PtrSafe to the Declare and substituting long with LongPtr will make the Declare statement works with both 32- and 64-bit
- **You are using SharePoint Server 2010 and want the Edit in Datasheet view.** You can continue to run the Edit in Datasheet view.

Microsoft 365 Apps

Even though Microsoft 365 Apps is a bit similar to other versions of Office, there are differences, containing Deployment differences and Licensing differences.

The main difference is that Microsoft 365 Apps is updated regularly, as often as monthly, with new features, unlike non-subscription versions of Office.

Microsoft 365 is a subscription in which you have updated productivity tools from Microsoft. There are Microsoft 365 subscriptions for home and personal use for small and mid-sized businesses, large enterprises, schools, and non-profit organizations.

Microsoft 365 plans for home or business contain the robust Office desktop apps you are familiar with.

With a subscription, you will have updated features, fixes, security updates, and tech support at no added cost. You can select to pay for your subscription monthly or yearly. The Microsoft 365 Family plan also allows you to share these subscription benefits with up to 5 additional people.

Most of the Microsoft 365 plans for businesses, schools, and non-profits include fully updated desktop apps, but Microsoft also provides basic plans with the online versions of Office, file storage, and email. You choose what works best for you: Small business, Enterprise, School, or Non-profit.

Deployment differences

- By default, Microsoft 365 Apps updates as one package. This means that all Office apps are linked to the computer. But   you can create the deployment to exclude or delete specific Office applications
- Because Microsoft 365 Apps uses a separate installation technology, called Click-to-Run, there is an alternate way to apply software updates. Microsoft 365 Apps are configured to install updates from the Office CDN on the internet. But   you can deploy form Microsoft 365 Apps to install updates from a location within your network, or you can control updates to Microsoft 365 Apps with Microsoft Endpoint Configuration Manager
- Microsoft 365 Apps also allows managing how often users get feature updates. For example, users can have new features to Microsoft 365 Apps as soon as they are ready or once a month
- Office 365 (and Microsoft 365) offers a web-based portal where users can install Microsoft 365 Apps. If users are not local administrators, administrator will have to install Microsoft 365 Apps for them

Licensing differences

- Users can have Microsoft 365 Apps on up to 5 different computers with a single Office 365 license if a user can have Microsoft 365 Apps installed on a computer in Office, on a laptop to have when traveling, and on a home computer. Users can also install it on up to five tablets and five phones
- Microsoft 365 Apps is provided as a subscription. If you remove your subscription, Microsoft 365 Apps goes into smaller functionality mode. In smaller functionality mode, users can open and view existing Office files but cannot use most of the other Microsoft 365 apps' other features

- To use Microsoft 365 Apps, a user should have an Office 365 account and have been dedicated to a license. If the user's license or account is deleted, the user's installations of Microsoft 365 Apps go into smaller functionality mode

More information about Microsoft 365 Apps

- Users can keep the files they form with Microsoft 365 Apps on their local computers or anywhere on the network, such as a SharePoint site. Office 365 (and Microsoft 365) also offers cloud-based file storage options
- Microsoft 365 Apps are not the same as the web versions of the Office applications. The web versions let users open and work with Word, Excel, PowerPoint, or OneNote documents in a web browser. The web versions of this Office application are included with all Office 365 (and Microsoft 365) plans

Microsoft 365 Apps for Business

With constantly updated desktop, mobile, and online versions of Word, Excel, PowerPoint, and Outlook, as well as business intelligence solutions to make your job more enjoyable and help your company develop, Microsoft 365 Apps for Business and Apps for Enterprise let you work how you want, practically anywhere.

- Download the desktop versions of Office programs such as Outlook, Word, Excel, PowerPoint, and OneNote (plus Access and Publisher for PC only)
- Each user gets 1 TB of OneDrive cloud storage for file storing and sharing
- Use one license to cover five mobile devices, five tablets, and five PCs or Macs per user with fully installed Office programs
- Every month, automatically add new features and functionalities to your apps
- Access Microsoft's 24/7 phone and online support at any time

Always Available

A 99.9% uptime guarantee and a service-level agreement backed by money will provide you peace of mind that the services you have paid for are available.

Built-in security

Utilize cutting-edge, five-layer security and proactive monitoring to protect consumer data.

Easy to set up

No IT knowledge is necessary to deploy and manage Microsoft 365. Quickly add and delete users.

24/7 Customer Support

For setup and quick solutions, rely on Microsoft support for answers through call or chat, how-to guides, and connections with other Microsoft 365 users.

Microsoft 365 Apps for Enterprise

The most efficient and secure Office experience for organizations is Microsoft 365 Apps for business, which enables your teams to collaborate easily from anywhere, any   time.

Built for Teamwork

With Microsoft 365 Apps for enterprise, you can enable your teams to collaborate easily across geographical boundaries. Give users the means to securely share files, collaborate in real-time, and simply interact with coworkers.

Stay Connected

Utilize your iOS, Android, or Windows device from anywhere. You may send emails from your tablet or phone and view, edit, and share documents.

Power of AI

Utilize technologies you already know and the intelligent cloud to complete more tasks. With the support of Microsoft 365 Apps for business, you can write better in Word and Outlook, get insights in Excel, and make presentations in PowerPoint.

Security

Protect your data and identities, recognize internal and external dangers faster, and make sure that third-party apps and macros work with Microsoft 365 Apps for business.

Features

Monthly updates

Get the most recent features and functionalities with fully installed and up-to-date versions of Outlook, Word, Excel, PowerPoint, Teams, Access, and Publisher for Windows or Mac (PC only).

Self-service Business Intelligences

With Get & Transform (Power Query), find and connect to data, model and analyze with Power Pivot, and visualize insights with new maps and charts.

1TB secure cloud storage

With 1 TB of OneDrive cloud storage, you can edit and share documents, photographs, and more on all of your devices from anywhere.

Office on the web

Create and edit documents in Word, OneNote, PowerPoint, and Excel, right from a browser.

Works across multiple devices

Get the Office programs fully installed on several PCs, Mac, tablets, and mobile devices (running on different operating systems like Windows, iOS, and Android).

Professional digital storytelling

With Sway, you can quickly and easily create and distribute interactive, web-based reports, presentations, newsletters, training, and more from your smartphone, tablet, or browser.

Activating Microsoft 365

To get and activate a product key, Microsoft 365 Apps communicates with the Office Licensing Service and the Activation and Validation Service. The machine connects to the Activation and Validation Service daily or when the user logs on to check the licensing status and extend the product key. Microsoft 365 Apps

continue to work flawlessly as long as the machine can connect to the internet at least once per 30 days. Microsoft 365 Apps enters a reduced functionality state until the next time a connection can be made if the computer is offline for longer than 30 days.

The user can connect to the internet and enable the Activation and Validation Service to reactivate the installation to make Microsoft 365 Apps fully functional. However, in some circumstances, the user must log in first.

Managing Activated Installations

A user is permitted to install Microsoft 365 Apps on a maximum of five desktop computers, five tablets, and five mobile devices per Microsoft 365 Apps license. The user manages installments through the Office 365 site.

The device that has not been used the most often is disabled immediately if a user downloads Microsoft 365 Apps on more than 10 devices. On the inactive device, Microsoft 365 Apps enter a reduced capability mode. Please take note that, at this time, only Windows-based devices are supported for this automatic deactivation.

Improvements in Licensing and Activation

The following enhancements were added in Microsoft 365 Apps 1910 and later:

- Users are not required to deactivate Microsoft 365 Apps on previous devices to install them on a new one. The device that has not been used for the longest period of time is automatically terminated if a user has more than 10 devices with Microsoft 365 Apps active.
- A new user can successfully activate Microsoft 365 Apps on a device after Microsoft 365 Apps have been deactivated there due to the portal or the removal of a license.
- The activation report in the Microsoft 365 admin center shows both activations when a user enables Microsoft 365 Apps on a device and a second user logs in to that device.

Lab 16-01: Deploy Microsoft 365 Apps from the Cloud

Follow the steps to deploy Microsoft 365 Apps to client computers from the Office CDN using the ODT.

Before you begin

Ensure your users have local admin privileges on their devices. If that is not the scenario, then you must use your standard deployment tools and processes to install Office.

Step 1: Download the Office Deployment Tool

1. From the shared folder **Server****Share****M365**, assign read permissions for your users.

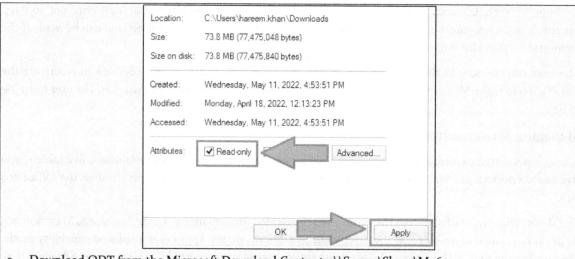

2. Download ODT from the Microsoft Download Center to \\Server\Share\M365.

Thank you for downloading Office Deployment Tool

If your download does not start after 30 seconds, click here to download manually

Installation note:
In the following Install Instructions, please start at the step after the mention of clicking the Download button.

 Install Instructions

3. After downloading the file, run the executable file with the ODT executable (setup.exe) and a sample configuration file (configuration.xml).

Step 2: Form a Configuration File for the Pilot Group

1. Go to Office Customization Tool and update the settings for your Microsoft 365 Apps installation. Select the following options:
   - **Products:** Microsoft 365 Apps.

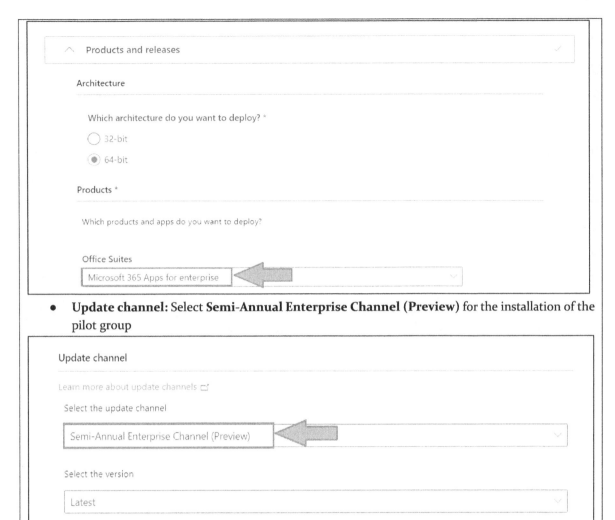

- **Update channel:** Select **Semi-Annual Enterprise Channel (Preview)** for the installation of the pilot group

- **Language:** Select all the language packs you plan to deploy. Select **Match operating system** to automatically install the same languages the OS uses.

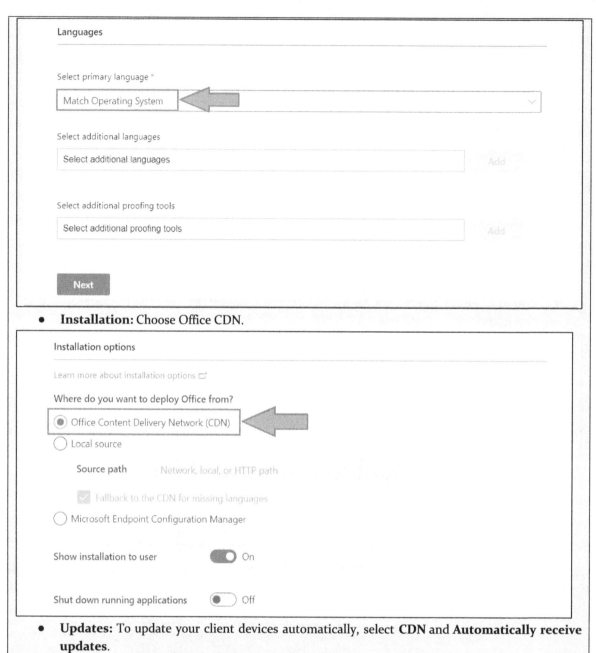

- **Installation:** Choose Office CDN.

- **Updates:** To update your client devices automatically, select **CDN** and **Automatically receive updates**.

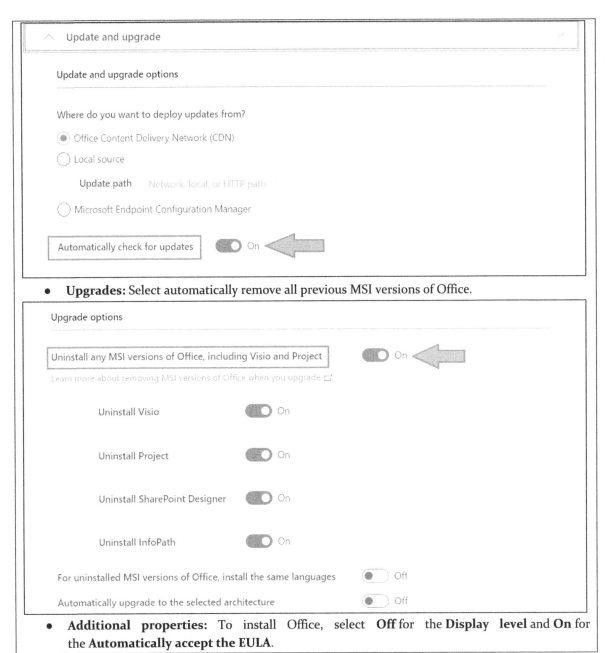

- **Upgrades:** Select automatically remove all previous MSI versions of Office.

- **Additional properties:** To install Office, select **Off** for the **Display level** and **On** for the **Automatically accept the EULA**.

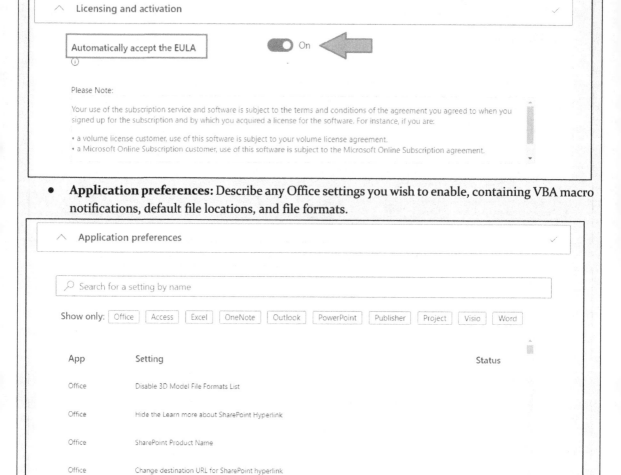

- **Application preferences:** Describe any Office settings you wish to enable, containing VBA macro notifications, default file locations, and file formats.

2. When you finish the configuration, select **Export** and save the file as **config-pilot-SECP.xml** in the **Server\Share\M365** folder.

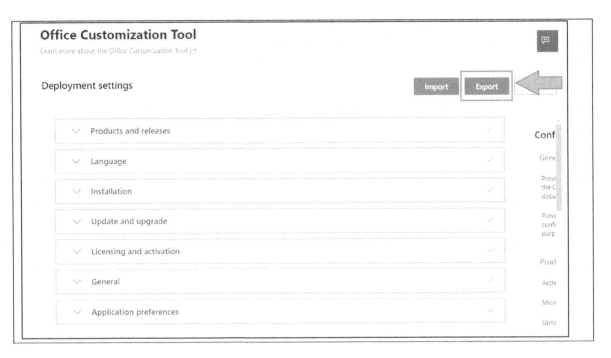

Step 3: Make a Configuration File for the Broad Group

1. Go to Office Customization Tool and update the desired settings for your Microsoft 365 Apps installation. It is recommended to match the same points as the pilot group in Step 2, except for the below change:

   - **Update channel:** Select **Semi-Annual Enterprise Channel** for the installation package for the broad group.

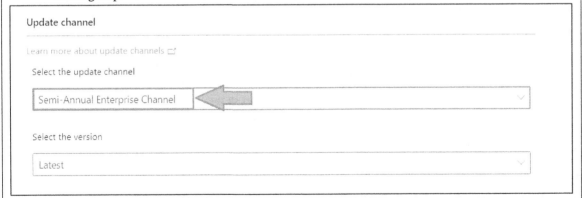

2. When you finish the configuration, click **Export** and keep the file as **config-broad-SEC.xml** in the **\\Server\Share\M365** folder.

Office Customization Tool

Learn more about the Office Customization Tool 🗗

Deployment settings

[Import] [Export]

∨ Products and releases	✓
∨ Language	✓
∨ Installation	✓
∨ Update and upgrade	✓
∨ Licensing and activation	✓
∨ General	✓
∨ Application preferences	✓

Conf

Gene

Provi
the C
docu

Provi
confi
purp

Prod

Archi

Micr

Upda

This file is used to download and install Office installation files to the broad group.

Step 4: Deploy Office to the Pilot Group

To deploy Office, offer commands that users can run from their client's system. The commands run the ODT in admin mode and concerning the configuration file, which describes what version of Office to install on the client computer. Clients who write these commands must have local admin privileges and read permissions to the share.

From the computers for the pilot group, run the following command from a command prompt with admin privileges:

\\Server\Share\M365\setup.exe /configure \\Server\Share\M365\config-pilot-SECP.xml

```
C:\Users\hareem.khan>\\Server\Share\M365\setup.exe /configure \\Server\Share\M36
5\config-pilot-SECP.xml
```

After running the command, the Office installation must start immediately.

Step 5: Install Office to the Broad Group

After you have finished testing Office with the pilot group, you can deploy it to the broad group. Run the below command from a cmd with admin rights:

\\Server\Share\M365\setup.exe /configure \\Server\Share\M365\config-broad-SEC.xml

```
C:\Users\hareem.khan>\\Server\Share\M365\setup.exe /configure \\Server\Share\M36
5\config-broad-SEC.xml
```

After running the command, the Office installation must start immediately.

Mind Map

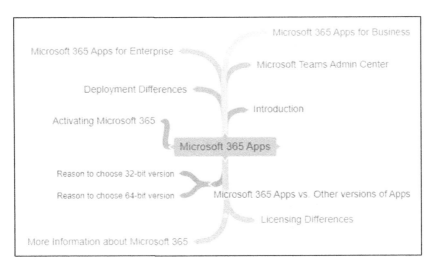

Figure 16-01: Mind Map

Practice Questions

1. Microsoft 365 Apps is available in the _____ version.
   A. 32-bit
   B. 64-bit
   C. Both of the above
   D. None of the above

2. Computers running _____ versions of Windows generally have more resources, such as processing power and memory.
   A. 32-bit
   B. 64-bit
   C. Both of the above
   D. None of the above

3. Users can install Microsoft 365 Apps on up to _____ different computers with a single Office 365 license.
   A. Two
   B. Three
   C. Four
   D. Five

4. _____ applications can access more memory.
   A. 32-bit
   B. 64-bit
   C. Both of the above
   D. None of the above

5. Microsoft 365 Apps is updated _____.
   A. Regularly
   B. Weekly
   C. Monthly
   D. Yearly

Answers

Chapter 01: Introduction to Microsoft 365

1. **Answer: A**

Explanation: The most recent Windows operating systems are Windows 10 and 11. You might be familiar with Windows. Windows 365 is not quite an operating system and is not set up on your computer like Windows. You may build and manage PCs remotely using Windows 365, a business subscription service.

2. **Answer: B**

Explanation: Policies are used across the Microsoft Teams service to ensure the end-user experience conforms to the organization's needs. A **policy package** is a collection of predefined policies and settings.

3. **Answer: A**

Explanation: A cloud-based subscription service called Microsoft 365 includes a portfolio of integrated goods like Office applications, Teams, Windows, top-notch security, and more. Any size organization, including yours, may benefit from Microsoft 365. It represents the workplace of the future. Whether at home, in the office, out in the field, or on the go, these Microsoft 365 features help enhance productivity, collaboration, and communication securely across numerous devices. Microsoft 365 ensures a trustworthy, secure, and contemporary experience for every employee at any time and everywhere while integrating everyone into the digital revolution.

4. **Answer: C**

Explanation: Your gateway and guide to everything Microsoft 365 are Microsoft 365 Fundamentals. Three learning routes make up Microsoft 365 fundamentals, introducing you to the platform's many features through its range of products and services.

5. **Answer: B**

Explanation: Messaging policies control which chat and channel messaging features are available to users. Admins can configure policies for Teams, including Meeting policies, Messaging policies, Updating policies, creating Policy packages, and more.

6. **Answer: A**

Explanation: Secure sign-ins with Multi-Factor Authentication (MFA) and built-in security features to guard against malware, malicious attacks, and data loss.

7. **Answer: B**

Explanation: Select Set up E5 subscription from the Microsoft 365 E5 developer profile page to access the E5 subscription.

8. **Answer: A**

Explanation: Microsoft 365 Fundamentals offers 4 types of options:

- Microsoft 365 Home
- Microsoft 365 Education
- Microsoft 365 for Business
- Microsoft 365 Enterprise

9. **Answer: A**

Explanation: Policies are used across the Microsoft Teams service to ensure the experience end-users receive conforms to the organization's needs, among which meeting policies control the features available to participants in meetings.

10. **Answer: B**

Explanation:

Instant Sandbox: Microsoft Teams, SharePoint, Outlook, and Office are already pre-provisioned in the immediate sandbox. You receive pre-installed data and are unable to change the domain name.

Configurable Sandbox: You must add sample data to the configurable sandbox, which is initially empty. The provisioning of this sandbox may take up to two days. Your domain name can be modified.

11. **Answer: A**

Explanation: To learn more about Microsoft 365, enroll in the Microsoft 365 Developer Program. You can use the program's Microsoft 365 E5 developer subscription to build your sandbox and develop solutions. Your production environment has no bearing on this program. The program has a 90-day duration and 25 user licenses. Using Microsoft Graph, the SharePoint Framework, Power Apps, and other tools, you may create Microsoft Teams apps, Office add-ins for Word, Excel, PowerPoint, Outlook, or SharePoint add-ins.

12. **Answer: B**

Explanation: The program has a 90-day duration and 25 user licenses.

13. **Answer: A**

Explanation: Under **Users,** administrators can configure settings for **Guest access** and **External access.**

External access, formerly known as a **federation,** lets Teams users communicate with users outside your organization.

Guest access lets individuals outside your organization access teams and channels.

14. **Answer: C**

Explanation: External access, formerly known as a **federation,** lets Teams users communicate with users outside your organization.

15. **Answer: C**

Explanation: IaaS uses virtualization technologies to supply cloud computing infrastructures, such as servers, networks, operating systems, and storage. IaaS clients have total control over the entire infrastructure as these cloud servers are often made available to the company through a dashboard or an API. Without the need for all of it to be physically maintained or managed, IaaS offers the same technologies and capabilities as a typical data center. Although everything is outsourced to a "virtual data center" in the cloud, IaaS clients can still access their servers and storage directly.

16. **Answer: D**

Explanation:

PaaS is designed to facilitate the fast development of web or mobile apps for developers without the need to take concern over the setting or maintaining the underlying server, storage, network, and database infrastructure needed for development.

17. Answer: A

Explanation: Software as a Service (SaaS) is considered the largest and most popular use of cloud computing today. It continues to grow as it replaces traditional on-device software with web-based alternatives. Rapidly moving programs to the cloud, often using a subscription-based model, and making the software browser-accessible, eliminates the need to install client software and, in many cases, makes it cross-platform and accessible on the broad set of devices that we use today. Some examples include Gmail, Google Drive, Power BI, Microsoft Office 365, etc.

Chapter 02: Productivity Solutions in Microsoft 365

1. Answer: B

Explanation: Initiation of a cohesive file-sharing experience: OneDrive cloud storage helps us share and access files easily anywhere.

2. Answer: A

Explanation: Working smartly with business-class email and calendaring: Get a customized inbox, an organized way to read and engage with email, and automated event recording on your calendar via Exchange.

3. Answer: B

Explanation: **Staying on the right track seamlessly**: Through Project, you can easily organize your projects with dynamic scheduling depending on the effort required, project length, and allocated team members.

4. Answer: C

Explanation: To assist you in completing tasks more quickly and producing outstanding content, connected experiences assess your material and make recommendations to help you better your job. For example, design advice from PowerPoint Designer, editing and proofreading suggestions from Word Editor, and automated bibliography updates from Word Researcher.

5. Answer: D

Explanation: The features of connected experiences include using built-in intelligence capabilities like Microsoft Editor and Researcher to produce amazing documents and enhance your writing.

6. Answer: B

Explanation: With sophisticated tools like Presenter Coach and PowerPoint Designer, PowerPoint can help you produce professional presentations that stand out effortlessly.

7. Answer: C

Explanation: OneNote may assist you with your note-taking requirements by arranging your notes into tabs and subsections, resulting in a single digital notebook.

8. Answer: A

Explanation: Work management solutions from Microsoft 365 enable your employees to work the way they want, providing companies with the outcomes they want. Project, Planner, Bookings, and To Do are among the job management tools provided. Each tool is built with unique characteristics to allow you to select the ideal tool to assist you in managing your specific sort of job.

9. Answer: C

Explanation: Project is a strong project management application for complicated work initiatives. Microsoft's current cloud-based work and project management option is Project for the Web. Project for the Web offers easy, robust work management tools that can be tailored to most needs and roles. Take on little undertakings as well as huge efforts. Regardless of team size, project managers and team members may utilize Project for the Web to plan and manage work involving dynamic scheduling, subtasks, and/or dependent tasks.

10. Answer: A

Explanation: Create visually attractive interactive dashboards with Power BI to see every part of the project at a glance.

11. Answer: A

Explanation: Because Project is developed on the Power Platform, it is extensible with other platform apps and data.

12. Answer: B

Explanation: Planner is an easy-to-use, collaborative task management application that allows users to plan, organize, and accomplish task-based activities. Planner allows teams to plan their work straightforwardly and visually. The Planner is a web-based application accessible from anywhere and has a mobile app for iOS and Android.

13. Answer: A

Explanation: Bookings is an appointment scheduling and management system accessible over the internet. Bookings make it easier to schedule and manage appointments. It features a web-based booking calendar and interacts with Outlook to optimize your staff's schedule and allow your clients to book at a time that works best for them.

14. Answer: C

Explanation: To Do is a smart task management program that helps you plan and organize your day. To Do is a better, more personal, and intuitive method for individuals to remain organized and make the most of their days. It works with Outlook and Planner and is powered by Office 365 Exchange Online. To Do is accessible via iOS, Android, Windows, and the web. To Do encourages you to do the most critical tasks you need to get done every day, whether for work, school, or home.

15. Answer: B

Explanation: Microsoft Exchange Online is a cloud-based messaging system that provides the functionality of the Microsoft Exchange Server. It allows users to access email, calendar, contacts, and tasks from PCs, the web, and mobile devices all in one location. It fully interfaces with all other Microsoft 365 workloads, making management simple.

Chapter 03: Collaboration Solutions in Microsoft 365

1. Answer: B
Explanation: Teams allow people to chat one-on-one quickly or in a group and host voice or audio meetings.
2. Answer: A
Explanation: Viva includes four modules – Viva Connections, Viva Insights, Viva Topics, and Viva Learning.
3. Answer: C
Explanation: You can share files with users inside and outside your organization.
4. Answer: B
Explanation: You can create Team sites, Communication sites, and Hub sites in SharePoint.
5. Answer: C
Explanation: Yammer, Teams, and Stream will allow you to use different types of content and host a major online event.
6. Answer: A
Explanation: Power BI in Teams can empower your organization to collaborate with data to improve outcomes.
7. Answer: C
Explanation: Viva Connections offers added functionality through three primary components.
8. Answer: C
Explanation: Yammer supports both internal and external networks to help users communicate and collaborate.
9. Answer: A
Explanation: An internal network is restricted to users inside the organization.
10. Answer: B
Explanation: An external network is open to users outside the organization's domain.

Chapter 04: Endpoint Modernization, Management Concepts, and Deployment Options in Microsoft 365

1. Answer: C
Explanation: Configuration Manager manages on-premises infrastructure, and Intune manages cloud-based functions.
2. Answer: A
Explanation: Windows 365 and Azure Virtual Desktop are virtual desktop solutions, also known as Desktop-as-a-Service.
3. Answer: B

Explanation: Windows-as-a-Service is a new model for Windows. Instead of a major release every three or four years, features are released more frequently, such as semi-annually.

4. Answer: B

Explanation: Monthly Enterprise Channel receives feature updates once a month, on the second Tuesday of the month.

5. Answer: C

Explanation: Azure Virtual Desktop, a Virtual Desktop Infrastructure (VDI) solution, allows you to quickly deploy virtual desktops and apps to enable secure remote work.

6. Answer: B

Explanation: Windows 365 is available in two subscription offerings.

7. Answer: B

Explanation: With Windows clients, there are two release types.

8. Answer: C

Explanation: A typical ring structure uses three deployment groups.

9. Answer: C

Explanation: There are three types of deployment categories or methods.

10. Answer: B

Explanation: Microsoft provides each update channel with two other updates released on the second Tuesday of every month.

Chapter 05: Analytics Capabilities in Microsoft 365

1. Answer: A

Explanation: Viva Insights is a tool that helps people and businesses thrive with data-driven, privacy-protected insights and recommendations to improve productivity and wellbeing.

2. Answer: B

Explanation: Viva Insights provides personal insights, insights for managers, and organizational insights for business leaders.

3. Answer: C

Explanation: The two reports in the Microsoft 365 admin center are Productivity scores and usage reports.

4. Answer: B

Explanation: View audit logs and sign-in activity reports in the Azure Active Directory admin center.

5. Answer: B

Explanation: There are two kinds of reports visible in the admin center.

Chapter 06: Security and Compliance Concepts

1. Answer: A

Explanation: In the shared responsibility model, the customer organization is responsible for its data, including information and data relating to employees, devices, accounts, and identities.

2. Answer: B

Explanation: Multifactor authentication is an example of defense-in-depth at the identity and access layer.

3. Answer: C

Explanation: Encryption at rest could be part of a security strategy to protect stored employee data.

4. Answer: B

Explanation: Data, particularly personal data, is subject to the laws and regulations of the country/region in which it is physically collected, held, or processed.

5. Answer: C

Explanation: The Zero Trust model has three principles that guide and underpin how security is implemented. These are: verify explicitly, least privilege access, and assume breach.

6. Answer: D

Explanation: The six elements are the foundational pillars of the Zero Trust model.

7. Answer: B

Explanation: There are two top-level types of encryption: symmetric and asymmetric.

8: Answer: A

Explanation: Symmetric encryption utilizes the same key to encode and decode the data.

9: Answer: B

Explanation: Asymmetric encryption uses a public key and private key pair.

10. Answer: B

Explanation: Hashing is used to store passwords. When a user enters their password, the same algorithm that created the stored hash creates a hash of the entered password.

11. Answer: A

Explanation: This is one of the multiple roles you can use to get into the Compliance Center.

12. Answer: C

Explanation: Both your organization and Microsoft work together to execute these controls.

13. Answer: A

Explanation: Compliance Manager offers admins the capabilities to understand and improve their compliance score to ultimately enhance the organization's compliance posture and help it stay in line with its compliance requirements.

14. Answer: A

Explanation: Compliance Manager is an end-to-end solution in Microsoft 365 compliance center to allow admins to manage and track compliance activities.

15. Answer: B

Explanation: A compliance score calculates the overall compliance posture across the organization, which is available through the Compliance Manager.

Chapter 07: Identity Concepts

1. Answer: B

Explanation: With single sign-on, a user signs in once and can access several applications or resources.

2. Answer: C

Explanation: Federated services use a trust relationship to allow access to resources.

3. Answer: A

Explanation: Authentication is verifying that a user or device is who they say they are.

4. Answer: D

Explanation: Identity infrastructure can be organized into four fundamental pillars that organizations should consider when creating an identity infrastructure.

5. Answer: B
Explanation: The authentication pillar describes the story of how much an IT system needs to know about identity to have sufficient proof that they are who they say they are.
6. Answer: C
Explanation: The authorization pillar is about verifying the incoming identity data to determine the level of access to an authenticated person.
7. Answer: D
Explanation: The auditing pillar tracks who does what, when, where, and how. Auditing contains in-depth reporting, alerts, and governance of identities.
8. Answer: A
Explanation: Authentication is providing that a person is who they say they are. When someone purchases an item with a credit card, they may be required to show an additional form of identification.
9. Answer: B
Explanation: Authorization determines the level of access or the permissions an authenticated person has to your data and resources, and authorization is sometimes shortened to AuthZ.
10. Answer: C
Explanation: Federation lets the access of services across organizational or domain boundaries by establishing trust relationships between the respective domain's identity providers.

Chapter 08: Threat Protection with Microsoft 365 Defender

1. Answer: A
Explanation: Microsoft Defender for Office 365 safeguards against malicious threats from email messages, links (URLs), and collaboration tools.
2. Answer: C
Explanation: Through the Data Security pillar, an admin can identify and control sensitive information and respond to classification labels on content.
3. Answer: B
Explanation: Microsoft Defender for Identity is a cloud-based security solution that identifies, detects, and helps you investigate advanced threats, compromised identities, and harmful insider actions directed at your organization.
4. Answer: B
Explanation: A secure score in the M365 Defender portal will give a snapshot of an organization's security posture and provide details on how to improve it.
5. Answer: B
Explanation: Microsoft Defender for Office 365 is accessible in two plans.

Chapter 09: Describe the Security Capabilities of Microsoft Sentinel

1. Answer: B
Explanation: A SIEM/SOAR solution uses to collect, detect, investigate, and respond to identify and protect your organization's network perimeter.
2. Answer: A

> **Explanation:** Using the Microsoft Sentinel integration with Azure Monitor Workbooks lets you monitor data and offers versatility in forming custom workbooks.
> **3. Answer: B**
> **Explanation:** A SOAR system gets alerts from many sources.

Chapter 10: Describe The Compliance Management Capabilities In Microsoft Purview

> **1. Answer: A**
> **Explanation:** This is one of the multiple roles you can use to view the compliance portal.
> **2. Answer: C**
> **Explanation:** Your organization and Microsoft work together to implement these controls.
> **3. Answer: A**
> **Explanation:** Compliance Manager offers admins the capabilities to understand and improve their compliance score so that they can eventually recover the organization's compliance posture and help it to stay in line with its compliance necessities.

Chapter 11: Service Trust Portal and Privacy at Microsoft

> **1. Answer: A**
> **Explanation:** Saving the document to the My Library section of the Service Trust Portal will ensure you have the latest updates.
> **2. Answer: A**
> **Explanation:** The foundation of Microsoft's approach to privacy is built on the following six principles: customer control, transparency, and security, strong legal protections for privacy, no content-based targeting, and benefits to customers from any data we collect.
> **3. Answer: D**
> **Explanation:** Microsoft Cloud services are built on trust, security, and compliance.
> **4. Answer: D**
> **Explanation:** Microsoft's approach to privacy is built on six principles.
> **5. Answer: B**
> **Explanation:** Microsoft Priva helps you meet challenges so you can achieve your privacy goals. Priva's capabilities are available through two solutions.

Chapter 12: Pricing, Licensing, and Billing Options Available in Microsoft 365

> **1. Answer: A**
> **Explanation:** The Cloud Solution Provider (CSP) model provides your subscription through an expert CSP partner.
> **2. Answer: C**
> **Explanation:** You modify the payment method and frequency of your Microsoft 365 subscription in the Microsoft 365 admin center.
> **3. Answer: B**

> **Explanation:** Microsoft 365 Business is built for companies with under 300 employees.
> **4. Answer: D**
> **Explanation:** The Enterprise Agreement offers the best value to organizations with 500 or more users or devices.
> **5. Answer: B**
> **Explanation:** There are two types of add-ons.

Chapter 13: Describe Support Offerings for Microsoft 365 Services

> **1. Answer: C**
> **Explanation:** Your organization can receive on-site support, a dedicated technical account manager, and access to advisory services through premier support.
> **2. Answer: B**
> **Explanation:** Your organization should submit a claim to Microsoft, and Microsoft will then review your claim for approval.
> **3. Answer: C**
> **Explanation:** You can view the current health status of your Microsoft 365 services and tenant through the Microsoft 365 admin center.
> **4. Answer: C**
> **Explanation:** Microsoft product teams will see your ideas and discuss them with you through the feedback web portal.
> **5. Answer: B**
> **Explanation:** Microsoft will provide two different types of notifications.

Chapter 14: Describe the Service Life Cycle in Microsoft 365

> **1. Answer: C**
> **Explanation:** The General Availability (GA) phase is the release version of a product.
> **2. Answer: B**
> **Explanation:** Under the Modern Lifecycle Policy, Microsoft gives a minimum of 12 months' notice before ending support for products.
> **3. Answer: B**
> **Explanation:** The three phases that a feature has in the Microsoft 365 Roadmap are In development, Rolling out, and Launching.
> **4. Answer: C**
> **Explanation:** The roadmap groups the features into three update phases.
> **5. Answer: C**
> **Explanation:** A product or service lifecycle typically has three phases.

Chapter 15: Mobile Device Management

> **1. Answer: C**

Explanation: Android and iOS devices must be manually enrolled to MDM using the Company Portal app.

2. Answer: B

Explanation: Only users assigned an Intune license can enroll their supported device types in   Intune.

3. Answer: C

Explanation: When a DEM enrolls a device, no user is associated with the device, and the device has no assigned user.

4. Answer: C

Explanation: A DEM account can only be used for device enrollment.

5. Answer: A

Explanation: To control access to company resources, organizations can configure either a Security policy in Microsoft 365 or a Conditional Access policy in Intune. These policies can be configured only to access company resources from enrolled devices.

6. Answer: B

Explanation: Apple DEP is only available for iOS devices that an organization purchases through either Apple or an authorized reseller to provide to employees. Once the devices are purchased, DEP automates the enrollment and configuration of the iOS devices to MDM.

7. Answer: C

Explanation: An organization can use the Configuration Manager console to change its MDM authority setting.

8. Answer: A

Explanation: Northwind's users can enroll their Apple devices in   MDM through the Company Portal app.

9. Answer: B

Explanation: This certificate is used to communicate with Intune, even if you are using Basic Mobility and Security (remember, Basic Mobility and Security is hosted by the Intune service and includes a subset of Intune services). The certificate is renewed automatically when the device communicates with Intune. If the certificate expires, the device is no longer managed by MDM. The device is automatically removed from Intune after 180 days if the certificate is not renewed.

10. Answer: C

Explanation: The Autodiscover service is configured when you create an alias (CNAME resource record type) in the domain DNS zone that automatically redirects enrollment requests to Intune servers.

11. Answer: A

Explanation: Conditional access is an Azure Active Directory capability included with an Azure AD Premium license.

12. Answer: C

Explanation: Organizations use Conditional Access policies with Microsoft Intune to control the devices and apps that can connect to an organization's email and company resources. When integrated, you can control access to keep your corporate data secure while giving users an experience that lets them do their best work from any device and location.

13. Answer: C

Explanation: If Windows 10 is a domain member, it may be operated by Group Policy and MDM simultaneously.

14. Answer: A

Explanation: Organization-wide device access settings enable an organization to specify whether it wants to allow or block access to Exchange mail for devices not supported by Basic Mobility and Security and which security groups should be excluded from access control.

15. Answer: C
Explanation: Remote actions are available in both Microsoft Intune and Basic Mobility and Security, although limited functionality is provided in Basic Mobility and Security.

16. Answer: B
Explanation: Devices that are not enrolled in MDM cannot have their compliance evaluated.

17. Answer: C
Explanation: When organizations create policies or profiles, they can only deploy them by assigning them to groups of users, and they cannot assign them directly to individual devices or users.

18. Answer: B
Explanation: Microsoft 365 includes two Mobile Device Management (MDM) services: Basic Mobility and Security and Microsoft Intune.

19. Answer: B
Explanation: Intune is Microsoft's gold-level standard for MDM solutions.

20. Answer: B
Explanation: Devices can be managed by MDM even if they are not members of a domain.

21. Answer: C
Explanation: By using MDM and MAM, an organization can deploy applications, manage their settings, and separate data created by personal and business apps.

22. Answer: C
Explanation: MDM is implemented by using an MDM authority and MDM clients.

Chapter 16: Microsoft 365 Apps

1. Answer: C
Explanation: Microsoft 365 Apps is available in 32-bit and 64-bit versions.

2. Answer: B
Explanation: Computers having 64-bit versions of Windows generally have more resources like processing power and memory.

3. Answer: D
Explanation: You can install Microsoft 365 Apps on up to 5 different computers with a single Office 365 license.

4. Answer: B
Explanation: 64-bit applications can access more memory.

5. Answer: A and C
Explanation: Microsoft 365 Apps is maintained regularly and monthly with new updates, unlike non-subscription versions of Office.

Acronyms

Azure AD	Azure Active Directory
AD	Active Directory
ADDS	Active Directory Domain Services
ADFS	Active Directory Federation Services
AI	Artificial Intelligence
APNS	Apple Push Notification Service
AVD	Azure Virtual Desktop
BPOS	Business Productivity Online Suite
BYOD	Bring Your Own Device
CapEx	Capital Expenditure
CASB	Cloud Access Security Broker
CDN	Content Delivery Network
CIA	Confidentiality, Integrity, Availability
CIs	Configuration Items
CPU	Central Processing Unit
CRM	Customer Resource Manager
CSP	Cloud Service Provider
DC	Domain Controller
DDoS	Distributed Denial of Service
DEM	Device Enrollment Managers
DEP	Device Enrollment Program
DR	Disaster Recovery
DSARs	Data Subject Access Requests
DSRs	Data Subject Requests DSRs
EA	Enterprise Agreement
EAS	Exchange ActiveSync
EFT	Electronic Funds Transfer
ERP	Enterprise Resource Planning

EXP	Employee Experience Platform
FAQs	Frequently Asked Questions
GA	General Availability
HTTPS	Hypertext Transfer Protocol Secure
IaaS	Infrastructure as a Service
ICD	Imaging and Configuration Designer
IDaaS	Identity as a Service
ID	Identity
IdP	Identity Provider
IoT	Internet of Things
ISV	Independent Software Vendor
JEA	Just-Enough Access
JIT	Just-In-Time
KPIs	Key Performance Indicators
MAM	Mobile Application Management
MDM	Mobile Device Management
MDT	Microsoft Deployment Toolkit
MEM	Microsoft Endpoint Manager
MFA	Multi-Factor Authentication
MOSP	
MPSA	Microsoft Products & Services Agreement
ODT	Office Deployment Tool
OOBE	Out-of-Box Experience
OS	Operating System
OpEx	Operational Expenditure
PaaS	Platform as a Service
PII	Personally Identifiable Information
RDS	Remote Desktop Services
SaaS	Software as a Service
SOAR	Security Orchestration Automated Response
SOCs	Security Operation Centers
SIEM	Security Information Event Management

SLA	Service Level Agreement
SLC	Service Life Cycle
SSO	Single Sign on
STP	Service Trust Portal
UPN	User Principal Name
USLs	User Subscription Licenses
VDI	Virtual Desktop Infrastructure
VL	Volume Licensing
WaaS	Windows-as-a-Service

References

https://docs.microsoft.com/en-us/microsoft-365/admin/security-and-compliance/set-up-multi-factor-authentication?view=o365-worldwide

https://docs.microsoft.com/en-us/deployoffice/about-microsoft-365-apps

https://www.microsoft.com/en/microsoft-365/microsoft-365-and-office-resources?rtc=1

https://support.microsoft.com/en-us/office/what-s-the-difference-between-microsoft-365-and-office-2021-ed447ebf-6060-46f9-9e90-a239bd27eb96

https://support.microsoft.com/en-us/office/choose-between-the-64-bit-or-32-bit-version-of-office-2dee7807-8f95-4d0c-b5fe-6c6f49b8d261

https://support.microsoft.com/en-us/office/what-s-new-in-microsoft-365-95c8d81d-08ba-42c1-914f-bca4603e1426

https://docs.microsoft.com/en-us/office365/servicedescriptions/office-365-service-descriptions-technet-library

https://docs.microsoft.com/en-us/learn/certifications/courses/ms-101t00

https://docs.microsoft.com/en-us/learn/units/introduction-to-mobile-device-management/

https://docs.microsoft.com/en-us/learn/units/introduction-to-mobile-device-management/1-introduction

https://docs.microsoft.com/en-us/learn/units/introduction-to-mobile-device-management/2-explore

https://docs.microsoft.com/en-us/learn/units/introduction-to-mobile-device-management/3-explore-mobile-device-management-services-microsoft-365

https://docs.microsoft.com/en-us/learn/units/introduction-to-mobile-device-management/4-examine-mobile-device-management-policy-settings-microsoft-365

https://docs.microsoft.com/en-us/learn/units/introduction-to-mobile-device-management/5-examine-how-email-document-access-are-controlled

https://docs.microsoft.com/en-us/learn/units/introduction-to-mobile-device-management/6-knowledge-check

https://docs.microsoft.com/en-us/learn/units/introduction-to-mobile-device-management/7-summary

https://docs.microsoft.com/en-us/learn/certifications/courses/ms-101t00

https://docs.microsoft.com/en-us/learn/units/deploy-mobile-device-management/

https://docs.microsoft.com/en-us/learn/units/deploy-mobile-device-management/1-introduction

https://docs.microsoft.com/en-us/learn/units/deploy-mobile-device-management/2-activate-mobile-device-management-services-microsoft-365

https://docs.microsoft.com/en-us/learn/units/deploy-mobile-device-management/3-configure-domains-for-mobile-device-management

https://docs.microsoft.com/en-us/learn/units/deploy-mobile-device-management/4-obtain-apple-push-notification-service-certificate

https://docs.microsoft.com/en-us/learn/units/deploy-mobile-device-management/5-manage-security-policies-for-mobile-device-managed-devices

https://docs.microsoft.com/en-us/learn/units/deploy-mobile-device-management/6-define-corporate-device-enrollment-policy

https://docs.microsoft.com/en-us/learn/units/deploy-mobile-device-management/7-knowledge-check

https://docs.microsoft.com/en-us/learn/units/deploy-mobile-device-management/8-summary

https://docs.microsoft.com/en-us/learn/certifications/courses/ms-101t00

https://docs.microsoft.com/en-us/learn/units/enroll-devices-to-mobile-device-management/

https://docs.microsoft.com/en-us/learn/units/enroll-devices-to-mobile-device-management/1-introduction

https://docs.microsoft.com/en-us/learn/units/enroll-devices-to-mobile-device-management/2-enroll-windows-10-android-devices

https://docs.microsoft.com/en-us/learn/units/enroll-devices-to-mobile-device-management/3-enroll-ios-devices-using-apple-device-enrollment-program

https://docs.microsoft.com/en-us/learn/units/enroll-devices-to-mobile-device-management/4-regulate-device-enrollment-by-using-enrollment-rules

https://docs.microsoft.com/en-us/learn/units/enroll-devices-to-mobile-device-management/5-examine-how-users-can-enroll-their-personal-devices

https://docs.microsoft.com/en-us/learn/units/enroll-devices-to-mobile-device-management/6-enroll-devices-using-device-enrollment-manager-account

https://docs.microsoft.com/en-us/learn/units/enroll-devices-to-mobile-device-management/7-examine-need-for-multi-factor-authentication-to-secure-enrollment

https://docs.microsoft.com/en-us/learn/units/enroll-devices-to-mobile-device-management/8-knowledge-check

https://docs.microsoft.com/en-us/learn/units/enroll-devices-to-mobile-device-management/9-summary

https://docs.microsoft.com/en-us/learn/paths/m365-licensing-service-support/

https://docs.microsoft.com/en-us/learn/modules/describe-service-life-cycle-microsoft-365/

https://docs.microsoft.com/en-us/learn/modules/describe-service-life-cycle-microsoft-365/1-introduction

https://docs.microsoft.com/en-us/learn/modules/describe-service-life-cycle-microsoft-365/2-private-public-general-availability

https://docs.microsoft.com/en-us/learn/modules/describe-service-life-cycle-microsoft-365/3-support

https://docs.microsoft.com/en-us/learn/modules/describe-service-life-cycle-microsoft-365/4-roadmap-portal

https://docs.microsoft.com/en-us/learn/modules/describe-service-life-cycle-microsoft-365/5-knowledge-check

https://docs.microsoft.com/en-us/learn/modules/describe-service-life-cycle-microsoft-365/6-summary-resources

https://docs.microsoft.com/en-us/learn/paths/m365-licensing-service-support/

https://docs.microsoft.com/en-us/learn/modules/describe-support-offerings-for-microsoft-365-services/

https://docs.microsoft.com/en-us/learn/modules/describe-support-offerings-for-microsoft-365-services/1-introduction

https://docs.microsoft.com/en-us/learn/modules/describe-support-offerings-for-microsoft-365-services/2-explore-support-options

https://docs.microsoft.com/en-us/learn/modules/describe-support-offerings-for-microsoft-365-services/3-explain-service-level-agreements

https://docs.microsoft.com/en-us/learn/modules/describe-support-offerings-for-microsoft-365-services/4-track-service-health-status

https://docs.microsoft.com/en-us/learn/modules/describe-support-offerings-for-microsoft-365-services/5-communicate-share-ideas-uservoice

https://docs.microsoft.com/en-us/learn/modules/describe-support-offerings-for-microsoft-365-services/6-knowledge-check

https://docs.microsoft.com/en-us/learn/modules/describe-support-offerings-for-microsoft-365-services/7-summary-resources

https://docs.microsoft.com/en-us/learn/paths/m365-licensing-service-support/

https://docs.microsoft.com/en-us/learn/modules/identify-licensing-options-available-microsoft-365/1-introduction

https://docs.microsoft.com/en-us/learn/modules/identify-licensing-options-available-microsoft-365/2-cloud-solution-provider-model

https://docs.microsoft.com/en-us/learn/modules/identify-licensing-options-available-microsoft-365/3-bill-management-options

https://docs.microsoft.com/en-us/learn/modules/identify-licensing-options-available-microsoft-365/4-license-management-options

https://docs.microsoft.com/en-us/learn/modules/identify-licensing-options-available-microsoft-365/5-knowledge-check

https://docs.microsoft.com/en-us/learn/modules/identify-licensing-options-available-microsoft-365/6-summary

https://docs.microsoft.com/en-us/learn/paths/m365-security-compliance-capabilities/

https://docs.microsoft.com/en-us/learn/units/describe-compliance-management-capabilities-microsoft/

https://docs.microsoft.com/en-us/learn/units/describe-compliance-management-capabilities-microsoft/1-introduction

https://docs.microsoft.com/en-us/learn/units/describe-compliance-management-capabilities-microsoft/2-describe-service-trust-portal

https://docs.microsoft.com/en-us/learn/units/describe-compliance-management-capabilities-microsoft/3-describe-microsofts-privacy-principles

https://docs.microsoft.com/en-us/learn/units/describe-compliance-management-capabilities-microsoft/4-describe-microsoft-priva

https://docs.microsoft.com/en-us/learn/units/describe-compliance-management-capabilities-microsoft/5-knowledge-check

https://docs.microsoft.com/en-us/learn/units/describe-compliance-management-capabilities-microsoft/6-summary-resources

https://docs.microsoft.com/en-us/learn/paths/m365-security-compliance-capabilities/

https://docs.microsoft.com/en-us/learn/modules/describe-threat-protection-with-microsoft-365-defender/

https://docs.microsoft.com/en-us/learn/modules/describe-threat-protection-with-microsoft-365-defender/1-introduction

https://docs.microsoft.com/en-us/learn/modules/describe-threat-protection-with-microsoft-365-defender/2-describe-services

https://docs.microsoft.com/en-us/learn/modules/describe-threat-protection-with-microsoft-365-defender/3-describe-defender-office

https://docs.microsoft.com/en-us/learn/modules/describe-threat-protection-with-microsoft-365-defender/4-describe-defender-endpoint

https://docs.microsoft.com/en-us/learn/modules/describe-threat-protection-with-microsoft-365-defender/5-describe-microsoft-cloud-app-security

https://docs.microsoft.com/en-us/learn/modules/describe-threat-protection-with-microsoft-365-defender/6-describe-defender-identity

https://docs.microsoft.com/en-us/learn/modules/describe-threat-protection-with-microsoft-365-defender/7-describe-microsoft-defender-portal

https://docs.microsoft.com/en-us/learn/modules/describe-threat-protection-with-microsoft-365-defender/8-knowledge-check

https://docs.microsoft.com/en-us/learn/modules/describe-threat-protection-with-microsoft-365-defender/9-summary-resources

https://docs.microsoft.com/en-us/learn/paths/m365-security-compliance-capabilities/

https://docs.microsoft.com/en-us/learn/units/describe-identity-principles-concepts/

https://docs.microsoft.com/en-us/learn/units/describe-identity-principles-concepts/1-introduction

https://docs.microsoft.com/en-us/learn/units/describe-identity-principles-concepts/2-define-authentication-authorization

https://docs.microsoft.com/en-us/learn/units/describe-identity-principles-concepts/3-define-identity-primary-security-perimeter

https://docs.microsoft.com/en-us/learn/units/describe-identity-principles-concepts/4-describe-role-identity-provider

https://docs.microsoft.com/en-us/learn/units/describe-identity-principles-concepts/5-describe-concept-of-directory-services-active-directory

https://docs.microsoft.com/en-us/learn/units/describe-identity-principles-concepts/6-describe-concept-federation

https://docs.microsoft.com/en-us/learn/units/describe-identity-principles-concepts/7-knowledge-check

https://docs.microsoft.com/en-us/learn/units/describe-identity-principles-concepts/8-summary-resources

https://docs.microsoft.com/en-us/learn/paths/m365-security-compliance-capabilities/

https://docs.microsoft.com/en-us/learn/unirs/describe-security-concepts-methodologies/

https://docs.microsoft.com/en-us/learn/unirs/describe-security-concepts-methodologies/1-introduction

https://docs.microsoft.com/en-us/learn/unirs/describe-security-concepts-methodologies/2-describe-shared-responsibility-model

https://docs.microsoft.com/en-us/learn/unirs/describe-security-concepts-methodologies/3-describe-defense-depth

https://docs.microsoft.com/en-us/learn/unirs/describe-security-concepts-methodologies/4-describe-zero-trust-model

https://docs.microsoft.com/en-us/learn/unirs/describe-security-concepts-methodologies/5-describe-encryption-hashing

https://docs.microsoft.com/en-us/learn/unirs/describe-security-concepts-methodologies/6-describe-compliance-concepts

https://docs.microsoft.com/en-us/learn/unirs/describe-security-concepts-methodologies/7-knowledge-check

https://docs.microsoft.com/en-us/learn/unirs/describe-security-concepts-methodologies/8-summary-resources

https://docs.microsoft.com/en-us/learn/paths/describe-microsoft-365-core-services-concepts/

https://docs.microsoft.com/en-us/learn/modules/describe-analytics-capabilities-microsoft-365/

https://docs.microsoft.com/en-us/learn/modules/describe-analytics-capabilities-microsoft-365/1-introduction

https://docs.microsoft.com/en-us/learn/modules/describe-analytics-capabilities-microsoft-365/2-describe-capabilities-of-viva-insights

https://docs.microsoft.com/en-us/learn/modules/describe-analytics-capabilities-microsoft-365/3-describe-capabilities-of-admin-center-user-portal

https://docs.microsoft.com/en-us/learn/modules/describe-analytics-capabilities-microsoft-365/4-describe-reports-available-admin-center-other-admin-centers

https://docs.microsoft.com/en-us/learn/modules/describe-analytics-capabilities-microsoft-365/5-knowledge-check

https://docs.microsoft.com/en-us/learn/modules/describe-analytics-capabilities-microsoft-365/6-summary-resources

https://www.computerworld.com/article/3205968/office-2021-vs-microsoft-365-office-365-how-to-choose.html

https://its.uiowa.edu/support/article/103425

https://www.sherweb.com/blog/office-365/microsoft-365-fundamentals/

https://docs.microsoft.com/en-us/learn/paths/describe-microsoft-365-core-services-concepts/

https://docs.microsoft.com/en-us/learn/modules/describe-endpoint-modernization-management-concepts-deployment-options/

https://docs.microsoft.com/en-us/learn/modules/describe-endpoint-modernization-management-concepts-deployment-options/1-introduction

https://docs.microsoft.com/en-us/learn/modules/describe-endpoint-modernization-management-concepts-deployment-options/2-management-capabilities-of-microsoft-365

https://docs.microsoft.com/en-us/learn/modules/describe-endpoint-modernization-management-concepts-deployment-options/3-compare-capabilities-of-windows-365-azure-virtual-desktop

https://docs.microsoft.com/en-us/learn/modules/describe-endpoint-modernization-management-concepts-deployment-options/4-describe-deployment-release-models-for-windows-service

https://docs.microsoft.com/en-us/learn/modules/describe-endpoint-modernization-management-concepts-deployment-options/4-describe-deployment-release-models-for-windows-service

https://docs.microsoft.com/en-us/learn/modules/describe-endpoint-modernization-management-concepts-deployment-options/6-knowledge-check

https://docs.microsoft.com/en-us/learn/modules/describe-endpoint-modernization-management-concepts-deployment-options/7-summary-resources

https://www.computerworld.com/article/3205968/office-2021-vs-microsoft-365-office-365-how-to-choose.html

https://its.uiowa.edu/support/article/103425

https://www.sherweb.com/blog/office-365/microsoft-365-fundamentals/

https://docs.microsoft.com/en-us/learn/paths/describe-microsoft-365-core-services-concepts/

https://docs.microsoft.com/en-us/learn/modules/describe-collaboration-solutions-microsoft-365/

https://docs.microsoft.com/en-us/learn/modules/describe-collaboration-solutions-microsoft-365/1-introduction

https://docs.microsoft.com/en-us/learn/modules/describe-collaboration-solutions-microsoft-365/2-workloads-teams-value-they-provide

https://docs.microsoft.com/en-us/learn/modules/describe-collaboration-solutions-microsoft-365/3-describe-core-employee-experience-capabilities-microsoft-viva

https://docs.microsoft.com/en-us/learn/modules/describe-collaboration-solutions-microsoft-365/4-describe-how-features-of-sharepoint-onedrive-promote-collaboration

https://docs.microsoft.com/en-us/learn/modules/describe-collaboration-solutions-microsoft-365/4-describe-how-features-of-sharepoint-onedrive-promote-collaboration

https://docs.microsoft.com/en-us/learn/modules/describe-collaboration-solutions-microsoft-365/6-knowledge-check

https://docs.microsoft.com/en-us/learn/modules/describe-collaboration-solutions-microsoft-365/7-summary-resources

https://www.computerworld.com/article/3205968/office-2021-vs-microsoft-365-office-365-how-to-choose.html

https://its.uiowa.edu/support/article/103425

https://www.sherweb.com/blog/office-365/microsoft-365-fundamentals/

2023 BONUS MATERIAL! FREE SURPRISE VOUCHER

1.   Get **350** UNIQUE Practice Questions (online) to simulate the real exam.

AND

2.   Get FREE **Exam Cram Notes** (online access)

Apply the Coupon Code: **BONUSMS900**

Link: https://ipspecialist.net/courses/ms-900-microsoft-365-fundamentals/

About Our Products

Other products from IPSpecialist LTD regarding CSP technology are:

 AWS Certified Cloud Practitioner Study guide

 AWS Certified SysOps Admin - Associate Study guide

 AWS Certified Solution Architect - Associate Study guide

 AWS Certified Developer Associate Study guide

 AWS Certified Advanced Networking – Specialty Study guide

 AWS Certified Security – Specialty Study guide

 AWS Certified Big Data – Specialty Study guide

 AWS Certified Database – Specialty Study guide

 AWS Certified Machine Learning – Specialty Study guide

 Microsoft Certified: Azure Fundamentals

 Microsoft Certified: Azure Administrator

Microsoft Certified: Azure Solution Architect

 Microsoft Certified: Azure DevOps Engineer

 Microsoft Certified: Azure Developer Associate

 Microsoft Certified: Azure Security Engineer

 Microsoft Certified: Azure Data Fundamentals

 Microsoft Certified: Azure AI Fundamentals

 Microsoft Certified: Azure Database Administrator Associate

 Google Certified: Associate Cloud Engineer

 Google Certified: Professional Cloud Developer

 Microsoft Certified: Azure Data Engineer Associate

 Microsoft Certified: Azure Data Scientist

 Ansible Certified: Advanced Automation

About Our Products

 Oracle Certified: OCI Foundations Associate

 Oracle Certified: OCI Developer Associate

 Oracle Certified: OCI Architect Associate

 Oracle Certified: OCI Operations Associate

 Kubernetes Certified: Application Developer

Other Network & Security related products from IPSpecialist LTD are:

- CCNA Routing & Switching Study Guide
- CCNA Security Second Edition Study Guide
- CCNA Service Provider Study Guide
- CCDA Study Guide
- CCDP Study Guide
- CCNP Route Study Guide
- CCNP Switch Study Guide
- CCNP Troubleshoot Study Guide
- CCNP Security SENSS Study Guide
- CCNP Security SIMOS Study Guide
- CCNP Security SITCS Study Guide
- CCNP Security SISAS Study Guide
- CompTIA Network+ Study Guide
- Certified Blockchain Expert (CBEv2) Study Guide
- EC-Council CEH v10 Second Edition Study Guide
- EC-Council CEH v12 First Edition Study Guide
- Certified Blockchain Expert v2 Study Guide

Made in the USA
Middletown, DE
31 October 2023